the WILD COAST 2

the WILD COAST 2

A KAYAKING AND RECREATION GUIDE FOR THE NORTH AND CENTRAL B.C. COAST

by John Kimantas

whitecap

Whitecap Books

Edited by Elaine Jones
Proofread by Joan E. Templeton
Cover by Michelle Mayne & Jacqui Thomas
Interior design by Jacqui Thomas
Typeset by Five Seventeen & Diane Yee
Photography and maps by John Kimantas (www.thewildcoast.ca)
Author photo by Iris "Zippy" Lancaster

Printed and bound in Canada

LIBRARY AND ARCHIVES CANADA CATALOGUING IN PUBLICATION

Kimantas, John
The wild coast 2 / John Kimantas.
Includes index.
ISBN: 1-55285-786-7
ISBN: 978-1-55285-786-1
1. Kayaking—British Columbia—Pacific Coast—Guidebooks. 2. Pacific Coast (B.C.)—Guidebooks. I. Title. II. Title: Wild coast two.
GV776.15.B7K552 2006 797.122'4'097111 C2005-906781-0

The publisher acknowledges the financial support of the Government of Canada through the Book Publishing Industry Development Program for our publishing activities.

Contents

Acknowledgements

Many people assisted in the compilation of information for this book including (in alphabetical order) Gus Angus, Harvey Bergen, Cliff Doiron, Raelene Dudoward, Alan Hobler, Larry Jorgenson, intrepid campsite finders Michael and James Luce, Andrew Martindale, Anne McCarthy, Ed McDonald, Stuart Millham, Serge Pare, Dennis Rose, Paul Tataryn and Jeremy Webb.

Government agencies lending assistance include B.C. Parks, Ministry of Forests and Range, Environment Canada Weather Office, Land Information B.C., B.C. Ministry of Energy, Mines and Petroleum Resources (B.C. Geological Survey) and Canadian Coast Guard Marine Communication and Traffic Services Centre in Prince Rupert.

Others assisted with the logistics of the summer-long kayak expedition behind this book, most notably Richard Antonchuk, Lou Pescarmona, Frank Kimantas, Carey Lockwood, Joe O'Blenis, Kitimat hosts Don Pearson and Wayne Pritchell and Prince Rupert host Joe Paolinelli. Peace of mind came courtesy of Bill and Joka Wright and Gerrit McGowan, who backed up my digital photos en route.

Several businesses were also kind enough to unconditionally support the 2005 coastal expedition:

- Alberni Outpost (the centre of the kayaking universe at **www.albernioutpost.com**)
- Seaward Kayaks (**www.seawardkayaks.com**)
- Northwater (**www.northwater.com**)
- Clif Bars (**www.clifbar.com**)

Mist near Cherry Islets, Squally Channel

Foreword

I PULLED MY KAYAK OUT OF THE WATER AT PORT HARDY, BRITISH COLUMBIA on September 2, 2005, 92 days after I first launched. I had paddled 3,404 km (2,115 miles)—or more than 6 times the distance between Port Hardy and Alaska. I had explored B.C.'s most secluded inlets and ventured out to some of the most remote archipelagos. During the trip I encountered 9-m (30-foot) swell, a bear standing on my kayak, a sleeping humpback whale and scenery too beautiful to describe. I was rained on for 13 days straight, blown down channels despite my best efforts to go in the other direction and went days, occasionally weeks, without seeing another soul. I travelled into areas where kayaks rarely go and discovered, for possibly the first time in my life, what it is like to be a pioneer.

Despite our shrinking planet, so much of the B.C. coast remains remote and unexplored.

I had several goals when I set out to write this book. First I wanted to provide an overview of the north and central B.C. coast through photographs, maps and descriptions—a shopping list, if you like, of possible destinations that others might one day like to explore.

A second goal was to demystify some aspects of the coast, particularly the idea that the Inside Passage is a difficult, distant and exclusive place to journey. I also wanted to raise the profile of the Outside Passage, about which very little has been written.

A third goal was to compile a list of camping opportunities along the coast. A reasonable network of campsites *should* exist by now; sadly it was still lacking when I ventured out in late spring of 2005. This information is critical for kayakers. Never did I encounter a group without at some point huddling down over a chart and sharing what little we knew about camping locations. I hope this book will take away some of the anxiety of where to set up camp while travelling the coast.

Last, wherever possible I wanted to share historical and ecological trivia to bring these regions to life. Not being a historian or an ecologist, I relied on other sources for this information. A great help was the province's coastal management plans and the various park management plans compiled by B.C. Parks. For specific navigation information I consulted *Sailing Directions*, published by Fisheries and Oceans Canada. The origin of place names was explained wherever possible courtesy of Land Information B.C.'s Geographical Name Information Service. Captain John T. Walbran's work *British Columbia Coast Names*, though now a century old, has never been superceded. It provided valuable backup.

More information on these publications and other sources is provided in the bibliography.

There were, of course, the many helpful people in government, tourism agents and individuals who enthusiastically passed on information and first-hand knowledge. Sharing information with people (however few) met on the coast also proved invaluable. My belief continues to hold true: there are no warmer people than those met on a cold, wet coast.

Introduction

THE B.C. COAST IS A PLACE SHROUDED IN MYSTERY, OFTEN SEEN AS STORMY, remote and inaccessible—beautiful but too perilous to explore. There are stories of fabled white bears, of yachtsmen who sailed into magically untouched coves surrounded by mile-high mountains, of places where waterfalls cascade in numbers too numerous to count and salmon run so thick grizzlies can scoop them out while standing on the shore.

We had to take their word for these stories, of course. Many of these places were truly a mystery. Major portions of the coast weren't charted until 1991. Small pockets remain uncharted today.

Occasionally a hardy soul would paddle the coast and return with epic tales of braving the elements by canoe or kayak—struggling against nature and eventually conquering the Inside Passage. We revelled in these stories about the wealth of nature along the coast and the difficulties entailed in reaching it.

While this pioneering spirit is still very much alive, the coast is undergoing a transformation. The doors are finally opening.

Perhaps more than anything else, B.C. Ferries has opened up the coast with its Inside Passage and Discovery Coast Passage routes, which provide vehicle, foot and even kayak access to remote communities such as Bella Bella, Klemtu and Ocean Falls. Through a wet-launch service, paddlers can now explore many points in between.

Resorts have popped up. Those like Hakai, Shearwater and Koeye River cater to wilderness lovers in areas otherwise the realm of fishing lodges only.

Old communities like Namu and Ocean Falls are returning to life. The First Nations communities of Klemtu, Hartley Bay and Metlakatla are embracing their past and diversifying their economy

Alaska
Portland Inlet
Dixon Entrance
Work Channel
Chatham Sound
PRINCE RUPERT
Skeena River
Terrace
Smithers
Telkwa
Granisle
Houston
16
37
KITIMAT
Porcher I.
HECATE STRAIT
Grenville Channel
Douglas Channel
Principe Channel
Pitt I.
Banks I.
Gardner Canal
Wright Sound
Nepean Sound
NORTH COAST
Princess Royal I.
Princess Royal Channel
Caamaño Sound
KLEMTU
Aristazabal I.
Laredo Sound
Roderick I.
SPIRIT BEAR
Milbanke Sound
Dean Channel
Burke Channel
BELLA COOLA
BELLA BELLA
King I.
Queen Charlotte Islands
QUEEN CHARLOTTE SOUND
Queens Sound
Fitz Hugh Sound
KATIT
Calvert I.
Rivers Inlet
Smith Sound
Continental Slope
CENTRAL COAST
Kingcome Inlet
QUEEN CHARLOTTE STRAIT
Vancouver Island Shelf
PORT HARDY
Port McNeill
Alert Bay
Johnstone Strait
Port Alice
Transition Pacific
Miles
40
80
Km
40
80
120
Vancouver Island
Zeballos

with travel and tourism packages, from kayak trips to cultural heritage tours. Water taxis provide access to areas once difficult to reach, and the growth in popularity of kayaking allows the exploration of areas considered too hazardous to navigate by deep-keeled boats.

Despite the opportunities, tourism in B.C.'s north and central coast is still in its infancy. Infrastructure consists of a few docks, fuelling stations and stores selling basic provisions—fewer services than the days when coal-powered steamships ran the coast. There are few coastal towns on the outer reaches, just Bella Bella, Klemtu, Hartley Bay and Lax Kw'alaams. The major communities of Prince Rupert, Kitimat and Bella Coola provide the only road access.

In other words, wilderness is still the backdrop for almost the entire B.C. coast.

FOR BOATERS

This is not a cruising guide, but rather an overview of the features of the coast. The intricacies of anchorages are well covered in guides that have done an excellent job for decades now. As a minimum I have included information on boat havens, those provincially recognized anchorages with official standing, plus a few key sites I know of and a few strategic anchorages detailed in *Sailing Directions*.

While the camping information provided in this book won't apply to most boaters, there is a growing but little-used opportunity to see the coast through boat camping. Fuel docks are numerous enough along the coast that a family or a group can travel by small motorized boat or dinghy to end the day on a beach. This is a cheap alternative to owning or renting a yacht. It allows just as much access to the coast as yachts and is comparable to kayaking in the amount of shore you can visit—and without having the same limitations in terms of speed.

This is an attractive option for families with young children, where kayaking isn't practical. Beaches will have more room than most cabin cruisers anyway, and kids can relax on the beach during the day while the dads go fishing for dinner. Light inflatable boats can be carried up the beach at night, and the speed of a motor eliminates many of the hazards that kayaks face, such as tides, currents and weather changes.

THE RULES OF THE COAST

Anyone who plans to spend time on the open B.C. coast should be prepared for the hazardous conditions. To minimize repeating the same information for each location in the book, certain hazards should be taken for granted. That is, they will be the norm rather than the exception.

- Currents in inlets will generally run into the inlet in flood (rising) tides and out of the inlet in ebb (falling) tides. This also holds true of most connecting channels. But there is no guarantee. Freshet—freshwater runoff from streams and rivers into the ocean—will very often alter the time of slack tides, shorten flood tides or even override the flood currents altogether. Whether this happens depends on many factors, including spring tides (see page 17), the time of year, the amount of recent rain and even the depth of the snowpack that accumulated over the winter on nearby mountains. This all means that particular conditions are difficult to calculate, but be prepared for the possibility of a more difficult journey into an inlet than out of it—outflow winds nothwithstanding.

- Inflow and outflow winds will affect most inlets and channels near major inlets. These winds are generated independent of prevailing ocean conditions and vary according to the differentiation of ocean and inland temperatures. This makes them unpredictable. Only one interior waterway, Douglas Channel, is given special consideration by Environment Canada in marine weather forecasts. The weather service will occasionally comment on the possibility of inflow or outflow winds near mainland inlets, but this is the exception, not the rule. This means you must generally rely on your own weather forecasting. In prevailing summer weather conditions, outflow winds will occur in the morning and then shift to inflow with the warming inland temperatures in the afternoon. The problem is prevailing weather conditions don't prevail as often as you might hope on the B.C. coast. Instead you may find inflow or outflow winds continuing unabated for days.

- Tidal currents can run at several knots in any channel and even in areas of open coast. Occasionally directions of currents are marked on charts. If they aren't, expect them to run in the same

Darby Channel, Rivers Inlet.

direction of other nearby currents, though there will be exceptions. Wherever possible tidal currents are explained in this book. In many areas currents are variable, unpredictable or so complex as to appear unpredictable. Be prepared that in many locations it may not be as simple as waiting six hours for the next tide change.

- Wind can build up surface currents that override tidal currents. This can mean if you wait out a change in tide in the morning to take advantage of a favourable current later in the day, you might find the rising afternoon winds worse than the tide you avoided.

- When wind opposes the tidal current, the result can be choppy water. If you find you are in a situation where the size and sharpness of the wind waves and the number of whitecaps seem out of all proportion to the strength of wind, you are probably experiencing this condition. Consider pulling out until slack tide. You will be surprised how quickly a tumultuous ride flattens into a serene waterway once the tide changes.

- When waterways collide, expect turbulence. This will occur whenever inlets, channels, sounds or the open ocean mix. The turbulence can be tidal rips, whirlpools, eddies, standing waves or just a general confusion of the waters. If these conditions are known for being particularly violent or dangerous, they will be mentioned in the description for that region; otherwise they are likely to be more alarming than dangerous. Note these conditions are usually quite localized and dependent on tides, winds and the height of swell. Conditions are usually more severe in stronger winds.

- Winds will rise in the afternoon. The prevailing weather pattern should be lightest winds in the morning and a series of increases until the highest winds in mid-afternoon. For this reason it is strongly advised that open water crossings are planned for the morning. A common mistake of novices is to enjoy a serene morning trip only to find adversely strong winds in the afternoon. The best strategy is to leave early in the morning and plan to be off the water or in a sheltered location near early afternoon. If the winds don't rise, keep going, but if you are counting on travelling in the afternoon you may find yourself in deteriorating conditions with no shelter nearby.

Naturally, the prospect of rising afternoon wind varies with particular weather conditions. Inlets may be prone to inflow or outflow winds independent of the prevailing coastal weather conditions. In poor weather conditions, winds may be strong at sunrise. If this is the case, it's a good indication to stay off the water. Monitor marine weather forecasts and pay attention to weather reports for nearby stations for the possibility that rough weather may be heading your way.

PRIMARY COASTAL FEATURES

Here are some general descriptions of features you'll see on the coast that may help with deciding where to travel.

Major inlets

These long inlets have long been the domain of cabin cruisers that can meander up the channels, anchor at some sheltered spot, then meander out again the next day. It is an ideal way to enjoy the waterfalls and mountain scenery.

Kayakers, on the other hand, face numerous hurdles. Inflow or outflow winds, funnelling of wind through the inlet, and tidal currents can hamper travel. The few beaches to be found in inlets will almost certainly be rough and rocky. Sediment is rare except at estuaries, which do not make for good camping. Estuaries tend to be mucky places to camp and, more importantly, from an ecological standpoint, are easily disturbed. Camping in inlets is generally limited to rough, rocky beaches and alongside creek beds. The good news is that once you have accepted the idea of less than ideal camping conditions, spots won't be difficult to find.

Spring tides—an important warning: Spring tides refer to the period when the sun, moon and earth are the closest to being in alignment. There are two types of spring tides—at the new moon when the sun and moon are on the same side of the earth, and at the full moon when the sun and moon are on opposite sides of the earth. The highest spring tides are at the full moon. The lowest tides, called neap tides, occur at quarter moons.

The term "spring tide" is unfortunate because it occurs year-round and has nothing at all to do with the spring season (it does have to do with the tides "springing" forth and back again). The term "maximum high tide" might better reflect the reality, but the accepted term is spring tide, and this book will follow the norm. The danger lies in someone misunderstanding the meaning and discounting the information about spring tide levels because he or she is planning a trip for late summer during the full moon, not during the spring.

As tide levels are exceptionally higher at spring tides, camps can be washed out and improperly stored boats or kayaks can be swept away. One kayaker near Butedale who misread the tide took the precaution of securing his kayak to a drift log on the beach. Unfortunately both his kayak and the log floated away. So paying attention to tide levels can be critical.

A campsite on a rough beach at Surf Inlet.

The highlight of inlets is the wonderful mountain scenery. Unfortunately, mountains attract cloud cover, and you may find the most attractive feature of your journey hidden for days on end.

Some travellers will be drawn to the beauty and seclusion of inlets, and to the challenge of completing a waterway to its head. Coupled with large rivers or portages into lakes, a journey by paddle can extend far inland into breathtaking areas such as into Kitlope Heritage Conservancy (see Chapter 7, Kitimat). These journeys will be of special interest to those who are willing to overlook the drawbacks of inlets for the sake of experiencing a wonderful portion of coast few are ever likely to visit. Other suggestions for rewarding trips into inlets include Work Channel and Quottoon Inlet near Prince Rupert (Chapter 9), Laredo Inlet or Surf Inlet in Princess Royal Island (Chapter 6) and Spiller Channel to Ellerslie Bay north of Bella Bella (Chapter 3).

Small inlets, coves and bays

A wonderful feature of the B.C. coast is the convoluted shoreline. Often shallow and reef-strewn, these areas are perfectly suited to exploration by paddle or small boat.

These sheltered shorelines have not been pounded into rock bluffs or scenic headlands by open ocean conditions and the scenery can be repetitive. The rock shoreline and thick, steep forest cover tends to have little variation. Still, many travellers enjoy exploring these nooks and crannies. The waters are often calm and the places magical, with moss-draped trees extending out over narrow, twisting passages. These routes are best for travellers who appreciate details. Viewed with an artist's eye, visitors won't leave disappointed.

Sea urchins marooned at low tide.

Lagoons

Lagoons are shallow bodies of water cut off from the sea and can range from tiny to huge, such as Wyclees Lagoon off Smith Sound or Elizabeth Lagoon north of Fish Egg Inlet.

The B.C. coast has numerous lagoons, including many on inlets. As most inlets are rarely explored, you can be sure the lagoons are virtually untouched.

Lagoons are usually connected to the ocean by a narrow channel, resulting in strong currents that can be dangerous. Tidal chutes—drops in elevation—and rapids are very common. Transit is safest at slack tide, and slack tides can be difficult to predict. Rarely do slack tide times coincide with the turn of the tide elsewhere in the region. Also, be strongly advised that passages may initially appear to be nothing more than river entrances, drawing you in, only to reveal tidal rapids farther along.

Tide change times for lagoons used in this book come from *Sailing Directions* if they are available.

Dean Channel.

Major channels and passages

Given their significance, these major routes are described in detail. Most are transit corridors used by ferries, cruise ships and commercial traffic of all types. Hazards are generally few, and problems are limited simply to the management of tidal currents, wind funnelling and boat traffic.

Anchorages and camping options in these waterways are generally good. They are listed for each location in the appropriate text.

Secondary channels and waterways

These are for more adventurous travellers who wish to stay away from major routes. These alternatives are most prevalent in the area around Bella Bella and near Kitimat. For instance, you can avoid the Inside Passage traffic of Lama Passage toward Bella Bella by taking Gunboat Passage. Or you can avoid the worst of the inflow winds Douglas Channel is famous for by taking Verney Passage, which is (arguably) a more scenic option anyway.

Archipelagos

Island clusters probably offer the best opportunities for exploring on the coast. The waters can be protected, the campsites better and the features are generally more varied.

The west and south shores of the clusters—the most exposed sides—will generally be the most appealing, with high rock bluffs and twisted, wind-battered forests above. The bluffs will become less prominent in inner channels, and the north and east extents of a cluster lose these features entirely, with shorelines akin to inland waterways and inlets.

The coastal archipelagos are generally covered detail in this book.

Narrows

These are areas where passages constrict, and the B.C. coast has a few famous ones. The constriction will almost certainly (but not always) mean a much faster tidal current and may even lead to dangerous conditions.

The most prominent on the Inside Passage is Heikish Narrows north of Klemtu (see Fiordland, Chapter 5). Its location on a main route has earned it its own entry in the *Canadian Tide and Current Tables Volume 7, Queen Charlotte Sound to Dixon Entrance*. Oddly, the current rarely exceeds 2 knots and is not of much greater velocity than the neighbouring channels. It does, however, provide a base for calculating slack currents for the secondary stations also listed in the current tables, those being Draney Narrows (Chapter 1), Perceval Narrows (Mathieson Channel, Chapter 5) and Porcher Narrows (Chapter 9). Narrows such as those

A tidal rapid at Man Trap Inlet, Fish Egg Inlet.

in Jackson Passage (Chapter 5) and Union Passage (Chapter 8) are not listed in the tide guide. See the entry for each location for more information.

If you are visiting Nakwakto Rapids (Chapter 1), it has its own current table in *Canadian Tide and Current Tables, Volume 6, Discovery Passage and West Coast of Vancouver Island*.

There are also a few passages with narrows that become significant tidal rapids. They are Gale Passage (Bella Bella, Chapter 3), Griffin Passage (Fiordland, Chapter 5) and west of Philip Island (Prince Rupert, Chapter 9). They are generally passable only at slack high water and because of the complexity are considered adventurers' routes only.

Smith Sound.

Sounds

A sound is defined as a long, relatively wide body of water considered larger than a strait or a channel, or simply a long, wide ocean inlet. It is a definition loosely applied. As a result sounds are difficult to categorize. For instance, we have an Estevan Sound west of Campania Island and a larger Squally Channel on Campania Island's east side. Or contrast Smith Sound with the nearby and larger Rivers Inlet. The tiny waterway just south of the McNaughton Group is called Cultus Sound, whereas other larger bodies of water go unnamed.

If you find yourself in a sound that appears to be an inlet (such as Fitz Hugh Sound), treat it as such when you are trying to determine its characteristics. Major sounds such as Queens Sound have a personality all of their own. See the individual text for more details.

ABOUT THE WEATHER

A little honesty up front might be in order. If the success of your holiday relies on warm weather and sunshine, travel elsewhere. Pick up a brochure for trips to Tahiti, because the B.C. coast probably isn't for you.

While prolonged sunny stretches can and do happen on the coast, they are rare. More likely a series of low-pressure systems will blow in, bringing clouds and rain. And even if you do get good weather, there is a general pattern that may not sound appealing. Mornings will most often begin with fog or cloud cover. This will bring the possibility of morning showers or drizzle. Then a general clearing will take place through the rest of the day. This could mean partly sunny skies, clouds with sunny breaks or even clear sunshine. If you do get sunshine, it is astonishing how quickly it can come. I remember crossing Fitz Hugh Sound into Namu and seeing one tiny patch of sunshine on the hills behind the town. It was the only sunlight as I passed outlying Kiwash Island. By the time I reached the dock at Namu 15 minutes later all the clouds had somehow lifted and I was in bright sunshine. I have no idea how or where the clouds went, but go they did.

The outer coast: The two major coastal routes are the Inside and Outside Passages, but there is a third option: the outer coast or offshore route. It is an attractive place to travel for the same reason it is avoided—the untamed open ocean.

Untamed does not mean unvisited. A few areas of the outer coast are among the more heavily used. Fishing resorts have picked key locations, meaning high concentrations of boat traffic in areas where you would expect seclusion. This is definitely the case for outer Aristazabal and Athlone islands, where resorts make the concentration of boat traffic about the highest on the coast during the fishing season.

Outer Banks Island is probably the least travelled. A trip involves 80 km (50 miles) of difficult coastline; with few campsites or anchorages it is suitable only for the most experienced and adventurous travellers. For this reason the offshore route is not suggested as a formal kayaking route. Some ocean sections can be paddled in a day, such as Dundas Island, the Dufferin Group, the Goose Group and portions of Hakai. These are covered in more detail, as they can be safely enjoyed if weather conditions are closely monitored.

Naturally, all areas of open coast are prone to swell and the full brunt of ocean weather. The upside is the wind doesn't funnel. I can say this is truly a blessing after having been stopped dead by wind many times in interior inlets while the marine weather was recording low winds elsewhere on the coast. It's another example of my belief that all portions of the coast are safe if navigated in the correct circumstances.

If the sun shines, expect to see wisps of cloud on the horizon in the afternoon. These may drift in as the day continues, giving patchy or hazy sunshine.

On many days, the cloud cover will remain over mountains the entire day—either as small fluffy halos capping the mountain peaks or as thick cloud cover. It's quite possible to be in brilliant sunshine on the outer coast and see the nearby inner coast obscured in heavy clouds.

Fog or clouds will generally re-form overnight, and the cycle will begin again.

A cool, wet and heavily overcast day on Princess Royal Channel—typical coastal weather.

Of course, for every generalization there are as many exceptions. After spending 92 days on the coast in 2005, I tabulated the weather I experienced and found there were just 3 days with complete horizon-to-horizon sunshine. That meant 89 days with some cloud cover and 42 days in which some rain fell. For 40 days there was no sunshine to speak of at all.

In tabulating the prevailing weather each day, I would say that 31 days were generally rainy, 31 cloudy and 30 could be categorized as mostly sunny. That's a little subjective, though, as on many days it was a toss-up between whether it was mainly sunny or mainly cloudy.

At its worst I encountered 13 days with rain in a row. The longest stretch during that was 100 hours without a break in the rain. (I was a tad wet and cranky when I pulled up at Butedale at the tail end of the 100 hours in a row.)

The accompanying map shows the weather stations used by Environment Canada in VHF marine weather forecasts. The chart cross-references averages for each station. Additional weather information is provided under the station headings.

The Wild Coast, Volume I referred to daily average temperatures in the weather summaries. That statistic is a bit misleading, as it simply averages out the highs and lows for any given day; this volume instead refers to average daytime maximum and minimum temperatures. These should be more useful, as they indicate the warmest temperature you can expect on any given afternoon and the coolest point overnight.

Wind speed "averages" are the only way wind is recorded. Weather stations take note of wind speed and direction several times a day and average those readings. That means if the morning is calm and the winds rise progressively to 55.5 km/h (30 knots), then fall progressively to calm the next morning, the daytime average will be 27.8 km/h (15 knots). Since averages are not a way to predict field conditions, the usefulness of this statistic probably lies in comparing various stations. The results shouldn't be a surprise, as the most exposed stations have the highest average wind.

	Egg Island	Addenbroke Island	Dryad Point	Bella Coola	McInnes Island	Boat Bluff	Kitimat	Bonilla Island	Prince Rupert	Green Island
RAIN (mm)										
June	124	158	138	64	131	219	89	102	123	108
July	78	100	104	53	100	166	66	81	114	105
August	103	136	133	62	131	218	95	102	155	153
September	168	246	207	115	197	358	204	164	244	240
Annual (cm)	256	328	252	165	259	502	273	212	259	244
LOW TEMPS (°C)										
June	9.3	9.8	9.8	9.3	9.6	9.0	9.5	9.3	8.0	9.8
July	11.0	11.7	11.8	11.4	11.5	10.8	12.0	11.1	10.1	11.7
August	11.3	12.1	12.1	11.3	12.0	11.1	12.1	11.7	10.3	11.9
September	9.4	10.1	10.3	8.0	10.6	9.5	8.9	10.5	7.6	10.0
HIGH TEMPS (°C)										
June	14.0	15.7	16.9	19.5	14.7	16.7	19.0	13.3	14.2	15.4
July	15.7	17.7	18.9	22.1	16.5	18.7	21.9	15	16.1	17.2
August	16.1	17.9	19.2	22.0	16.9	19.0	21.8	15.6	16.7	17.3
September	14.5	15.7	16.6	18.1	15.4	16.4	17.3	14.3	14.9	14.5
WIND (km/h)										
June	16.2	14.2	8.5	10.8	15.0	7.1	-	23.7	11.3	-
July	14.5	13.1	7.7	11.0	13.5	6.3	-	22.4	9.6	-
August	14.2	13.1	7.3	9.2	12.9	6.0	-	-	9.6	-
September	15.1	12.8	8.0	7.1	-	7.1	-	-	10.8	-
Prevailing (summer):	NW	N	SW	W	NW	SE			W/SE	-
Highest:	137	97	109	83	130	85	40	143	93	157
DAYS OF MODERATE RAIN*										
June	7.6	8.6	8.5	4.4	7.7	9.9	6.0	6.5	8.1	6.5
July	4.8	5.6	6.2	3.7	5.8	8.2	3.9	4.8	7.6	6.4
August	6.2	7.3	7.8	4.2	6.7	9.5	5.8	6.0	8.5	8.2
September	7.8	9.8	10.5	6.5	9.5	12.1	8.8	8.6	11.1	11.4

*Moderate rain = 5 mm /0.2 inches or more

For further reading, consider Environment Canada's *Living with Weather along the British Columbia Coast* by Owen S. Lange. It and other weather-related publications can be viewed at **www.weather office.pyr.ec.gc.ca/promotion/default_e.html**.

ABOUT CHARTS

GPS units equipped with electronic charts are gaining popularity for aiding marine navigation, but they cannot be relied upon as the sole source of chart information. Standard Hydrographic Service of Canada charts designed for boats should still be the primary source of navigation information, as cumbersome as they may be.

For those who do use GPS units for navigation, a handy addition to this volume are waypoints for camping locations. Most GPS units are capable of pre-programming waypoints. By adding the waypoints to your GPS before departing you can greatly reduce the mystery and stress of locating campsites.

The charts you are likely to need are shown in the accompanying map. On my three-month-long kayak trip I took mostly the small-scale maps (those marked in pink), as smaller-scale maps cover a larger area. A few large-scale maps (those in blue outline) filled the gaps where necessary, and on a few areas I went with faith and a reliance on my GPS. For instance, I did not pack chart 3724 so I did not have Dewdney Island on paper. Naturally, the electronic GPS chart failed early in the trip, so for a few areas I was actually navigating by the rough drafts of the maps used in this volume (not recommended at all). Fortunately I found my way home eventually anyway.

On the attached chart list I added U.S. chart 17441 as an option for the Prince Rupert area, as it does a slightly better job of the Prince Rupert approaches than Canadian chart 3927. Other charts than those shown may be available, as this selection just represents an overview of the main charts you may need.

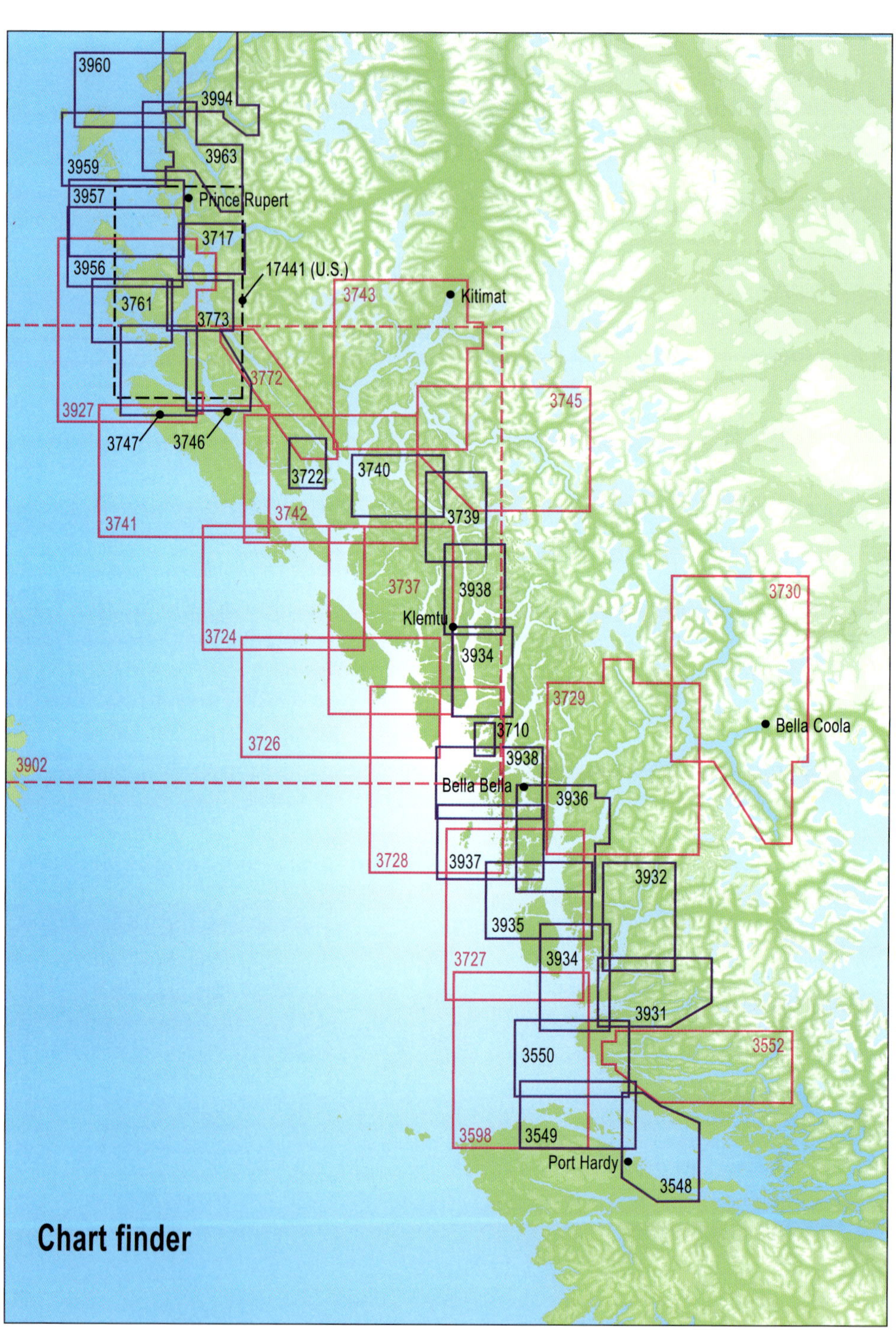
3960
3994
3963
3959
3957
Prince Rupert
3717
3956
17441 (U.S.)
3761
3773
3743
Kitimat
3772
3745
3927
3747
3746
3722
3740
3739
3741
3742
3737
3938
Klemtu
3724
3934
3730
3729
3726
3710
Bella Coola
3902
3938
Bella Bella
3936
3728
3937
3932
3935
3727
3934
3931
3550
3552
3598
3549
Port Hardy
3548
Chart finder

ABOUT THE *WILD COAST* MAPS

As regions are not necessarily the correct shape for the rectangle of page sizes, overlaps tend to appear on most maps in *The Wild Coast*. White lines mark the divisions. Anything outside the white line falls into the realm of a different chapter or region. Orange text on the edge of the map indicates where to look for adjoining maps.

For the record, it's worth stating the following.

- Most chapters have additional regional maps, but not all. If there is no regional map, look to the main map accompanying each chapter to locate areas discussed in the text.
- Regional maps are shown on the main map for each chapter and are marked with a corresponding page number.
- Icons are only placed on the main chapter maps if there are no regional maps. Otherwise look to the regional maps for the campsite and anchorage markers.
- Elevation markers are provided where possible on regional maps. In most cases, elevations were verified for named mountains. For other peaks, elevations were estimated through contours on topography maps. These markers are rounded to the nearest 100 m (328 feet), and actual elevations may be slightly higher—as much as 99 m.

MAP SYMBOLS

Rest area: This denotes a beach that may be used as an emergency campsite or a place for a picnic or break. While camping *may* be possible, the site did not meet my criteria for a desirable campsite.

Spring tide campsite: The blue tent indicates a campsite with a developed camping area in the uplands or a high-backed beach that will withstand spring (highest) tides.

Undeveloped campsite: The red tent icon is for beaches that have not yet been developed and may not be useable during a spring tide in their current state. These were picked as the best choice, of possible camping beaches in the area.

Marine trail site: Purple tent icons mark campsite locations indicated in the B.C. Ministry of Forests' marine trail audit. These are sites that did not overlap my inventory. See page 38 for details.

Anchorage: This icon is used to indicate the location of recognized all-weather anchorages. It is not comprehensive, as this guide is not intended to replace cruising guides.

Launch site: This icon indicates locations suitable for launching small boats or kayaks from road access.

Lighthouse: This symbol is used for manned lighthouse locations. It does not indicate lighted buoys or navigation beacons.

Marina: This icon shows the location of docks, either privately owned for public use or government wharfs.

Trail: Purple dotted lines indicate recognized hiking routes. Most coastal routes are not maintained and may be overgrown and in some cases impassable. See the text for details.

Cabin: This icon denotes a public-use cabin. The Haisla in the Kitimat region have created a considerable number that are free for public use. The Heiltsuk have also built a fair number, with most available to the public. The Kitasoo Xai'xais have a cabin rental program. See the text for details.

Bird nesting area: Seabird nesting locations.

Parkland: Orange land indicates provincial parkland or an ecological reserve. Marine areas and some terrestrial areas that are protected are indicated by a hatched orange line. Solid orange parkland and hatched outlines are used interchangeably. The reason for this is practical: hatched lines can be difficult to see in some situations, while solid orange can obscure details such as elevation contours. Note that the Kitasoo Spirit Bear designated area on Princess Royal Island is marked, though it is not yet a park.

Municipality: Grey areas outlined in purple indicate municipalities (towns, villages or cities). First Nations communities are not marked in this way, as they are on reserve property.

Indian Reserve: The pink on maps indicates First Nations (Indian) land as allotted generally in the 1880s. It is likely that within the next decade the amount of reserve land will increase substantially as land settlements are reached. Reserve land should be treated as private property. *Map numbers*: The coloured numbers set inside boxes on maps refer to pages with more detailed maps for the area indicated within the box.

Map numbers: The coloured numbers set inside boxes on maps refer to pages with more detailed maps for the area indicated within the box.

CAMPING ON THE COAST

Many of the best kayak trips aren't just about where you paddle. They're also about where you end up at the end of the day. To me the ideal campsite is a beautiful beach overlooking a mountainous passage or looking out between reefs and headlands to an open ocean. The beach should have a smattering of driftwood logs to use as furniture. The sand should be clean—the type you enjoy walking upon at the surf line.

Unfortunately, this is exceedingly rare in some portions of the coast, and finding suitable campsites can be a major hurdle to kayaking (or boat camping). The problem isn't necessarily a lack of beaches. It can simply be the tides.

If you look at a typical shoreline of inner coast you'll see the treeline ends in an almost perfectly straight line. Green branches may hang down below rocks, over beaches and above intertidal grasses, but no matter the situation, the dryland greenery will drop down to an almost perfectly uniform edge. This straight line marks the highest tide line.

This can be hard to appreciate, as you may travel past the shore at the day's high tide and see the water is still many feet away from the treeline. This is because all tides are not equal. As well as operating on roughly a 25-hour cycle, tide heights vary over the course of the month (see page 17).

Tide levels also vary along the B.C. coast. For instance, at Bella Bella the spring tide is about 5 m (17 feet) during the summer. In Prince Rupert, it is about 7 m (23 feet). But be assured that come the full moon, no matter the regional tide level, the result is the same: the high water will rise to where the upland's vegetation ends.

At the July 23, 2005, spring tide at Elbow Point in Petrel Channel I tied my kayak up to trees at the very top of the beach. Had I been paying attention I would have noticed the water line on the trunk. The moss on the trees my kayak was sitting upon led me astray (in retrospect the moss, usually a dryland feature, was actually an alga), so I misjudged the tide by over a metre (four feet), waking up in the middle of the night to find my kayak ready to sail without me. Thankfully it was tied up.

All too often the beach ends at steep, rocky upland capped with impenetrable forest. Venturing into the forest is just about impossible, let alone finding a clear, level campsite.

Contrast this with open-ocean beaches where surf is the norm. Waves from storms have battered the shoreline, built up the sand on the beach and driven back the upland vegetation. This usually allows for great camping right on the sand. Protected inner channels, on the other hand, get no such storms. This means at spring tides the treeline and tide will meet, submerging the entire beach and leaving exceedingly few camping choices.

In researching a campsite network for this book I found myself stopping at innumerable beaches and picking through the forest cover hoping to find a clearing. Occasionally—much to my delight—I did find an established and/or useable tent clearing. Most often, though, I would walk along a beach and find no evidence that anyone had ever camped there before at spring tides. It was a constant reminder of the pioneering nature of exploring the B.C. coast. Strategic camping locations—points vital to transiting the coast—still had no developed tent areas. It begs the question: what have people been doing? The short answer is getting by however they can, even if that means sleeping on logs.

Random camping is often encouraged to avoid concentrating the impact of camping in just a few locations. While it may sound like wisdom, it is simply not practical on the B.C. coast. Campsites protected from spring tides are rare, and for these to evolve it requires clustering. Besides, good campsites can also evolve into wonderful places—where the moss, forest, drift logs and fallen trees combine to create natural, comfortable backdrops for low-impact, no-trace camping. If sited away from sensitive estuaries or wetlands, the environmental impact is limited to the ground cover—usually bushes that will grow back all too quickly if the site isn't maintained.

As much as I would have liked to deliver a complete network of established campsites in this book, it simply doesn't exist yet. So where no established campsites could be found, my role was limited to suggesting appropriate beaches where camping is possible. This prompted the creation of two types of icons on the maps. A blue tent icon designates locations with a developed upland to escape spring tides, while a red tent icon designates camping beaches where the upland is not yet clear.

A third icon, the purple tent, indicates a marine trail campsite (see page 38).

Blue icons were used occasionally where sufficient room was available to escape a spring tide on the high backing of a beach. This was only done where such clearance was beyond question. Many other beaches may have high backing, but I erred on the side of caution. An incorrect assessment of the tide clearance could lead to someone's camp being washed away come a full moon. If I hear back from enough people that a beach has spring tide protection, the icon should change to blue in the next edition (contribute your experiences to **www.thewildcoast.ca**). Many of these high-backed areas might seem unappealing, as they will be small squares set back in among trees, bushes or drift logs. The great thing about spring tides, though, is the high tide occurs in the middle of the night (usually about 2:30 a.m.). This means you have full use of the beach during the day, and need only pack up your belongings and stash them carefully before bed. I even left up my tarp in many cases, securing it with ties fastened to rocks that would be submerged at night but still be in place on a dry beach in the morning.

Another consideration was the number of beaches where camping was possible but not ideal. There were hundreds of these locations. Rather than designating them possible but marginal camping areas I decided upon another category: picnic sites, with a corresponding picnic icon on maps. Picnic sites are areas that could be campsites, but aren't choice. The beach might have been too grubby, lacked a view, was too exposed or was simply too near a better site. But they are worth knowing about for using as lunch stops, pee breaks or emergency campsites. Who knows, you may even like some as much as the campsites I chose.

The list of campsites is not exhaustive. Not every beach is listed, just those that appear better suited for a break or are in a strategic location to create a marine trail system. In cases where there are many beaches, the best-of-the-best are listed. In areas with few beaches, any or all options are listed.

While the tent site icons on the maps are meant to be helpful, it is worth reading the corresponding text to ensure the stop is appropriate for your group. Some sites may not accommodate large groups, for instance.

The campsite selection presented here, in many cases, is just the first step in creating a complete marine trail system for the upper

B.C. coast, not the last. When a true marine trail system evolves over the next 20 years or so, it could appear very different from what I'm proposing. Some good sites will have been missed from this list. Some that I dismissed may be another person's favourite. In areas where no established campsites yet exist, some people may find better beaches than those I chose to present here. For that reason, and many others, a website will be running by summer 2006 as an adjunct to *The Wild Coast* series that will list updates about camping opportunities. As campsites are improved, created or discovered, readers are invited to share their experiences to keep the campsite network up to date. Also, check for updates before planning a holiday. The website is **www.thewildcoast.ca**.

CAMPSITE TERMINOLOGY

Rather than invent different ways of describing the same thing, the descriptions for campsites and beaches in this book have been standardized for clarity. While sand is generally easily understood, some other terms are open to interpretation. To be consistent, here is a description of each type of beach listed in this book.

Atop the clamshell beach at Fin Island.

A "grubby" beach at south Troup Narrows—a mixture of stones, muck and seaweed but no large rocks, which makes this better than many rough beaches.

High-backed

This term is used to identify beaches that will remain partially exposed at spring tides. High-backed beaches will provide camping at all tide levels.

Upland

This describes the dryland vegetated or forested areas that lie above spring tide levels. Contrary to some other definitions, in this book "upland" describes all land above sea level.

Pebble

This indicates wave-rounded stones generally up to 2.5 cm (1 inch) in size.

Cobble

A cobble beach indicates wave-rounded stones generally 2.5 cm (an inch) in size to as large as 8 to 10 cm (3 to 4 inches) but sometimes as large as 15 cm (6 inches). Both cobble and pebble beaches make ideal campsites.

Grit

This indicates a sediment more coarse than sand. It is generally grey and mixed with stones. Despite sounding unappealing, grit beaches are ideal for camping. They form the majority of the best camping beaches on inner channels and inlets, where sand is rare.

Clamshell

These beaches are probably the best for camping. There is no sediment to track into tents or shoes, it is fairly soft for sleeping on and insects are few. The clamshells are usually crushed into small bits and wave-rounded to a foot-friendly smoothness. They are an appealing white and most often pile at or above the high tide line. Lower tide levels may be grit, stone, rock or clam beds.

Clamshell beaches can be found on the inside of many small islets that sit close to other larger land masses. The islets will become joined by a sand or grit bar with crushed clamshell on the highest portions. These are generally beautiful beaches in areas where beaches with sediment are rare. Several of these islets form the backbone of this book's campsite network in Fitz Hugh Sound and Fisher Channel as far as the entrance to Cousins Inlet. Usually a portion of these beaches will be high-backed, but the area may only be large enough to accommodate one or two tents at or near spring tides, making them unsuitable for larger groups unless there is also a developed upland (which is rare).

Stones

These are small rocks, generally no larger than 8 cm (3 inches), and are not wave-rounded. Large stones are 8 to 15 cm (3 to 6 inches) in size. Stone beaches are generally suitable for camping. On many beaches small stones are found at the higher levels with rocks at lower levels. Sand patches may be found at the highest portions of the beach.

Rocks

These are stones larger than 15 cm (6 inches). Rocky areas are almost always unsuitable for camping, though rock beaches can often have smaller rocks or stones at the high tide level, making them useful for emergency haulouts as the stones can be camped upon. Steep beaches and/or wave action can make landings on rock beaches difficult and

The B.C. Marine Trail concept:

The marine trail concept dates back to about 1996 with the creation of the B.C. Marine Trail Association. An inventory of campsites on the south B.C. coast was completed, and the association even managed to create a designated marine campground at Blackberry Point on Valdes Island in the Gulf Islands.

The ultimate goal is to establish a network of campsites within 16 km (10 miles) of one another along the coast as a marine link between Washington State and Alaska. The B.C. government picked up on the initiative, but hasn't exactly run with it. A marine trail audit was undertaken in 2001 by the Vancouver Forest District and revised in 2002. But the end report was never formally approved by the Ministry of Forests. And so now it sits collecting dust.

It was a case of a good idea at the wrong time. In 2002 the B.C. government had a change in strategy and decided to close forest recreation sites instead of adding more. More recently, the whole forest recreation site concept has been handed over to the Ministry of Tourism, which hopefully gives the concept a chance for reconsideration.

The shelved marine trail audit was a good start, but it was just that—a start. It only listed potential campsites as far north as the Central Coast. First Nations interests were not considered in the selection. Fieldwork was limited to two days on a float plane for an aerial assessment of sites. Because the project was cancelled in midstream, many of the sites were not inventoried at all.

After an initial chance to review part of the report, the ministry declined to release it in its complete form, as it was never formally approved. But an inventory report, however incomplete, is better than none. I have included some limited information from the marine trail site report in the text, identifiable by the phrase "marine trail site(s)." On the maps, some selected marine trail sites that might be useful and did not overlap my own inventory have been included. They are identified with a purple icon. I am unable to comment on the suitability of these sites, so proceed duly warned. Feedback is welcome at **www.thewildcoast.ca**.

sometimes perilous. Loading kayaks on rock beaches at falling tides is also a cause for misery. Many otherwise ideal sand beaches can become rock at lower tide levels. For this reason campsite options are more numerous when your arrival and departure coincide with high tides.

Clam beds

Found only at lower tide levels, clam beds are characterized by a gently sloping mud base, often interspersed with rocks. Both the clamshells and rocks can be covered with a gritty barnacle-type growth that is harmful to fibreglass hulls. Due to the gentle slope of these beaches, low tides can extend a considerable distance—a problem when the beds are particularly mucky. The lowest extent may be eelgrass. Often clam beds are the price to be paid for enjoying the perfect crushed

A makeshift campsite above a rock beach at Fisher Channel. This campsite didn't earn even a picnic icon in this book.

clamshell or sand beach above. Loading a kayak in a falling tide on a clam bed is to be avoided if possible. It pays to wait for the return of higher tides before launching from a clam bed beach.

Intertidal grasses

Beaches with intertidal grasses create frustratingly illusionary campsites. From a distance these alluring locations promise level and clear areas, a soft base to camp on and protection above high tides. In reality the grass usually hides rocks unsuitable for camping. The grasses are most often intertidal, and the presence of this green strip is no indication of the height of spring tides. In some cases there will be a green buffer of dryland grasses before the forest, but it is rare. Grass beaches should be a last resort for campsites unless you see that the top level of grass is interspersed with other plants, such as wildflowers. That's a good clue the grassy area at the top is dryland grass.

The *Queen of Chilliwack* passes Cascade Inlet.

MANAGING KAYAKS ON FERRIES

The advent of B.C. Ferries' Discovery Coast Passage service was a huge leap forward for both tourism on the coast and the ferry service itself. Never has a B.C. Ferries service been as flexible, including altering routes to view a pod of passing whales and dropping off kayakers at requested locations.

The drop-off service has been instrumental in opening up destinations normally difficult to reach. And yet it is underused, with just 50 kayakers requesting to be dropped off in the 2005 season. That's a ridiculously low number, considering the service it provides. Obviously the word has yet to get out.

The *Queen of Chilliwack* covers the Discovery Coast Passage route from the beginning of June to early September. Ports of call include Port Hardy, Bella Coola, Bella Bella, Shearwater, Ocean Falls and Klemtu.

The *Queen of Chilliwack* can hold 85 cars and 250 passengers. There is no current limit on the number of kayaks. The vessel has unloaded as many as 12 kayakers at a time, an endeavour that took just 20 minutes. The transition hasn't always been so speedy. One kayaker took 45 minutes to load his kayak because he brought canned goods in a barrel, and chose to load them into his kayak one can at a time.

It's a lesson to be prepared and be as fast as possible. The system works like this.

You can make your ferry reservations through the main B.C. Ferries service at **1-888-223-3779**, but it's best to contact the Port Hardy (Bear Cove) ferry terminal to make particular arrangements for the wet launch (call **250-949-6722**). The launches are always at the captain's discretion, and are dependent on weather and available light. The ferry will not drop off a kayaker in darkness, which is important when planning a trip. Drops that are possible in June when the days are longer won't be possible in August.

If darkness is a problem, the ferry will most likely continue until sunrise, then drop you at the first possible location nearest to your requested location. If weather is a factor, you may end up having to go to the next ferry terminal, so it's best to build some flexibility into your schedule and carry charts for the entire region.

At the ferry terminal, proceed to the baggage area to load your kayak onto a kayak dolly. You can then park your car in the terminal's long-term parking.

Once on the ferry, make contact with the staff. The captain will review your request for the wet launch and give it the official yea or nay. One common problem is requesting a drop-off point not on a particular ferry's route, as the route changes over the course of a week.

About an hour before the wet launch it is time to get ready. That means preparing your gear and kayak at the stern vehicle deck of the ferry. When the time comes the stern door is opened and a special platform designed for kayaks is lowered to sit just below the water level at the outer edge of the vehicle deck. The kayak is set on the platform for loading and the kayaker can paddle away when all is ready.

Pickup service—or wet loading—is also available. The process works in reverse but is usually simpler because there is less food and water on the kayak. A piece of carpet is placed over the edge of the ferry's vehicle deck door to minimize damage to the kayak when it is lifted over.

During the launch or load, two of the ferry's four engines are shut down. The two on the far end are used to keep the ship in station, with the ship placed to provide lee protection in the stern where the launch is taking place. The ferry is highly exposed with the stern door down. A wave washing up the ferry could capsize it.

Missing a launch isn't nearly as critical to an agenda as missing a wet landing. With a missed wet launch you can simply be dropped off at the next terminal. But missing a wet landing means you may have to wait for the next ferry. In the case of locations near Klemtu, that could be a week. For this reason many people request a wet launch and paddle over the course of their trip to a ferry terminal for transit home, arriving well in advance for peace of mind.

To plan your journey, see the schedule at **www.bcferries.com**. Since that doesn't necessarily make it clear where the ferry will be at any given time during the week, the schedule is discussed in more detail on page 55, with tips on how to use it to your advantage as a kayaker.

Something to keep in mind is that you will be charged the distance to the next port, even if you're dropped partway there. If, for instance, you request to be dropped off at Egg Island on a Thursday, you will be charged for the distance to Bella Coola. If you are dropped off on a Tuesday, you will be charged only to Bella Bella—a much cheaper journey, though your time aboard the ferry is the same in both cases.

If you choose to launch or land at a ferry terminal, be aware that at present the Bella Bella terminal is several miles south of town at McLoughlin Bay. The beach is rough rock and not well suited for landing or launching. Meanwhile, nearby Shearwater has a concrete boat ramp next to the terminal. Shearwater is also near facilities including laundry, a store, accommodation and—perhaps as a reward for a journey safely completed—a pub. In the planning stage by B.C. Ferries is a launch ramp specifically constructed for kayakers at McLoughlin Bay. Until that time it is probably better to meet the ferry in Shearwater.

The most popular drop-off points are Lama Passage, Middleton Point on Nalau Island and Sea Otter Inlet at Hakai.

MANAGING SHIPPING TRAFFIC

One daunting part of the coast is the prospect of meeting ship traffic. Many cruise ships now travel the Outside Passage to avoid narrow, congested portions of the inner route. They can be encountered in Laredo Channel, Squally Channel, Estevan Sound, Principe Channel and even tiny, twisting Lewis Passage. These huge ships are quick and quiet, and encountering one unexpectedly can be a shocking

A freighter passes through narrow and busy Grenville Passage.

experience for boaters and kayakers alike. Kayakers, of course, are more at risk, as they are slower-moving, less visible and don't show up on radar.

In cases of clear sightlines, encounters shouldn't be a problem. However, fog can occur at any time on the coast, and heavy rain can act like fog to obscure visibility. It can even be worse, as the sound of the rain can hide engine noise—or replicate it.

The good news is that shipping traffic along the coast is monitored. North of Cape Caution, control is managed by Canadian Coast Guard's Marine Communications and Traffic Services (MCTS) Centre in Prince Rupert. That station monitors two main frequencies. South of Baker Inlet to Cape Caution it is Channel 11. North of Baker Inlet it is Channel 71. South of Cape Caution is the jurisdiction of Comox Marine Communications and Traffic Services Centre (Channel 71).

Ships are required to contact traffic control at designated points and instruct the traffic control station on the estimated time of arrival at the next designated point. For instance, at Fog Rocks near Burke Channel ships must call in and give an estimated time for arriving at Dugout Rocks at Rivers Inlet. Anyone with a marine radio operator's licence can contact Prince Rupert vessel control on Channel 11 and request traffic information for that area. MCTS only asks that you have cause (such as fog or sightline concerns) to avoid spurious calls that could tie up the frequency.

Here is how it might work. If you call Prince Rupert MCTS as a kayaker crossing Fitz Hugh Sound at Hakai Passage, you may be alerted that a ship has just passed Fog Rocks and will be at Dugout Rocks in two hours, meaning it is likely to pass by your area in an hour. Given that it is 10 km (6 miles) from the entrance at Hakai Passage to Koeye River (your fictional destination), you will likely be mid-channel in an hour. So it would not be wise to proceed in fog on what could be a collision course. Even with good visibility, many kayakers may also wish to wait until the ship has passed to avoid being in the same general area.

A list of call-in points is included with the weather station map on page 25.

Most ships monitor Channel 11 and Channel 16 for emergency communication. Should you be in mid-channel and see a ship coming toward you, it might be wise to simply ask via marine radio, "Do you have me in sight?" You can be sure if they didn't see you before you called, the ship's crew will be searching for you with binoculars afterwards. MCTS advises you give an accurate description of yourself and the vessel you are trying to reach to avoid miscommunication. You don't need every ship on the coast suddenly on alert for a kayak.

Keep in mind the illusion that from several miles away in a 10-km-wide (6-mile) channel all vessels will seem to be heading straight for you. As they get closer it's easier to read the line of the hull, and it's not uncommon for ships to pass a half a mile (or almost a kilometre) distant when a collision seemed imminent 10 minutes before.

If you are truly in danger, radio communication may not be the best use of your time. If a ship looms out of the fog or appears suddenly from around a corner it wouldn't be wise to put down your paddle and start fiddling with the radio. It's not like the ship could turn to avoid you anyway, so paddle as fast as you can out of the way. The good news is ships are not that wide. A ship might be 30 m (100 feet) wide, and that is not a great distance to clear. At 2 m/s (4 knots) you can travel that distance in under 15 seconds. At 15.4 m/s (30 knots), the ship will cover just 235 m (256 yards) in that 15 seconds, or not even twice the length of one of the B.C. Ferries Spirit-class ferries, which is 167 m (549 feet). Assuming you sight the ship more than two ship lengths away, you should be fine. It might pass too close for comfort, but if you get away unscathed it's a happy ending.

If you are concerned about traffic but too shy to call Prince Rupert MCTS, you can always simply monitor channels 71 or 11. Ships will have to report at all call-in points, so it won't take long before you have a pretty good idea of what the traffic situation is like in your area.

MANAGING INSECTS

There were several areas of the coast I was warned to avoid due to bugs. Having visited them all, I can say that no particular region was worse than others. The problems seemed to be seasonal. Early June was almost bug-free. Then no-see-ums plagued the mornings and lasted several weeks (going onto months). Following them came what I call sand flies—insects smaller than but similar to house flies but with a propensity to bite and a likelihood to be found on sand beaches. (There are about 800 species of sand flies, and I was unable to find a scientific name for the species that I encountered. Indeed, they might not even be truly named sand flies, but you'll probably identify them quite easily. An obvious characteristic is their slowness. Once they start to bite they are rarely quick enough to escape a swat, whereas the much larger blackflies are frustratingly quick.) Then they disappeared, and by the tail end of August I was spending sunny, warm afternoons and evenings free of bugs.

In my experience, the no-see-ums liked dry evenings and mornings after nightfall and before first light. They were worst in the morning before dawn when I was attempting to tear down camp by headlamp. They were attracted to the light, which meant a cloud wherever I looked. A big mistake was putting on a headlamp one night before leaving my tent. This brought dozens inside the tent as I opened the door to get out.

Mosquitoes were worst in shady, windless areas or in the evenings, which worked well for me because I tended to be asleep in the early evening for a rise at first light. I saw very few mosquitoes, though I was in the great outdoors the entire summer.

Blackflies showed up on hot, sunny afternoons for a few hours, then disappeared for the day. They were only around for a few weeks and were more prevalent near estuaries.

Sand flies tended to like sandy beaches and warm weather. The flies were worst on warm, sunny evenings, often making dinner hour a trying time. They could be a problem when launching in the morning, and would swarm the kayak well out into the water.

Some locations were generally bad no matter what time of day it was. I didn't camp at estuaries for environmental reasons, but grassy, sheltered, inland intertidal areas were the worst for bugs whenever I was near one. Short of those locations it was difficult to anticipate what type of area might attract these pests. The beach south of Jewsbury Peninsula on Campania Island had a bad sand fly problem while I was there. The same style of sand beach at Wolf Beach on Calvert Island was insect-free.

Toward August tiny spiders began to outnumber insects—perhaps accounting for the lack of insects. These spiders were inoffensive and easily removed if they got inside the tent by carrying them out on one of their strings.

The worst pest wasn't an insect at all. Amphipods are tiny prehistoric creatures known as beach hoppers that live at the waterline in the millions. They look like a cross between a miniature shrimp and a maggot and hop in indiscriminate directions; they are as likely to jump under your feet or into your sandals as they are to jump away from danger. I would gladly have traded amphipods for insects. They jumped into the kayak cockpit and hatches and anywhere else they could manage to get in, but invariably couldn't get back out.

Their worst characteristic, though, is a propensity to seek shelter anywhere they can find it. They head up to higher levels on the beach in rain, and this can bring them up to tent level.

My worst pest encounter during the entire trip occurred when I left my kayak deck bag open under the vestibule of my tent all night during a rainstorm at Safety Cove on Calvert Island. In the morning I zipped it up, and didn't unzip it again until out on the water at Grief Bay. Suddenly, there in the midst of open water and swell, I was greeted by dozens—possibly hundreds—of hopping amphipods. Dozens more tried to stay sheltered inside the deck bag. It was like a scene from a horror movie. It took six dunks of the empty deck bag to get rid of the last amphipod. I can't tell you how many I had to flick off the kayak sprayskirt.

There is no magic answer to the insect question, but I can tell you there were an incredible number of evenings that were pest-free. So don't believe it when someone tells you a certain area of the coast is overrun by blackflies or other insects. Just take it under advisement. It may have been true for them at that precise location at that time of year, but it might not be true for your visit. You may have an entirely different problem to contend with.

Just be sure to turn off your headlamp before leaving your tent at night and never, ever leave your deck bag unzipped on the beach.

FIRST NATIONS OVERVIEW

No guide to the B.C. coast can ignore the link between the land and the First Nations people who lived here for thousands of years before the arrival of Europeans. It is a history still being played out as various groups work their way through a protracted process to reclaim lost rights through treaty negotiations. Six major groups have claim to lands on the north and central B.C. coast. They are the Tsimshian, Haisla, Heiltsuk, Nuxalk, Wuikinuxv and Gwa'sala-Nakwaxda'xw. Once forming the most populated region in North America north of Mexico, only a handful of First Nations communities are left on the coast: Lax Kw'alaams, Metlakatla, Kitkatla, Hartley Bay, Klemtu, Bella Bella, Bella Coola and Katit.

A First Nations painting adorns the longhouse at Koeye River.

Lax Kw'alaams
TSIMSHIAN
Metlakatla
Kitimaat Village
Kitkatla
HAISLA
Hartley Bay
Klemtu
Bella Coola
Bella Bella
NUXALK
HEILTSUK
WUIKINUXV
(OWEEKENO)
Katit
GWA'SALA-NAKWAXDA'XW
Modern communities
Reserve locations
KWAKIUTL
First Nations communities and territories
Territory boundaries were obtained from B.C. Treaty Commission Statement of Intent maps

The Tsimshian are the most widespread of the coastal First Nations, covering the area from the Alaskan border to near Bella Bella. Groups within the Tsimshian are the Gitga'at of Hartley Bay, the Kitasoo/Xai'xais of Klemtu, the Kitselas and Kitsumkalum of Terrace and the Metlakatla of Prince Rupert. Their presence over the centuries means thousands of cultural sites dot the coast. Visitors, and kayakers in particular, should be aware of this. There is a tendency to view reserves as First Nations land and everything else as public. Reserves, however, represent in most ways a purely artificial border contrived for the benefit of European settlers. Viewed with a historic eye, traditional First Nations lands include the entire area where water was the main form of transportation and where sites were inhabited in a pattern that shifted over time—whether over the course of a year as the group moved to follow resources or over the course of the centuries as political and economic boundaries shifted.

Kayakers in particular should be aware of the scope of the heritage landscape because of the need to camp on land. Beaches ideal for campsites have been ideal as such for hundreds of years, so if you can camp there, chances are others have many times before. You may be sleeping on a heritage site, potentially of some importance. This necessitates having a light footprint, not just for the sake of wilderness but for the sake of history.

Fortunately most camping is low-impact by nature and won't necessarily disturb the remaining archaeological features, the most prominent of which are things like fish traps and middens. Sites on the coast have reached the stage where any remaining artifacts are buried. The days of pushing into bushes to see remnants of longhouses are over. So activities that can harm a heritage site are those such as fires that can interfere with carbon dating and digging.

It is illegal to dig into or otherwise disturb archaeological sites in B.C. Many sites also have a cultural or sacred significance that extends beyond archaeological evidence, so known cultural sites where permission is not granted to camp should be avoided.

One problem with camping on the coast is that the cultural inventory is not advertised, so you don't necessarily know what to avoid. The list has been suppressed on the basis that it could lead to exploitation by self-guided tourists and facilitate looting. This posed a significant dilemma in writing *The Wild Coast* series. On the one hand I have been asked to self-censor to respect the sanctity of cultural sites, while on another level I am trying to put the land into a meaningful historical context, which means making specific ethnographic references. I have to argue that information by nature—and access to it—is not dangerous. Rather, the key lies in having both the information and the education for dealing with it. For instance, you can have a hundred kayakers camp unaware they are on a cultural site and the site will likely suffer some disturbance. Tell a hundred kayakers that it is a cultural site and how to behave properly around it and chances are they will become unofficial custodians, watching out for anyone who may disturb it.

At least that is my hope. Unfortunately it takes only one looter to prove me wrong.

To ward off the latter we can all play a part. If you see behaviour that you suspect is unethical, illegal or constitutes looting, it is worthwhile to notify the nearest band office so they can investigate. What you saw may be a sanctioned archaeological dig, or perhaps even drilling for mineral samples. But if we, as visitors, can add our collective eyes to the protection of cultural resources we can play a beneficial role rather than a destructive one.

For those who wish to learn more about culture of the various First Nations groups on the coast, the Internet allows these nations to tell their own stories. For Tsimshian culture, an excellent site is **www.sd52.bc.ca/fnes/tsimshian/tsim_index.html**. The Kitasoo/Xai'xais have a comprehensive site at **www.kitasoo.org**. The Kitasoo tourism website, **www.klemtutourism.com**, has a useful section under "tourism services" that includes a trip planning guide, minimum impact guidelines and a visitor's code of ethics. Anyone travelling through their traditional territories should follow this code and the guidelines.

The official Heiltsuk site is **www.heiltsuk.com**. It includes a useful historical section—"who we are"—plus news, references and links. The Haisla site is **www.haisla.ca**. It's in an earlier stage of development, with an interesting movie on Kitlope that can be viewed. The Nuxalk site is **www.nuxalk.org** and contains a good deal of historical and political information. There was no Gwa'sala-Nakwaxda'wx website as of 2006.

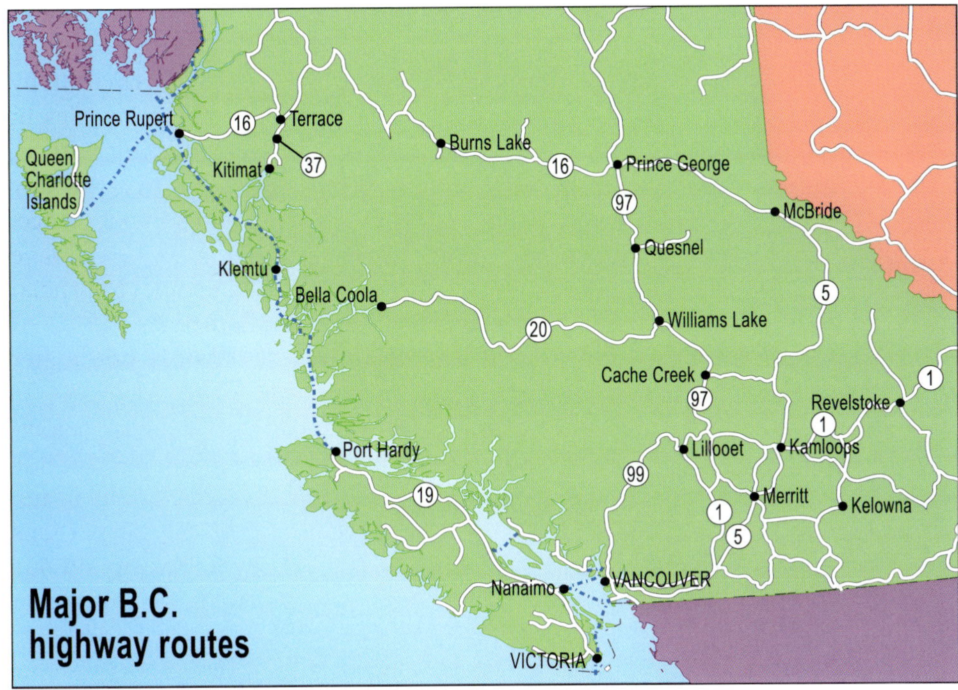

GETTING TO THE COAST

There are four major road accesses to the upper B.C. coast: Prince Rupert, Kitimat, Bella Coola and Port Hardy. Those three communities are served by B.C. Ferries. More information about getting to these locations is covered in the introductions to the three main sections of this book.

Kilometres
10
Spiller Channel
Don Peninsula
Return Channel
Roscoe Inlet
Cascade Inlet
Ocean Falls
Dean Channel
Labouchere Channel
BELLA COOLA
North Bentinck Arm
Bardswell Group
Athlone I.
Dufferin I.
BELLA BELLA
Gunboat Passage
Shearwater
King Island
Burke Channel
South Bentinck Arm
Campbell I.
Denny I.
Lama Passage
Codville Lagoon
Kwatna Inlet
Hunter I.
Goose Group
122 BELLA BELLA 3
Queens Sound
150 BELLA COOLA 4
Namu
Kildidt Sound
Hakai Luxvbalis Conservancy Area
Fitz Hugh Sound
Hardy Inlet
Wannock IR
Qwikeno L.
Rivers Inlet
Fish Egg Inlet
Calvert Island
Penrose Island Marine Park
Draney Inlet
2 HAKAI 98
Rivers Inlet
Boswell Inlet
Smith Sound
Smith Inlet
Queen Charlotte Sound
THE CENTRAL COAST
Cape Caution
Alison Sound
Belize Inlet
Nakwakto Rapids
Bramham I.
Seymour Inlet
Eclipse Narrows
Pine I.
Queen Charlotte Strait
Shelter Bay
God's Pocket Marine Park
VANCOUVER ISLAND
Port Hardy
1 CAPE CAUTION 66
Miles
5

PART ONE

The Central Coast

IF YOU SPEND ANY AMOUNT OF TIME ON THE WATER HERE YOU'LL QUICKLY become familiar with the marine weather forecasts for the central coast, "from McInnes Island to Pine Island." That serves as a way to define the geographic boundaries of the central coast, and in this book, the central coast section ends at the northwest extent of Seaforth Channel, the same latitude as McInnes Island.

On the south border it is a little more complicated. Pine Island is in the middle of nowhere at the entrance to Queen Charlotte Strait. To give a strategic starting point, I've stretched the central coast to include Port Hardy. This doubles up on some areas covered in *The Wild Coast, Volume 1*, so the compromise is to present what you need to know to get you started at Port Hardy while leaving the details of the region in *Volume 1*.

GETTING HERE

By road

There are two highway links to the central coast: Port Hardy and Bella Coola. Both locations are connection points for B.C. Ferries' Discovery Coast Passage.

Port Hardy is probably the closest starting point geographically for most visitors, but it requires getting to Vancouver Island, and that can mean an additional ferry if you're arriving from the mainland. Your options are the Washington State (Anacortes) ferry service to Victoria, the Vancouver (Tsawwassen) ferry to Victoria or the Vancouver (Horseshoe Bay) ferry to Nanaimo. The B.C. Ferries routes are busy and can have long weekend lineups and delays. Reservations are recommended. Call **1-888-223-3779** or visit

www.bcferries.com. For the Washington State ferry call **1-888-808-7977** in Washington or **206-464-6400** elsewhere for reservations, or visit **www.wsdot.wa.gov/ferries**.

Once on Vancouver Island, it is 391 km (243 miles) to Port Hardy from Nanaimo (4½ hours), and 502 km (312 miles) from Victoria (6 hours).

Bella Coola solves the problem of a ferry connection to Vancouver Island, but it has different challenges. One is the distance. It is about 1,000 km (600 miles) from Vancouver to Bella Coola, and not all of it is on paved road. No matter where you start, your trip to Bella Coola by car will take you to Williams Lake. Williams Lake is accessible from Vancouver via Highway 97 through Cache Creek or from Alberta via Highway 1 West or via Highway 5, then 97 North. And that's just the start of the journey. From Williams Lake, Highway 20 leads 450 km (280 miles) west through the Chilcotin region of B.C. and Tweedsmuir Provincial Park—an area so beautiful you may want to stop and spend your holiday there. Be prepared that much of the road between Williams Lake and Bella Coola is gravel and dirt. The good news is it is well-packed.

The highlight, of course, is The Hill. The Hill is the twisting, single-lane, dirt road that leads from Tweedsmuir park down into the Bella Coola Valley. Grades are as high as 18 per cent. With steep cliffs alongside, it has more in common with a goat trail than a provincial highway. It is also used by trucks, RVs and offloading ferry traffic. But as hair-raising as it may be, it is an extraordinary route to take.

Not surprisingly, The Hill was actually a pack horse trail for many years as the government wouldn't finance a proper road between the Bella Coola Valley and Anahim Lake due to the steep terrain. The citizens of Bella Coola eventually took the matter into their own hands, building it themselves. The official opening was in 1955.

Once you reach either Port Hardy or Bella Coola, a great option for kayakers is to take the Discovery Coast Passage ferry to the point where you want to begin your trip. The distance is best managed by treating the driving as an integral part of your holiday. Vancouver Island has many attractions along its route, as does the Bella Coola Valley, Tweedsmuir and the Chilcotin region. If you can, spread the driving over several days and enjoy the scenery and attractions of B.C. along the way.

By ferry

Once at Bella Coola or Port Hardy you can take the B.C. Ferries' Discovery Coast Passage service that connects with Bella Bella (McLoughlin Bay), Shearwater, Ocean Falls and Bella Coola. Service is also available to Klemtu (see page 171) and Prince Rupert from Port Hardy (see page 236).

The Discovery Coast Passage is covered by the *Queen of Chilliwack* from the beginning of June to the beginning of September. There is no off-season service, though all the stops except for Bella Coola are picked up by the Inside Passage ferry over the winter. The Discovery Coast Passage route changes over the course of a week, offering a chance to create your own itinerary. Ferry users can jump from destination to destination, staying overnight or longer at various ports of call before continuing on.

This is one of the most flexible routes offered by B.C. Ferries, as well as one of the most scenic and relaxed. For instance, the route out of Port Hardy is at the whim of the captain, who may travel through Gordon Channel on a normal day but could choose Goletas Channel or Richards Channel if conditions warrant it. If any whales are reported in the area, the route may be changed to view them. Passengers will also be given a chance to view the historic writing at Mackenzie Rock, and a side trip may lead up Cascade Inlet to view the incredible waterfalls.

All route information is available online at **www.bcferries.com**, but here's a little extra detail that may help with trip planning. The week begins Monday at 8 a.m. when the *Queen of Chilliwack* leaves Bella Coola for a direct run to Port Hardy via Burke Channel, arriving at 9 p.m. It lays over Monday night at Port Hardy, leaving Tuesday at 9:30 a.m. The ferry then travels Fitz Hugh Sound into Lama Passage for the first stop at Bella Bella (McLoughlin Bay) at 7:30 p.m. It leaves the bay at 9:15 p.m. to cross the short distance to Shearwater, arriving at 9:45 p.m. The ship leaves Shearwater at 11 p.m. and travels back down Lama Passage, then up Dean Channel to arrive overnight at Bella Coola Wednesday at 6:30 a.m.

The stop is brief at Bella Coola. An hour later the ship is back down Dean Channel in a reverse of the previous route, arriving at Shearwater at 2:30 p.m. on Wednesday, leaving at 4:30 p.m., arriving at McLoughlin Bay at 5 p.m., leaving at 7:45 p.m. and finishing at Port Hardy Thursday at 7:45 a.m.

At 9:30 a.m. Thursday the ship leaves Port Hardy for the non-stop trip to Bella Coola, arriving at 10:30 p.m. via Burke Channel.

On Friday it will leave Bella Coola at 8 a.m. and head down Dean Channel for a stop in Ocean Falls at 2 p.m. The layover in Ocean Falls is three hours, time enough for a good exploration, and at 8:30 p.m. the ship arrives in Shearwater. After an hour it heads to McLoughlin Bay, arriving at 10 p.m. and leaving at 11 p.m. It then heads out overnight to arrive in Port Hardy Saturday at 9 a.m.

Here the crew gets a break and doesn't leave again until 9:30 p.m. on the Saturday. The next leg is the long trip where some passengers will be spending two nights aboard. The first night is spent transiting to McLoughlin Bay for an arrival at 7:30 a.m. Sunday. After waiting an hour it heads to Shearwater to arrive at 9:15 a.m.

It's quite common for kayakers to have a wet launch on the Sunday morning, as the trip will take the ferry past areas like Kwashua Channel and Sea Otter Inlet in the ideal early morning hours. For more about wet launches, see page 40.

After an hour in McLoughlin Bay the ship leaves for Klemtu, arriving at 2:15 p.m. The layover in Klemtu is four hours. At 6:15 p.m. the ship heads for Ocean Falls, arriving at 1 a.m. After an hour the ship heads up Dean Channel to arrive at Bella Coola at 7 a.m. Monday. An hour later the ship leaves to begin the week over again.

This schedule presents wonderful opportunities for people to explore the coast and its communities, by foot alone or assisted by car. One popular option is a circle route from Port Hardy to Bella Coola, completing the mainland portion by car.

By air

Scheduled flights are available to Bella Bella, Bella Coola, Shearwater and Ocean Falls. Options originate from Vancouver or Port Hardy to Bella Bella. For the most up-to-date information on service providers or schedules for Bella Coola, please contact Cariboo Chilcotin Coast Region travel information at **1-800-663-5885**. For Port Hardy, call the Port Hardy and District Chamber of Commerce at **250-949-7622** or visit **www.ph-chamber.bc.ca/trans.html**. A main service provider to Port Hardy, Bella Bella and Bella Coola is Pacific Coastal Airlines. Phone **1-800-663-2872** or visit **www.pacific-coastal.com**.

By boat

Boat havens can be found across most areas of the central coast. The Cape Caution area has recognized anchorages at Shelter Bay (Queen Charlotte Strait), Miles Inlet in Bramham Island and Treadwell Bay in Slingsby Channel.

On the mainland side of Nakwakto Rapids boat havens are located at Strachan Bay in Mereworth Sound and Peet Bay in Alison Sound.

North of Cape Caution, boat havens can be found at Jones Cove, Millbrook Cove and Finis Nook (Boswell Inlet) in Smith Sound. Options in Rivers Inlet are Home Bay, the northwest corner of Ripon Island next to Walbran Island and the Penrose Island coves called Schooner Retreat.

Numerous boat havens are located along Fitz Hugh Sound and Fisher Channel. From south to north they are Safety Cove on Calvert Island, Green Island Anchorage just outside Fish Egg Inlet, Goldstream Harbour at Hakai Passage, Kwakume Inlet, Sea Otter Inlet and Crab Cove, Rock Inlet near Namu, Fougner Bay at the entrance to Burke Channel and The Trap at Clayton Island near Lama Passage.

For those boaters venturing into Hakai, boat havens are located at Keith Anchorage in Kwakshua Channel and Bremner Bay in Kildidt Sound.

Convenient to Bella Bella are Kynumpt Bay and Troup Narrows anchorages.

Boat havens en route to Bella Coola are Cathedral Point, Boukind Bay at Ocean Falls and Eucott Bay.

By kayak

Thanks to B.C. Ferries you and your kayak can be dropped directly to Shearwater/Bella Bella or you can request a wet launch. See page 40 for wet launch details. Or you can begin your journey at the two road-accessible options: Bella Coola or Port Hardy. Entering the central coast via Port Hardy will entail a route suitable for veteran kayakers only.

Highlights worth exploring are the sand beaches of the outer islands, the trails of Calvert Island, the strangeness of ghost towns like Namu and Ocean Falls, the hot springs at Eucott Bay and the beauty of Ellerslie Falls. And that's just for starters.

Central coast kayaking routes

Distances are in kilometres and represent probable marine travel distances, not direct distance as shown.

RECOMMENDED KAYAKING TRIPS

The recommended minimum time: For those taking the Discovery Coast Passage ferry for a launch at Bella Bella/Shearwater, the ferry arrives Sunday morning, Tuesday night, Wednesday afternoon and Friday night. Visitors starting from Port Hardy will likely want to arrive on the northbound ferry on either the Sunday or Tuesday and return leaving Bella Bella/Shearwater Wednesday or Friday on the direct southbound route. Visitors from Bella Coola will want to do the opposite—arrive Wednesday or Friday and leave Sunday or Tuesday—keeping in mind leaving Sunday will mean an extra night on the water due to the diversion through Klemtu.

At a minimum someone could arrive at Bella Bella from Port Hardy on Tuesday evening and leave Wednesday afternoon. Really, though, the shortest reasonable agenda to justify the distance would be about four days on the water. Such a trip might be to leave Port Hardy Saturday night, head out onto the water at Bella Bella Sunday and return on the Wednesday afternoon ferry.

Naturally there are a few shorter options available. Trip recommendations are for time spent on the water and do not include travel time.

- *If you have two days*: An overnight trip without ferry links could be a trip to Tallheo Hot Springs from Bella Coola. This would take you through impressive mountain scenery with a reward at the far end.

- *If you have four days*: You might consider a wet launch at Kwakshua Channel Sunday morning, overnighting at Wolf Beach and Superstition Point to reach Bella Bella or Shearwater on Wednesday. Another option is a circle route anywhere around Bella Bella. My suggestion is a trip down Hunter Channel to any of the campsites to the south of the Bardswell Group, with a stop as exotic as the McMullin or Goose group, if possible, and a return by Joassa Channel. An option avoiding a ferry connection would be an exploration of Cape Caution. Consider a crossing to Shelter Bay and a trip northwest to Wilkie Point, returning by the same route or by cutting across via Pine Island to overnight at Balaclava Island before returning to Port Hardy (there are nice campsites on the south end of Balaclava Island. See *Volume I*).

- *If you have five days*: With this much time you have the opportunity for a run of Dean Channel between Bella Coola and Bella Bella. The question is which way to go—Bella Bella to Bella Coola or Bella Coola to Bella Bella? Early in the summer you can take advantage of the favourable current and probably beat the summer inflow winds by leaving from Bella Coola. In August you might want to try the reverse to avoid fighting the summer inflow winds. Stops along the way should be Eucott Bay, Rattenbury Point, Port John and Rainbow Island. Another option is a wet launch from the *Queen of Chilliwack*. Consider Kwakshua Channel to Wolf Beach, Superstition Point, Goose Group, Kynumpt Harbour and then your ferry connection.

- *If you have a week*: With this much time you can really sink your teeth into an area. Depending on your anticipated daily travelling distance you can mix and match campsite connections on the accompanying map, but consider an adventurous option. Take the ferry to Shearwater then return to Port Hardy by running Cape Caution. A suggested itinerary would be campsites near the McNaughton Group, Wolf Beach, Penrose Island, Smith Sound, Wilkie Point, Shelter Bay and a return to Port Hardy. A more sedate option would be a leisurely run between Bella Coola and Bella Bella with a side trip to Ocean Falls. The traditional way to spend a week in this region is in Hakai. Consider adding Koeye River and Namu to an exploration of that area. You can launch from Shearwater or take advantage of a wet launch. A more relaxed week would be an exploration of the Bardswell Group. The non-traditional trip is to Ellerslie Falls. Plan for some time on Ellerslie Lake if you can manage the distance and the portage.

- *The ideal trip*: My ideal itinerary would be a launch from Bella Coola, a run down Dean Channel, a side trip up to Ellerslie Falls, a return down Spiller Channel to Bella Bella, a run down Joassa Channel to the McMullin Group and Goose Group, an exploration of Hakai, a run across Fitz Hugh Sound to Namu, then down the coast via Koeye River, Penrose Island, Dsulish Bay, Wilkie Point and Shelter Bay for an arrival in Port Hardy. The length of this trip would depend on the miles the party could average, but three weeks is recommended; two is possible but pushing it. Either way this would be a world-class paddle bordering on an adventure. Once in Port Hardy you could take the ferry back to your vehicle at Bella Coola. The direction could also be reversed.

GEOLOGY AND ECOLOGY

This is the land of the temperate rainforest—a world with a mild and wet climate where trees have the potential to grow to huge sizes but are often dwarfed and left clinging to life on steep bedrock mountain-sides or exposed oceanside bluffs.

B.C. has about half the world's temperate rainforests. In the central coast the dominant tree type is western hemlock, with Douglas-fir common south from Dean Channel below roughly N53° and most common in drier areas. Amabilis fir is common at higher elevations or, along with yellow-cedar, at wetter locations. Lodgepole pine is common at wet, boggy sites. Red alder can be found at logged areas, with black cottonwood along floodplains. Sitka spruce can be found in floodplains and exposed beaches, becoming more common in the north.

The scrubby, poor forests that line much of the outer coast are usually yellow-cedar, shore pine and mountain hemlock. Dead or spiked treetops are typical. This is believed to be due to a calcium deficiency.

The shrub layer is typically Alaskan blueberry, red huckleberry and salal. There is usually a prominent moss layer—most commonly Oregon beaked moss (*Kindbergia oregano*), *Rhytidiadelphus loreus* and *Hylocomium splendens*.

Salmon is central to the life cycle here, and most rivers and streams support spawning. This and the vegetation, particularly berries, provide sustenance for a high concentration of grizzly and black bears. Rivers supporting grizzly habitat include Bella Coola, Kimsquit (head of Dean Channel), Kwatna (Burke Channel), Koeye (Fitz Hugh Sound), Clyak (Moses Inlet/Rivers Inlet), Kilbella/ Chuckwalla (Kilbella Bay, Rivers Inlet) and Draney (Draney Inlet/ Rivers Inlet).

Other animals sharing this environment include river otter, mink and a variety of birds. The oolichan (also called eulachon, or candlefish) feeds seals, sea lions, gulls and bald eagles each spring as it reaches the lower levels of many coastal rivers.

Other common mammals on the coast here are the black-tailed deer and grey wolf. The small, rocky coastal islands provide habitat for nesting seabirds. Even mountain goats descend to lower forested cliffs near sea level during winter. At other seasons they inhabit the Coast Mountains, which often rise sharply to more than 1,600 m (1 mile) from the deeper fiords.

A major step forward in protecting central coast wildlife was made in December, 2005, when the Raincoast Conservation Foundation bought trophy hunting licences covering 200,000 square kilometres (77,200 square miles) and retired them. The $1.35 million purchase effectively turns most of the central coast into a conservation area without the need for legislation or public funding. Now protected are the area's grizzly bear, black bear, kermode bear, wolf, cougar and wolverine.

The Coast Mountains run about 1,600 km (1,000 miles) down the B.C. coast to the Fraser River and stretch 200 km (125 miles) into the interior. They were formed by uplift and erosion; glaciers moving down the valleys during the Pleistocene period (as recently as 10,000 years ago) carved the cliffs and created an intricate pattern of channels and inlets. Granite is the primary bedrock of these mountains, forming the largest connected granite outcropping in the world.

Glaciers can still be found at higher elevations near the coast. It is considered a young mountain range, but rather than volcanoes, hot springs are common. In the central coast region they are most prevalent near Bella Coola.

On the central coast no entire watershed is fully protected. Tweedsmuir Provincial Park protects 54 per cent of the Bella Coola River watershed. That could change as designated areas become parkland (see page 207).

FIRST NATIONS OVERVIEW

Four groups formed the First Nations population of the central coast: the Wuikinuxv (Oweekeno) of Rivers Inlet; the Nuxalk of upper Dean Channel, Bentinck Arms and the Bella Coola valley; and the Heiltsuk of Bella Bella, Fitz Hugh Sound and lower Burke and Dean channels. The Gwa'sala-Nakwaxda'xw made their home in north Queen Charlotte Strait and Smith Sound. They are considered kin of the Kwakwaka'wakw (Kwakiutl). For more information on the latter, see *The Wild Coast, Volume 1.*

Gwa'sala-Nakwaxda'xw

Now centred in Port Hardy, with 27 reserves spread throughout their traditional territory, this First Nation is a merging of three others in 1964—the Quawahelah, Nakwakto and Kwawkewith bands. They split in 1981, dividing into the Tsulquate and Kwawkewith. In 1985 the Tsulquate changed their name to the Gwa'sala-Nakwaxda'xw First Nation. Their traditional territory centres around Smith Inlet to the north and Belize and Seymour inlets to the south. They currently have no permanent communities in their traditional territories.

Wuikinuxv (Oweekeno)

Archaeological evidence shows the Wuikinuxv, formerly Oweekeno, have lived in the Rivers Inlet and Owikeno Lake area for about 9,000 years, and they are believed to have been at one time the largest of the mid-coast nations, numbering as high as 2,000. Their language is Oowekyala, similar to Heiltsuk and part of the Northern Wakashan language division. Their name is believed to be derived from "portage makers" or "those who carry on the back"—a reference to the travel between Rivers Inlet and Owikeno Lake. Another more recent translation is "right-minded people."

The Wuikinuxv concentrated on inland resources, inhabiting seaside villages less often than other coastal groups. The advent of logging and canning in the late 19th century centralized the population at Katit—the last Wuikinuxv village—at Wannock River at the top of Rivers Inlet. A fire in 1935 devastated the community and its longhouses and other historic artifacts.

Nuxalk

The Nuxalk First Nation is part of the Salishan language group, and is quite distinct from the nearby neighbours, the Wuikinuxv, though they participated in each other's winter ceremonies. Blessed with such an abundance of food in the area of the Bella Coola valley and upper Dean Channel, the Nuxalk didn't have to move throughout the year. Trade moved through the Nuxalk-Carrier grease trail, where eulachon grease was transported through the Coast Mountains for use in the interior. It was this trail that Alexander Mackenzie used to reach the Pacific Ocean in 1793.

European contact brought disease and a drop in the Nuxalk population, forcing them to regroup in one village at Bella Coola at the head of North Bentinck Arm in the 1920s.

Heiltsuk

Centred today in Bella Bella, the Heiltsuk once spread into Fitz Hugh Sound and the lower portions of Burke and Dean channels in over 50 major villages and many more seasonal camps. Their history is believed to extend back almost 10,000 years. The Hailhzaqvla language of the Heiltsuk is part of the Northern Wakashan linguistic group, and is related to Kwakiutl and Haisla.

The word Heiltsuk, or Hailhazakv, means "to speak or act correctly."

Known for their finely crafted canoes and utensils, the Heiltsuk survived by fishing, harvesting shellfish and hunting mammals. At pre-contact times the Heiltsuk were estimated to number 1,600, but that dropped to 204 due to disease by the mid-1800s.

European contact was heightened in 1833 with the construction of Fort McLoughlin on Campbell Island; the Heiltsuk concentrated there at a village called 'Qlc between 1860 and 1890. Several tribes united to settle at Waglisla (Bella Bella) around 1890, where they remain centred today.

Cape Caution

CHAPTER ONE

EVERY JOURNEY HAS TO HAVE A STARTING POINT, AND FOR B.C.'S INSIDE Passage that point is Cape Caution.

The cape itself is really just a small point of land, but it represents much more—a large region of open coast between the shelter of Queen Charlotte Strait and the southern entry to B.C.'s Inside Passage. It is an area with tumultuous seas and yet renowned for its sweeping beaches. Miles of sand can be found here, but it is not a place to linger. Reefs and swell are steepened to a sharp point by the shallow ocean floor, and it can be an intimidating stretch of coast, even on a day when the swell is low. Most other travellers tend to treat Cape Caution as an area to transit, not a destination in its own right. Both mariners and kayakers alike will hurry north to Penrose Island Marine Park in Rivers Inlet, an anchorage with a beautiful clamshell beach and camping area. Smith Sound has its own attractions, particularly Dsulish Bay with its string of beaches. Nor can Nakwakto Rapids be ignored as a visual highlight, with its 16-knot currents that place it among the fastest tidal rapids in the world.

Providing access to it all is Port Hardy on Vancouver Island. The city is a launching point, a ferry terminus, the northern limit of the Island Highway and one of the few vehicle-accessible gateways to the north and central B.C. coast.

Cape Caution may be a difficult stretch of coast, but few worthwhile ventures are easy. Navigating it is considered a badge of honour for mariners and kayakers alike, so if you travel past here, wear the badge of honour proudly.

80
69
Elizabeth L.
Kiltala IR
Hardy Inlet
Moses Inlet
Kilbella Bay
Katit IR
Owikeno L.
KATIT
Elizabeth Lagoon
Illahie Inlet
Wannock Cove
McPhee Bay
Addenbroke I.
Fish Egg Inlet
Sandell L.
CALVERT I.
FITZ HUGH SOUND
Darby Channel
Johnston Bay
WALBRAN I.
Penrose Island Marine Park
Draney Narrows
RIVERS INLET
Draney Inlet
Halowis IR
Robert Arm
Open Bight
Goose Bay
See Hakai, page 97
Shipping route
Caroline L.
Walkum Bay
Kelp Head
Dsulish Bay
Boswell Inlet
Naysash Inlet
Margaret Bay
Burnt I.
Burnt Island Harbour
Barrier Group
Smith Inlet
SMITH SOUND
Takush Harbour
GREAVES I.
Ahclakerho Channel
Wyclese IR
Table I.
Broad Reach
Egg I.
Leonora L.
Wyclees Lagoon
Long L.
Hoop Bay
Neck Ness
Blunden Bay
Chief Nollis Bay
CAPE CAUTION
Silvester Bay
Baker Range
Mereworth Sound
Alison Sound
Peet Bay
Belize Inlet
Burnett Bay
Miles
2
4
Km
4
6
Fraser Range
Richards Channel
Kequesta IR
Nugent Sound
Slingsby Channel
Seymour Inlet
Fox Is.
BRAMHAM I.
Murray Labyrinth
Emily Group
Reid Its.
Naiad Its.
Duke of Edinburgh Ecological Reserve
STORM ISLANDS
Southgate Group
Tinson Is.
Tree Its.
Pine I.
Shelter Bay
Ripple Passage
Bright I.
Prosser Rock
NIGEI I.
Gordon Channel
Walkers Group
Marsh Bay
Blunden Harbour
Balaclava I.
Raynor Group
GOLETAS CHANNEL
Deserters Group
God's Pocket Marine Park
Gordon Is.
QUEEN CHARLOTTE STRAIT
Hardy Bay
Shipping route
PORT HARDY
See The Wild Coast, Volume 1
See The Wild Coast, Volume 3

QUEEN CHARLOTTE STRAIT

Northern Queen Charlotte Strait is a crossroads for the B.C. coast—the border between the well-travelled and sheltered waters inside Vancouver Island and the wilder and more secluded open ocean of Queen Charlotte Sound. Attractions include numerous island clusters. Those nearest Vancouver Island are covered in *The Wild Coast, Volume 1*, where Port Hardy is also discussed in detail. Some information is provided here to get you started and across the strait.

This is a prime area to see marine mammals; common visitors include gray whales, harbour porpoises, Pacific white-sided dolphins and killer whales.

Place names: Queen Charlotte was the wife of King George III (1738–1820), the German princess Charlotte of Mecklenberg-Strelitz. She bore the king 15 children.

Port Hardy

This full-service community is the southern limit of the two B.C. Ferries routes that provide access to the north and central B.C. coast: the Discovery Coast Passage and Inside Passage routes. More information about Port Hardy and the immediate vicinity can be found in *The Wild Coast, Volume 1*. For the most current list of services available at Port Hardy, visit **www.ph-chamber.bc.ca** or call **250-949-7622**.

Fishing boats lie at rest at a Port Hardy dock.

Launches: Launches are possible from both the east and west sides of Hardy Bay. My favourite is from Bear Cove on the east side of the bay. From the Island Highway follow the Bear Cove Highway north by turning right at the wooden Welcome to Port Hardy sign. The boat launch is located just before the ferry terminal. Parking is available along the nearby roadside. Kayakers may prefer to use the older, decommissioned boat ramp to avoid the boat traffic using the newer, paved ramp.

On the west side of Hardy Bay south of the downtown is Fisherman's Wharf, where both a launch and parking are available for a fee. Kayakers may also prefer to launch from the beach behind Rotary Park in downtown Port Hardy next to the Visitor Information Centre. While centrally located, it has the disadvantage of an extensive beach at low tide.

God's Pocket Marine Park

This wonderful little group of protected islands offers a logical stopping point for any transit of Queen Charlotte Strait. A good anchorage is located in Harlequin Bay on the northeast side of Hurst Island, while camping is available in Harlequin Bay or on a clam beach on the south end of Bell Island. Look for it opposite the channel between two neighbouring islets.

Paddling across Queen Charlotte Strait: The daunting 32-km (20-mile) trip from Vancouver Island to the B.C. mainland can easily be broken into parts, thanks to the various island clusters between Port Hardy and Shelter Bay, though it is an achievable one-day trip in the right conditions. The most logical route is from Port Hardy to God's Pocket, then through the Deserters and Walker groups to Shelter Bay. The best camping en route is at God's Pocket Marine Park at about 16 km (10 miles) from the launch sites in Port Hardy. If you can make the crossing in one day, the campsite at Shelter Bay is ideal. In the event of high winds, camping just outside Hardy Bay in Goletas Channel or at God's Pocket Marine Park is recommended. Like any open water crossing, it is advisable to leave early when the winds are low and plan to be off the water if the winds rise in the afternoon.

Deserters and Walker Group

The majority of these islands located in the middle of Queen Charlotte Strait have rock shoreline with correspondingly few beaches. The best beach area is in the cove behind Hosford Island, which is used most often as an anchorage. Enter from the south side of Hosford Island, as the north entrance runs dry at low tide. Another good anchorage

Hoop Bay
Bertha L.
Leonora L.
Wyclees Lagoon
Toksee IR
Neck Ness
Coast Nipple
Mount Robinson
Mereworth Sound
Indian Cove
Blunden Bay
CAPE CAUTION
Strachan Bay
Tsai-kwi-ee IR
Village Cove
Silvester Bay
Baker Range
Westerman Bay
Raynor Pt.
Wilkie Pt.
Burnett Bay
Lassier Bay
Helm I.
BELIZE INLET
Bowley Bay
Nakwakto Rapids
Fraser Range
Bremner Pt.
Vigilance Pt.
Johnson Pt.
Treadwell Bay
Kequesta IR
Buccleugh Pt.
Slingsby Channel
Butress I.
Nugent Sound
Fox Is.
SEYMOUR INLET
Schooner Channel
Cougar Inlet
McEwan Pt.
BRAMHAM I.
Bramham Pt.
Miles Inlet
Richards Channel
Murray Labyrinth
Allison Harbour
Ellis Bay
STORM ISLANDS
Emily Group
Duke of Edinburgh Ecological Reserve
Rogers Is.
SOUTHGATE GROUP
71
Southgate I.
Harris I.
Knight I.
Tinson Is.
Arm Is.
Pine I.
Tree Its.
Annie Rocks
Westcott Pt.
Shelter Bay
See The Wild Coast, Volume 1
Wallace Is.
See The Wild Coast, Volume 3
BUCKLE GROUP
Bright I.
Herbert I.
Prosser Rock
Ripple Passage
WALKER GROUP
Kent I.
Hosford I.
Blunden Harbour
Marsh Bay
Miller Group
Staples I.
NIGEI I.
DESERTERS GROUP
Gordon Channel
Deserters I.
Wishart I.
Balaclava I.
God's Pocket Marine Park
QUEEN CHARLOTTE STRAIT
GOLETAS CHANNEL
Bell I.
Hurst I.
Gordon Is.
Miles
2
4
Km
4
6
Hardy Bay
PORT HARDY

is located between Wishart and Deserters islands in the Deserters Group. Camping options are generally poor here.

Shelter Bay

Shelter Bay is conveniently located at the north end of Queen Charlotte Strait. Mariners will appreciate the protected anchorage before or after crossing Cape Caution, while kayakers can use it for shelter after crossing from Vancouver Island. The rocky shoreline of the bay encloses a wonderful sand beach and some commercial fish farms and First Nation shellfishing. Nearby Annie Rocks is used by black oystercatchers as a nesting site.

Camping: N50°58.61'/W127°27.64'. A white sand beach is set back in the shelter of a small cove behind some islets just east of Westcott Point. The islets provide a good breakwater and also hide the beach; it may not be easily seen from Shelter Bay. Behind the beach some campsites have been created in the forested upland, but you probably won't need them as camping on the beach is good at most tide levels. At low tide a sand spit connects the beach to the closest islet. This is a wonderful campsite in a strategic location for crossing Queen Charlotte Strait from Port Hardy.

N50°58.66'/W127°28.07'. Just west of Westcott Point is a long, narrow cove backed by a beautiful white sand beach. It is problematic

Light breaks through the cloud cover over Queen Charlotte Strait.

on two counts: the angle of the cove makes the beach open to westerlies, to which this area is prone, and there is no clear upland area to avoid spring tides. But it is picturesque enough to consider if you pass by at the right time.

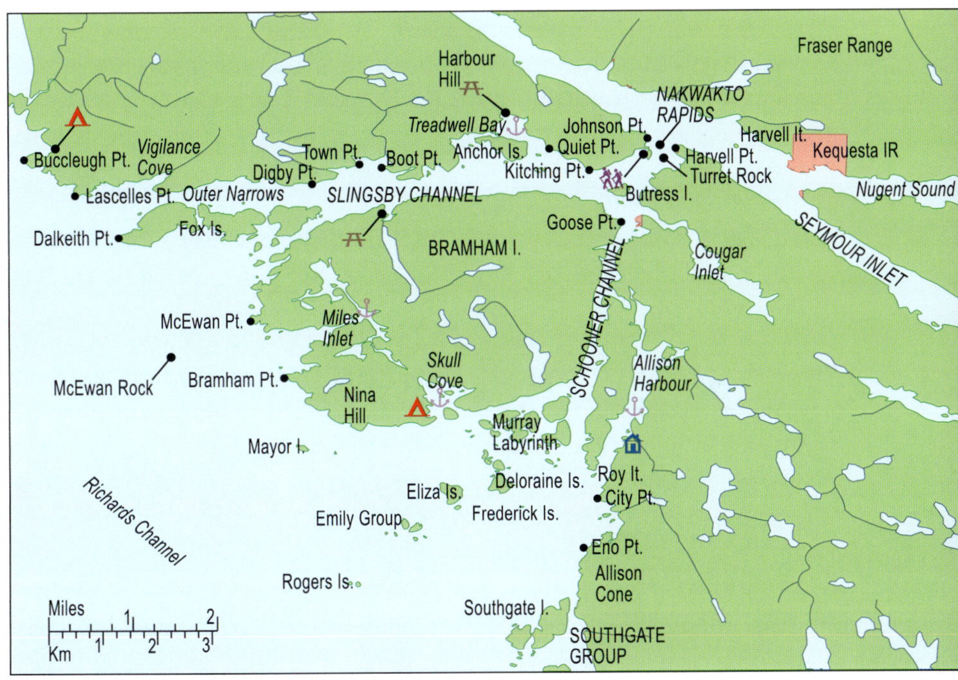

Allison Harbour

Used now mainly as an anchorage, Allison Harbour was once a small community. Some ruins, including the footings of the dock, can still be seen on a point near the southeast end of the harbour. The point directly to the north of the ruins is home to a very tidy and well-built cabin offered by its owners, a cooperative, for use by the general public. There is no beach access to the cabin, just rock shoreline.

Place names: Mr. Allison was manager of the logging operations at the Smith-Dollar Lumber Company in the early 1920s. The harbour also went by the old names of False Bay and False Schooner Passage—a hint to keep your eyes open if you intend to head to Schooner Channel instead.

Schooner Channel

Schooner Channel runs 5.5 km (3.4 miles) along the east side of Bramham Island, providing the main route for marine traffic passing through Nakwakto Rapids. Much of that traffic is log barges. The width along Schooner Channel constricts to as little as 60 m (200 feet), which creates currents as strong as 6 knots. Kayakers will want to travel with the current, which floods north and ebbs south.

Near the south entrance to the channel are a number of island groups. The ecological highlights are the Emily Group and Rogers Islands, which are nesting sites for black oystercatcher and pigeon guillemot. McEwan Rock is also a breeding site. The other islands, particularly Murray Labyrinth, might be interesting to explore due to the complex shoreline, but the islands are rocky with just a few rough beaches.

Camping: N51°02.96'/W127°33.78'. Skull Cove on the south side of Bramham Island offers arguably the best beach in the area. On the southwest side of the cove is a grit and rock beach with a grassy bank. A squatter's cabin is located on the nearby point. A marine trail campsite is indicated in Miles Inlet.

Nakwakto Rapids

All the tidal waters of Seymour Inlet, Belize Inlet and Nugent Sound must squeeze through this small passage, creating a current as strong as 16 knots—one of the fastest tidal rapids in the world. (*The Guinness Book of World Records* has listed it as the fastest navigable tidal rapid in the world, though fans of Skookumchuck Rapids at Sechelt Inlet will be quick to point out the current there has been recorded at 17 knots.)

There are three islands in the immediate vicinity of the rapids. Toward Bramham Island is Butress Island. Once north of Butress Island, continue only with extreme caution, as the current will get stronger. In mid-rapid is Turret Rock, remarkable for the many wooden signs nailed to trees. A popular excursion is to be dropped off at Butress Island at slack tide and picked up at the next slack. It gives the opportunity of feeling the rock tremble as it is beaten by the rapids.

To the immediate west of Turret Rock is a large but unnamed island that doesn't quite connect with the mainland. On the west side of this island is a rock shelf—the northernmost of two—where

A tug takes a load of logs through Nakwakto Rapids at slack tide.

small boats can tie up. A trail leads from here across the island to a treetop platform for viewing the rapids. The rock shelf where you must tie up is in the tidal current and very close to the tidal rapid that runs between the unnamed island and the mainland at Johnson Point, so use caution here.

Nakwakto Rapids has its own entry in the *Canadian Tide and Current Tables, Volume 6, Discovery Passage and West Coast of Vancouver Island*. Refer to the listed current table when visiting. The period of slack time, which lasts just five minutes, is quite different from the tide change elsewhere in the region. This anomaly affects Schooner Channel and Slingsby Channel as well.

Travel notes: Visitors in small boats and kayakers will want to visit the rapids by travelling Schooner Channel on a favourable flood tide. If you time your visit to arrive at the rapids at or near slack tide your journey will be simpler. You can tie up at the trailhead without having to worry about a current. You can then watch the rapids as the ebb current builds, using the favourable ebb current to leave the area when you are ready. If you arrive too early, be aware that the strong current can outpace paddlers and even small boats. If you pass north of Butress Island and run into trouble—that is, find the current pulling you along too quickly—you can find safety in a calm spot in the middle of the unnamed island. Aim for the island's centre and wait out slack tide, if necessary.

Place names: Nakwakto Rapids was home to the Nakwaxda'xw, a people of Kwakiutl descent. They lived here until their relocation to Tsulquate Indian Reserve in Port Hardy in 1962. Nakwakto is an anglicization of Nakwaxda'xw.

Seymour and Belize inlets

These two long waterways lie on the mainland side of Nakwakto Rapids. Joined to them are a number of sounds and bays; all are connected to the ocean via the rapids. A quick look at the extent of these waters should give an idea of why Nakwakto Rapids has such strong currents. Seymour Inlet lies north of the rapids and runs 53 km (33 miles) until it reaches Eclipse Narrows. From there it turns north and continues for another 21 km (13 miles). Belize Inlet extends 40 km (25 miles) east into the B.C. interior from the northwest end of Seymour Inlet. Tidal currents are low in both inlets, as not all the water can escape the inlets before the tide changes. This means fluctuations are as little as 1.2 m (4 feet) when tides run about 4.25 m (14 feet) elsewhere in the region.

These waters are rarely visited, primarily due to the barrier of the rapids, and the area was not even charted until 1987. One remarkable feature at Alison Sound's Chief Nollis Bay is a cliff with ochre pictographs depicting an early European encounter. (Not all of these inlets and sounds are on the regional map; a more complete view is offered on the main map for this chapter on page 66 and on the central coast map on page 52.)

Anchorages: There are two provincial boat havens in Belize and Seymour inlets—one in a cove to the southwest of Strachan Bay off Mereworth Sound (north of Belize Inlet) and the other in the southwest cove of Peet Bay at Alison Sound, on the east side of Belize Inlet.

Place names: Belize is the capital of Honduras. It was a British colony in the 1800s, and Frederick Seymour (Seymour Inlet) was its governor before being appointed British Columbia governor in 1864.

A pocket beach lies hidden north of Buccleugh Point.

Slingsby Channel

Slingsby Channel runs along the north end of Bramham Island, with a boat haven/anchorage at Treadwell Bay near Nakwakto Rapids. A few rough beaches are located along the length of the channel. Currents can run as high as 9 knots but will usually be much less. More troubling is the turbulence at the channel's mouth on an ebb tide. Standing waves and rips are likely where the outflow current meets Queen Charlotte Sound near Vigilance Point. Since travellers are likely to want to ride the ebb tide out of the channel, hitting the turbulence is likely.

The Outer Narrows, north of Fox Islands, is the only place in the northern straits where the Arctic cookie star (*Ceramaster arcticus*) is found.

Place names: Sir Charles Slingsby was the 10th and final baronet of Scriven Park, Yorkshire.

Camping: N51°05.10'/W127°37.59'. Some visitors may want to pull out on the rough beaches at Treadwell Bay or on Bramham Island, but if you're looking for sand consider the beach just north of Buccleugh Point. It can easily be passed by since you have to turn into the cove north of the point and look back to see it. Between the point's headland and an outlying reef is what I consider to be one of the prettiest beaches on the coast. It comes with a catch, however. The beach is open to northwest swell, which can crash off the headland and the nearby reef to block most of the entry to the beach with foaming water. Conditions are accentuated at low tide. Expect the possibility of a surf landing or launch under moderate conditions. In ideal conditions, though, this spot is highly recommended.

Storm, Pine and Buckle islands

These remote islands are part of the Duke of Edinburgh Ecological Reserve, and are key marine bird habitat—the second most important seabird area in B.C. See *The Wild Coast, Volume I* for more details.

Burnett Bay

This area is remarkable for its long sand beach, but the bay is exposed. High breaking surf is common, limiting its recreational use. If you are lucky enough to arrive on a calm day, be sure to take a stroll. Not many people get the chance.

Camping: N51°08.44'/W127°43.58'. The ideal location for camping in this area is north of Burnett Bay between Wilkie and Raynor points. Rocks and an islet reduce the amount of surf reaching the beach. Enter via the east side of the islet. A ring of reefs complicated by crashing swell on the west side of the islet makes entry hazardous.

Cape Caution

The cape represents one of the toughest stretches of open water along the B.C. coast. Unfortunately the tough conditions tend to hide the intriguing coastline of beaches, dramatic rock formations and prominent headlands.

The problem is the convergence of water from Queen Charlotte Strait, Queen Charlotte Sound and Smith Sound. The shallow water around the cape exaggerates swell, while the steep granite shoreline leads to strong rebound waves. Crossings are best undertaken in the morning before the swell and wind have a chance to build.

Blunden Bay, tucked in the north shore of the cape, is known for its sand beach, but reefs and rocks offshore make access difficult. The reefs worsen north of Hoop Bay, where they extend north in a line from Neck Ness. It is next to impossible to navigate between the reefs with any swell, so it is advisable to keep to the outside. This means travelling well offshore until you can enter Smith Sound. Blunden Bay, Indian Cove and Neck Ness have been tagged as B.C. marine

Crashing waves create their own fog at Cape Caution.

trail campsites. My experience is you would not want to approach these beaches in any kind of swell without local knowledge. This portion of coast is simply too temperamental.

Travel notes: My first crossing of Cape Caution entailed 9-m (30-foot) swell complicated by wind waves, rebound waves and turbulence. It was as if my kayak was in a bucket being shaken by an angry child. When the wind waves and rebound waves met under the stern they crashed together like an explosion under the kayak. There was no way to anticipate this because the waves were coming from behind. Stopping at any of the beaches around the cape was simply not an option on this day. The swell wasn't even noticeable because of all the other troubles until I crested one particular wave and looked up to see a huge valley of water ahead of me with the crest of the next wave approaching in the distance like something out of *The Perfect Storm*. Riding up the side of it was the only time I have ever had my stomach do an elevator-lurch in a kayak.

The second crossing was in far lighter conditions, but the size of the swell was still formidable. Conditions tended to be worst around Hoop Bay, where the shallow ocean shelf amplified the waves to about 3.5 m (12 feet). These would steamroll onto the reefs in an impressive blast of white water. Elsewhere the swell was closer to 1.2 m (4 feet). The spray from waves pounding against the rocks created instant fog, especially at the cape, and thick banks would quickly develop and drift by. Even as a veteran kayaker I would not have considered stopping at any of the most exposed beaches along this stretch. The surf sounded like a freight train as it worked its way down the length of the beach at Burnett Bay. Anyone camping overnight when conditions are ideal should prepare for the possibility of a change in the weather the next day. That could mean a high surf launch.

Place names: The hazard presented by Cape Caution was recognized by Captain Vancouver and reflected in the name he gave it in May 1793. His ship, *Discovery*, was nearly shipwrecked on a rock about 15 miles southeast of the cape on August 6, 1792. He wrote that it is "a conspicuous cape, terminating in rugged rocks, low hummocks, that produce some dwarf pine, and other small trees and shrubs. This cape, from the dangers navigating in its vicinity, I distinguish by the name of Cape Caution."

A rarely visited beach at Penrose Island Marine Park.

RIVERS INLET

The region surrounding Rivers Inlet includes Smith Sound and Fish Egg Inlet, and is best known for two features: secure anchorages—valuable after crossing the open waters around Cape Caution—and excellent fishing. Rivers Inlet is legendary for its 27-kg (60-pound) chinook. All five species of salmon are found here, and it is considered one of the premier fishing locations in B.C. The result is a choice of fishing resorts dotting the area and two fishing-based communities: Duncanby Landing and Dawsons Landing.

Both Rivers Inlet and Smith Inlet lead deep into the mountainous B.C. interior but are rarely visited by recreational traffic, perhaps because except for the backdrop of mountains, both inlets have few standout features. Kayakers tend to favour the passages around Penrose Island Marine Park. The park is also a popular anchorage.

Egg Island

Ferries and cruise ships on their way up the Inside Passage will pass west of here. Traffic bound for Smith Sound will want to use Alexandra Passage on the inside. A lighthouse was first built on Egg Island in 1898. The original tower was destroyed by a storm in 1948 and replaced with the current metal skeleton structure in 1949. The station is still staffed, and Egg Island provides weather updates for this region.

Weather: Though exposed, Egg Island is blessed with the relatively mild Pacific climate of the B.C. coast, with average daytime highs of just 14°C (57°F) to 16°C (61°F) through the summer months. The coolest portions of the day will be about 11°C (52°F) in July and August, dropping to 9°C (48°F) in June and September.

Temperatures rarely fall below freezing, with less than 10 days with freezing weather at any point during the day in January and less than eight days with temperatures below freezing in December. Rainfall tends to be lowest in July with an average of 78 mm (3 inches), compared to 124 mm (4.8 inches) in June and 103 mm (4 inches) in August. The wettest months are October at 305 mm (12 inches) and November at 366 mm (14.4 inches). The most rainfall in one day occurred on January 10, 1996, when the weather station on Egg Island recorded 199.9 mm (7.87 inches). Even during the summer months rain tends to fall more than half the days, with some rain recorded on average for 14 days in July, 16 days in August and 17 days in June. A moderate amount of rain, 5 mm (0.2 inches) or more, will fall about 5 days during July, 6 days in August and for about 8 days during June and September.

A boat left to rot, Smith Sound.

This area is prone to moderate winds, with the average wind speed at about 14 km/h (7.5 knots) in July and August, 16 km/h (8.5 knots) in June and 15 km/h (8 knots) in September. The prevailing wind is northwest in the summer and southeast the rest of the year. The highest recorded winds here were 74 knots (137 km/h) on February 12, 1999.

Smith Sound

Smith Sound lies 10 km (6 miles) north of Cape Caution and offers the first protected anchorage north of the cape at Jones Cove. The sound is just shy of 8 km (5 miles) wide between Macnicol Point to the south and Extended Point to the north. A variety of island groups are sprinkled around the sound, making for good exploration by kayak. The recreational highlight is the sand beaches of Dsulish Bay. Another very fine beach is found on the south shore of the sound near Chest Island. It is notable for the red sand, from which it gets its local name, Redsand Beach. Remarkably, Smith Sound is free of fish farms, resorts or development of any permanent nature.

Indian Island, now a reserve, was until recent times a winter village site; its heritage inventory includes middens, burial sites and a grave house. The nearby waters of Fly Basin, Broad Reach and Ahclakerho Channel are unremarkable, with mostly rough beaches.

Millbrook Cove is a boat haven, and a rough beach can be found on the north shore.

Place names: Smith Sound was first explored and named for reasons unrecorded by Captain James Hanna of the *Sea Otter* in 1786.

Camping: N51°15.35'/W127°42.81'. Just southeast of Chest Island, set back in a bit of a cove on the south side of the sound, is the remarkable Redsand Beach. On a high tide, cover can be found in the forest. Watch for the scuttled fishing boat in the westernmost of the two rivers that run through the beach. Despite its shelter the beach can be exposed to surf. Plan for moderate waves as high as 0.6 m (2 feet).

N51°20.31'/W127°40.57'. Dsulish Bay has two sandy beaches broken by a rock headland. Either beach is suitable for camping, and the rock bluffs provide protection from surf. This is a great place to stretch the legs.

Travel notes: On my arrival at Smith Sound I camped at the stone beach immediately northwest of Redsand Beach. I created a level area at the very top of the beach by pushing the stones flat to the top of a drift log for support on the bottom end. It was a near-spring tide but I expected adequate clearance. Later that night I was awoken by the sound of crashing surf very near my ear (there had been no surf when I landed). Moments later a wave smashed against the log my camp was built upon, shaking my tent. I stepped out to watch large breakers rolling onto the beach, with the largest breaking on the log by my tent, giving it a good outer soaking. Fortunately that was as high as the tide got that night, and the tent withstood the assault. It was the first time I had to consider the potentially disastrous combination of spring tides and surf.

Smith Inlet

Smith Inlet begins at McBride Bay and continues east for 32 km (20 miles), ending in Nekite River. Branching from the main inlet is Naysash Inlet and Wyclees Lagoon. The lagoon is protected by a

Driftwood lines the beach at Dsulish Bay.

narrows noted for its tidal chute. North of McBride Bay is Margaret Bay, which is often used as an anchorage. Ruins of an old cannery lie at the head. The Margaret Bay Cannery operated until 1938, and pilings, a boiler and other debris remain. Finis Nook, located near the mouth of Boswell Inlet, is a provincial boat haven.

Kelp Head

Between Extended Point on the north entrance of Smith Sound and Cranstown Point, which marks the south entrance into Rivers Inlet, there is 6.1 km (4 miles) of exposed shore. It is a rugged and rocky area. A beach at Extended Point is a good place to explore. Cranstown Point to the north is at the end of a notable headland with beaches on both sides of the narrow neck. The best protection is on the east side facing Open Bight. A short trail leads across the peninsula to the more exposed west-facing beach.

Camping: N51°22.31'/W127°46.41'. The beach facing Open Bight south of Cranston Point is a beautiful stretch and well protected thanks to the sand neck.

An islet with a view up Rivers Inlet.

Goose Bay

This deep inlet is a popular location for fishing resorts. Duncanby Landing offers showers, laundry, accommodation, a store, plus a pub and restaurant. The operation began in 1936 as a supply point for fishermen, loggers and trappers. It was operated as a public dock from 1993 to 2004, and is once again under private management. The landing monitors Channel 6.

Farther south is Goose Bay Landing, the site of an old cannery that operated until the mid-1950s. Regular service by the Union Steamship Company continued even after the cannery's closing. The buildings of the cannery still stand, and the Goose Bay Cannery remains one of the best examples of the heyday of canning when there were 17 operations in Rivers Inlet. The ruins of other canneries dot the inlet; one is converted to a fishing lodge.

Draney Inlet

This inlet leads 25 km (15.5 miles) into the B.C. coast. Draney Narrows can have tidal rapids and a chute of whitewater around a rock at the entrance. Currents run 8 to 10 knots. For calculating slack times, Draney Narrows turns to flood 25 minutes after the Prince Rupert low tide and turns to ebb 25 minutes after the Prince Rupert high tide.

Place names: Robert Draney was the manager of the cannery and sawmill at the mouth of Wannock River in 1890 before moving on to run the Namu cannery.

Kilbella Bay

Two major rivers drain into Kilbella Bay to create the Chuckwalla/Kilbella Rivers Estuary. The estuary is key grizzly and waterfowl territory, with high use by bear, fish, heron, trumpeter swan and western grebe. Chinook arrive in June to kick off the sport fishing season in Rivers Inlet. The bay was also the site of two former Wuikinuxv (Oweekeno) winter villages. Used through the 1800s, by 1935 the residents had all moved to the Katit Reserve on Wannock River.

Katit

Located on the north bank of the Wannock River between Owikeno Lake and the head of Rivers Inlet, Katit is a community of about 80 residents, while another 300 Wuikinuxv band members live off the reserve. Archaeological evidence suggests 9,000 years of habitation in this area, and it was once the centre of the largest population of all central coast First Nations. Hatcheries and commercial fishing provide today's economic backbone for the community, which boasts a school, community hall, band office and drop-in centre. Electricity is supplied by generator. There are no facilities designed for visitors.

Owikeno Lake

This long lake is characterized by steep slopes, but those who venture as far as Sheemahant River on the north end will be rewarded with a hot spring. The river is developed with a bathhouse next to the logging road. The spring empties into a small creek that is diverted to a boiler where it is allowed to cool before being piped into the bathhouse. The portage to this lake from the ocean earned the Wuikinuxv their name (see page 63).

Moses Inlet

Logging, roads and an airstrip characterize the use of this inlet. It ends in Clyak Estuary, where wetlands form part of a major system used by juvenile salmon, grizzlies and waterfowl.

Walbran Island

Walbran is the dominant island of Rivers Inlet, and together with close neighbours forms a network of narrow inlets and channels. Kayakers will want to explore Magee Channel and Geetla Inlet. Magee Channel meanders between Ripon and Walbran islands. With the number of islands and passages it is easy to get lost—but that's part of the fun, of course. Geetla Inlet can be obstructed by a drying bank 0.8 km (about a half mile) north of the intersection with Magee Channel. Both it and Magee Channel have numerous rocks and shoals, keeping it the domain of kayaks and smaller boats.

Place names: Captain John T. Walbran was commander of the steamer *Quadra* from 1891 to 1903. His legacy is a tome of historical information republished recently as *British Columbia Coast Names, Their Origin and History* by Douglas and McIntyre, 1971. His observations are quoted extensively in *The Wild Coast* series—in part because Land Information B.C.'s Geographical Name Information Service also quotes Walbran extensively in its own historical archive, an indication of his key role as a place name historian for B.C.

Floating cabins compose downtown Dawsons Landing.

Dawsons Landing

The site of a former cannery, this resort has evolved into a small floating community driven by fishing resort business. Amenities include a public dock, post office, liquor store, general store, resort, showers, laundry and water. The resort monitors VHF channel 6.

Place names: Dawsons Landing was first named as a steamer landing in 1947, and was serviced by the Union Steamship Company. The post office opened in 1967 on a float.

Darby Channel

This picturesque channel runs along the northwest side of Walbran Island, and is, anecdotally, a calmer alternative to larger and more exposed Rivers Inlet. One highlight of Darby Channel is an abandoned cannery with a boiler, bricks and machinery still visible. Beaches provide access to the ruins, but level upland areas for camping are hard to find.

Place names: Originally called Schooner Passage, the name Darby Channel was adopted in 1947 to avoid duplication. Dr. George Darby operated out of Bella Bella as a medical missionary on the B.C. coast for 45 years. He maintained a summer hospital on Rivers Inlet, and used Darby Channel in his travels.

Rough, rock shoreline is typical of Penrose Island Marine Park.

Klaquaek Channel

This waterway separates Walbran and Penrose islands. The north entrance is known as Slaughter Alley, or Slaughter Illahee (Illahee means "place" or "land"). An island at the north entrance to Rivers Inlet was an important Wuikinuxv village until a Heiltsuk raid in the mid-1800s saw a great number of Wuikinuxv killed. The survivors fled up the inlet.

A boat haven is located off the northwest corner of Ripon Island off the east side of the channel. A marine trail campsite is indicated at the island on the southwest side of Klaquaek Channel. It is apparently a small but protected site.

Penrose Island

A number of fishing lodges have taken up residence in Finn Bay on the north half of Penrose Island. Finn Bay Retreat is a floating camp with showers, while Buck's Trophy Lodge is on the east shore. Other resorts dot nearby areas, such as Sleepy Bay and Sunshine Bay. Quoin Hill is Penrose Island's highest point, reaching 250 m (820 feet). The south side of the island is protected parkland, along with the associated archipelago. Penrose Island, Fury Island and a line of reefs and islets create a sheltered anchorage often referred to as Fury Bay (though the real Fury Bay is at Langara Island in the Queen Charlotte Islands; this one has no official name). The bay is one of several anchorages known collectively as Schooner Retreat. The retreat has several large historic sites nearby.

Fury Bay is lined by a beautiful clamshell beach known locally as Clam Beach. Another boat haven is at Frypan Bay. A marine trail campsite is indicated at Addenbroke Point at the north side of the entrance to Rivers Inlet.

Camping: N51°29.14'/W127°45.68'. Clam Beach is one of the few appropriate camping locations in this region. The beach is on the north side of Fury Island and extends to a few neighbouring islets. The choice campsite, on an open but exposed point on the very north end of Fury Island, offers views of both Fitz Hugh Sound and into the

Penrose Island Marine Park

Penrose Island Marine Park includes half the namesake island plus numerous smaller islands, channels and coves. It is a mixture best explored by kayak, though boaters commonly use several anchorages within the park, including the very pretty and protected cove north of Fury Island. Used traditionally by the Wuikinuxv for shellfishing, the clamshells they once harvested now form the backbone of the recreational highlight of the park at Clam Beach. A short trail links Clam Beach and a cabin. The park was created in 1982, and protects 1,079 ha (4.1 square miles) of marine area and 934 ha (3.6 square miles) of land.

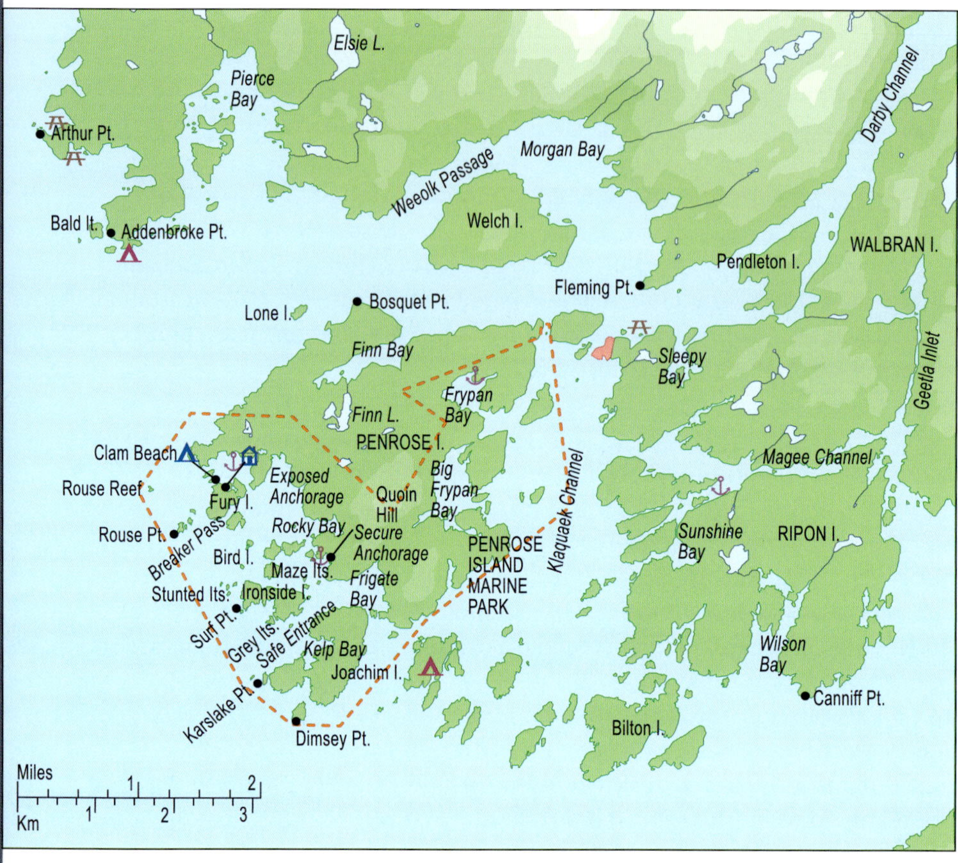

cove. More sheltered sites are found on the nearby beaches under the treeline. A cabin is set back a few yards in the forest. Wooden stairs and a plank ramp indicate the access to the trail. The cabin is dry but dark, and has a wood-burning stove, a table, chairs, bunks and shelving. Another beach lies just outside the anchorage on Fury Island. It is a wonderful spot, but finding it requires navigating rock-choked water. Adventurous kayakers may want to use it for the seclusion and views.

Fish Egg Inlet

This inlet has a growing reputation as a wonderful place to explore, by boat or by kayak. The multitude of coves, inlets and islands are best ventured into at low tide, when the rich subtidal ecology can be viewed. Watch for numerous species of anemones and sea cucumbers. Be sure to nose up to the tidal chutes at both Mantrap Inlet and

Reflections on perfectly calm water create fascinating patterns on the shore at Fish Egg Inlet.

Elizabeth Lagoon. The rapids are navigable at high-water slack tide by boats with a shallow draught.

Southwest of Green Island between two unnamed neighbouring islands is a basin that creates a protected anchorage and a provincial boat haven.

Outside of Fish Egg Inlet is a sizeable group of islands, with Addenbroke Island on the outer edge. The lighthouse on Addenbroke is still manned; a small beach just to the north allows visits. The original 1914 tower has been replaced twice now; the present skeleton tower was built in 1998.

Weather: Addenbroke Island experiences cool summers, with daytime highs averaging below 18°C (64°F) in both July and August. June and September are slightly cooler, with average daytime highs below 16°C (61°F). Temperatures will drop to a low of about 12°C (53°F) in July and August, and about 10°C (50°F) in both June and September. In winter, days will rarely remain below freezing.

Annual precipitation is 3,286 mm (130 inches). Expect about 100 mm (4 inches) to fall in July and 137 mm (5.5 inches) in August. That translates into 14 to 18 days per month with some amount of

Calm waters in the early morning at Fish Egg Inlet.

rain during the summer. Expect 5 to 10 days of moderate rain of 5 mm (0.2 inches) or more and 3 to 8 days with a good soaking of 10 mm (0.4 inches) or more each summer month.

The prevailing summertime wind is north—an indication of the funnelling of wind down Fitz Hugh Sound. Average wind speeds are lowest in September, at 12.8 km/h (6.9 knots), and mildly higher in July and August at 13.0 km/h (7 knots). Winds are highest in January, averaging 15.9 km/h (8.6 knots).

The windiest day recorded here was 96.9 km/h (52.3 knots) on January 22, 1981.

Camping: N51°33.99'/W127°47.61'. While Fish Egg Inlet has numerous beaches, they are invariably rough. The closest to being a sand beach is to the south of Fish Egg Inlet in Fitz Hugh Sound, partway between Fish Egg and Philip inlets. The best portion of beach is intertidal, however, and spring tide levels will likely force you onto the neighbouring stone beach instead.

Lighthouse etiquette: Staffed lighthouses are often the only inhabited and developed places on long stretches of the coast, and they tend to be a magnet for mariners. Some, like the Cape Scott lighthouse on northern Vancouver Island, are on a trail system and see a regular number of people. Most others, however, tend to be on exposed and isolated coastal locations—thus their usefulness as lights—and see very few visitors. Others are at locations that truly qualify for the definition "God-forsaken"—rocky, exposed islands on the remote outer coast that few would want to approach even in fair weather. And yet venture there they do. "There are many humorous stories about what happens to new keepers who think they can do their gardening in the buff, only to have a family of five show up and ask for a tour," says Dennis Rose, who shares duties as keeper of the Addenbroke lighthouse with his wife, Cynthia. They live on Addrenbroke Island with their children.

Addenbroke Island light station.

For that reason many lightkeepers prefer that you radio in first, which at the very least allows them to get out the cookie jar and put on a pot of coffee before you arrive (chances are you will be greeted warmly, and perhaps even offered accommodation). The Coast Guard, which oversees lighthouse operations, would prefer that you call first as well. Of course, every keeper has different preferences. "Some stations get so few visitors that you could sky-dive naked onto their front lawn and they'd invite you to lunch," Dennis says.

Lighthouses monitor 16, the emergency channel, and 82A.

Kwakume Inlet

This deep and convoluted inlet is a boat haven that provides a well-protected anchorage along most of its length. There are a few tiny beaches on the north end of the inlet that may be worth a picnic stop (such as N51°42.36'/W127°53.00'), though the islets slightly south of Kwakume Point offer a far finer camping opportunity.

Camping: N51°40.86'/W127°52.91'. About a mile south of Kwakume Point is a string of three islets strung together by a beautiful clamshell beach at lower tides. The main and cleanest stretch is between the mainland and the first and largest islet. Some limited camping opportunities are available here, though most of the clamshell bar will disappear at higher tides. A channel runs between the first and second (tiny) islet at most tides. A clamshell beach can be found among the rocks on the southeast side of the middle islet, giving access to it and the third islets. Flat rock ledges can be used for camping here and on the connected outer islet. There is also a flat area for a small tent on light vegetation on the middle islet. This is a beautiful spot with views clear up and down Fitz Hugh Sound. The really adventurous can set up on the flat rock ledge on the outside point of the outside islet.

A view down Fitz Hugh Sound from the islets south of Kwakume Point.

Shoreline on Calvert Island.

Hakai

CHAPTER TWO

WHEN I FIRST ARRIVED AT WOLF BEACH, THE FABLED KAYAKING DESTINAtion at Hakai, I was prepared for a crowd of kayakers. It was, after all, mid-August and the central coast's top kayaking stop.

Once I landed and began to explore, the tracks on the beach told the story. Wolves had been the only recent visitors, and their prints dotted the shoreline.

The next day two kayakers who had been sharing my itinerary off and on since Bella Bella showed up, but otherwise the incredible beaches along north Calvert Island were empty. When we left, Hakai once again belonged to the wolves.

Hakai Luxvbalis Conservancy Area is without doubt the highlight of the central B.C. coast, with a multitude of island groups, forests, mountains, anchorages, meandering inlets, tidal rapids, rarely visited lagoons and pure white sand beaches. Other areas to explore include the wave-battered shores of the Simonds and McNaughton groups, the intricate passages of Spider and Hurricane islands and—if you dare—the sprawling sand beaches of the outer reaches, from the Goose Group to west Calvert Island.

Despite its isolation from the nearest community with road access, Hakai is surprisingly easy to get to. The *Queen of Chilliwack* will drop off kayakers on its route along Fitz Hugh Sound at strategic points like Kwakshua Channel or Sea Otter Inlet. Lodges such as Hakai Beach Resort cater to backcountry coastal explorers who prefer luxury over tents. Fishing resorts dot inlets and coves.

Other nearby attractions are the icing on the cake. The ghost town of Namu and its cannery ruins beckon explorers. Historic Koeye River is also not to be missed, whether you are there to

STRYKER I.
CAMPBELL ISLAND
DENNY ISLAND
Fingal I.
Piddington I.
Lama Passage
McMullin Group
Tribal Group
Hunter Channel
See Bella Coola, page 149
Codville Lagoon MP
See Bella Bella, page 121
HUNTER ISLAND
KING ISLAND
Dodwell I.
Prince Group
Fisher Channel
107
Goose I.
GOOSE GROUP
Simonds Group
Sans Peur Pass
Kisameet Bay
Kildid Lagoon
McNaughton Group
Kinsman Inlet
De Cosmos Lagoon
BURKE CHANNEL
Gull I.
Duck I.
Gosling I.
QUEENS SOUND
Cultus Sound
Fougner Bay
Superstition Pt.
Goodlad Bay
Kildidt Inlet
Kiltik Bay
Harlequin Basin
Gosling Rocks
Shipping route
Rock Inlet
Spitfire Channel
Spider I.
Hurricane I.
NAMU
Namu L.
Kittyhawk Group
Watt Bay
Sea Otter Inlet
Kiwash Cove
Warrior Cove
Edna Is.
Mustang Bay
Manley I.
Uganda Pt.
Triquet I.
Leckie Bay
Serpent Group
Nalau Passage
Daedalus Pt.
115
Blenheim I.
Middleton Pt.
KILDIDT SOUND
Nalau I.
Koeye R.
Stirling I.
Bayly Pt.
HAKAI LUXVBALIS CONSERVANCY AREA
QUEEN CHARLOTTE SOUND
Breaker Group
Kelpie Pt.
Hakai Passage
Odlum Pt.
Kwakume Inlet
FITZ HUGH SOUND
Odlum I.
Kwakume Pt.
Surf I.
Adams Head
Hecate I.
Pruth Bay
Kwakshua Channel
Experiment Pt.
Illahie Inlet
Corvette Is.
Fish Egg Inlet
Addenbroke I.
Dublin Pt.
Bolivar It.
CALVERT I.
See Cape Caution, page 65
Safety Mountain
Safety Cove
Mark Nipple
Blackney I.
Cape Range
Chic Chic Bay
CAPE CALVERT
Miles
4
8
Km
4
8
12
Charley Is.
North Passage
Clark Pt.
Sorrow I.
Grief Bay
South Passage
100

photograph bears or to stay in the comfortable Heiltsuk-run lodge on the point.

And don't worry about the crowds. There is always space to spare in Hakai.

CALVERT ISLAND

The Inside Passage begins at the south end of Calvert Island, with Fitz Hugh Sound separating the island from the mainland by as much as 10 km (6 miles). Most traffic to Calvert Island tends to travel down Kwakshua Channel to Pruth Bay or Choked Passage. Here you will find good anchorages and the most accessible of the wonderful white sands of Hakai.

Fitz Hugh Sound

This vast passage lies between Calvert Island and the mainland, after which it transforms into Fisher Channel. It is the main route for most marine traffic heading north from Vancouver Island, and will include cruise ships, ferries, fishing vessels, barges and recreational boats. Kayakers travelling from the south will likely want to stay to the east side as they work up past Cape Caution. This gives access to attractions such as Penrose Island Marine Park and avoids an open and lengthy crossing. The east shore of Calvert Island has very few draws of its own, with the possible exception of a large waterfall that tumbles into Fitz Hugh Sound 2.4 km (1.5 mile) north of Truman Point. The logical crossing to Hakai for kayakers is at the narrowest section of open water at Addenbroke Island. Crossing later at Kwakume Point will double the distance of open water.

Tidal streams in Fitz Hugh Sound ebb south at as much as 2 knots, with a much weaker flood current north. These can be irregular or non-existent at neap (lower) tides when freshwater runoff is high.

For those who wish to visit south Calvert Island, be warned that the waters around Clark Point can be turbulent. If you travel this way, stop at the sand beach at Grief Bay. Most boaters, however, will simply continue north to the popular anchorage at Safety Cove. Despite the name, don't expect the shelter of a beach at Canoe Cove. It is just a jumble of rock.

Place names: Captain Hanna of the *Sea Otter* named this sound during his second visit between China and Nootka Sound in 1786. Captain Vancouver adopted the name on his chart when he explored here

See Queens Sound, page 115
Stirling I.
See Hunter Island, page 107
NALAU I.
Breaker Group
HAKAI PASSAGE
North Pointer Rocks
Kelpie Pt.
Umme Pt.
Goldstream Harbour
Barney Pt.
Whidbey Pt.
Kwakume Inlet
Kwakume Pt.
Odlum Pt.
Donald I.
Odlum I.
CHOKED PASSAGE
Rattenbury I.
HECATE I.
Starfish I.
Sandspit Pt.
Lower Is.
Adams Head
Meay It.
198
Stony Saddle
Surf Is.
Wolf Beach
Guise Pt.
Whittaker Pt.
Pruth Bay
KWAKSHUA CHANNEL
Experiment Pt.
Wedgborough Pt.
Keith Anchorage
183
(Tower trail)
FITZ HUGH SOUND
Corvette Is.
Dublin Pt.
CALVERT ISLAND
Mt. Buxton
1017
Addenbroke I.
HAKAI LUXVBALIS CONSERVANCY AREA
See Cape Caution, page 65
Bolivar It.
Truman Pt.
Safety Mountain
879
QUEEN CHARLOTTE SOUND
Safety Pt.
Safety Cove
South Pt.
Blackney I.
591
Cape Range
Mark Nipple
Herbert Pt.
Chic Chic Bay
Jennie I.
Canoe Cove
Stafford Pt.
Entry Cone
351
Miles
2
Km
2
4
Charley Is.
CAPE CALVERT
Harold Pt.
Grief Bay
Clark Pt.
North Passage
Sorrow Is.
South Passage

in 1792. Captain Duncan of the *Princess Royal* named it Sir Charles Middleton's Sound, but it never took.

Camping: N51°25.42'/W127°54.54'. Tucked in behind the shelter of Sorrow Islands is Grief Bay. The south-facing beach in the bay is composed of stones, but the west-facing beach is beautifully sandy—the sort of sand Calvert Island is famous for. If you sneak in from Fitz Hugh Sound you can enjoy the benefits of a beach typical of the outer coast without having to paddle the open ocean, though Clark Point can be a hurdle. Also, gales can make landings and launches difficult.

N51°31.81'/W127°56.19'. Safety Cove is backed by an extensive beach that is sandy on the southern end. Unfortunately the beach is low-backed, capped by low tree cover, dotted with rocks and dries a considerable distance at low tides. Those seeking a campsite in this area might want to consider the stone beach just to the north of the cove instead.

Kwakshua Channel

This is a more placid route than Hakai Passage when travelling from Fitz Hugh Sound to Pruth Bay or Choked Passage. The channel extends west to Pruth Bay, then turns north to join Hakai Passage. A few bluffs and waterfalls at the right time of year make this a pleasant route, but beaches are rough until you reach Pruth Bay.

The northern leg is the prettiest. Bluffs extend from the waterline on the west side. The bald hills of Stony Saddle provide a scenic backdrop on the east side, and there are some broad sand beaches on both sides.

Hakai Lodge, just one of a large number of fishing resorts in this area, is tucked into the shelter of a cove just north of Whittaker Point. Keith Anchorage is a provincial boat haven, and while there are beaches suitable for camping along the north leg of the channel, I recommend the extra distance to the beaches along Choked Passage instead. Some paddlers camp at the sand beach just north of Pruth Bay. Unfortunately this is a cultural site with a notable shell midden and should be avoided.

Hiking: A trail leads from Keith Anchorage to the distinctive bald cone hill with the microwave tower atop. The reward is panoramic views across the region. The trailhead is at the top of the west leg of Keith Anchorage. The trail takes roughly 40 minutes and can be overgrown. It is unofficially maintained by B.C. Parks but not sanctioned due to liability issues. It was not maintained at all in 2005. The trailhead is approximately N51°38.72'/W128°05.67'.

Pruth Bay

This bay is well used as an anchorage and by Hakai Beach Resort, recently renamed The Cliffs at Hakai Beach. It is located on the far end of Pruth Bay, conspicuous with its large buildings and a dock. The resort predates the creation of the park and covers 87 ha (215 acres) within the boundaries of the park, including an extensive portion—about 3.2 km (two miles)—of beachfront. A private trail leads from West Beach to the resort. Note that the resort is private property.

On Pruth Bay is a floating cabin for the park ranger for the Hakai Luxvbalis Conservancy Area. It is staffed infrequently, perhaps six or seven days a month during the summer season.

The drying mud flat off the north end of Pruth Bay is known as Goose Grass Bay. A trail connects it with Wolf Beach.

Hakai Passage

Kwakshua Channel is favoured over Hakai Passage by boaters, and the reason may be clear as soon as you nose into Hakai Passage. The passage is notorious for its swell due to the prevailing westerlies that blow in from Queen Charlotte Sound. There are also several shallow banks—at Breaker Ledge and Mainguy Rock—that accentuate conditions. For those crossing north-south between Kwakshua and Kildidt Sound, it will usually mean a journey sideways to the weather—fine in placid conditions but otherwise downright frightening. It's a crossing best planned for mornings before winds and swell can build. The tough conditions diminish east of the Breaker Group, but some swell is likely to be encountered as far as Kelpie Point, and rough westerlies can blow across Fitz Hugh Sound right into the cove at Koeye River.

Goldstream Harbour is a well-protected anchorage located just south of Kelpie Point off the southeast entrance to Hakai Passage.

Place names: Hakai means "wide passage" in Heiltsuk.

Camping: N51°43.54'/W128°00.45'. Good camping locations are few and far between on the Calvert Island side of Fitz Hugh Sound, but Goldstream Harbour offers a gravel beach backed by a forest. This is

Campers enjoy a meal while a fisherman tries his luck in Choked Passage.

a convenient spot at the entrance to Hakai Passage. Don't make the mistake I did and miss the campsite by entering from the northwest of Kelpie Point. If you enter the harbour from south of Kelpie Point there is indeed a beach suitable for camping.

Choked Passage

This is a popular fishing and kayaking area where the swell of Hakai Passage is broken by a line of islands and reefs. It is also a recreational playground, with trails and superb beaches. There are four main beaches on Calvert Island facing Choked Passage, and most are perfect for camping.

The first beach is a place called Sandspit Point, and is easily recognized by the large dock extending from the north end. The handrail is a work of art, made of driftwood resembling everything from elephants to giraffes. It belongs to Hakai Land and Sea, a cooperatively owned fishing lodge set back from the beach. It exists thanks to a forest-use permit grandfathered into the conservancy area, and, sorry, it doesn't shop for clients. Instead the owners fill the limited number of slots each summer. If you visit, be sure to ask for directions to a trail behind the lodge that leads to a fabulous lookout, or to view the paintings by Kayak Bill (see page 185).

Calvert Island's boggy interior is just another facet of Hakai.

Hakai Luxvbalis Conservancy Area: The Hakai Luxvbalis Conservancy Area protects 122,998 ha (475 square miles) in a massive collection of islands, islets and waterways. Many adjectives can be used to describe it, but suffice it to say the sweeping array of marine and land elements make this one of the prettiest and most varied parks in B.C.

First created as Hakai Recreation Area in 1987, it started with a fundamental flaw. The Heiltsuk First Nation was excluded from the park planning process. This created some temporary animosity. The park planning erred on a number of fronts, including creating five kayak-oriented campsites, two of which were on traditional Heiltsuk sites. Since then B.C. Parks has backed away from both advertising and maintaining the campsites.

Another key difficulty was the name "recreation area." Not surprisingly, the Heiltsuk did not feel their traditional lands should be made a recreation spot for holidaying tourists. In response a new process for the park's management was established, and in 1989 the name was changed to Hakai Luxvbalis (pronounced *looks-bal-ease*) Conservancy Area to better reflect the new reality. Integral to this new agreement is equal say for the Heiltsuk on park management decisions.

A new park management strategy is expected within the next year or two, and out of that kayakers should once again at some point be granted designated camping areas. The strategy, however, may only outline the process for designating campsites, so it could be years before a campsite network is established in Hakai. That means, of the various current camping options, McNaughton Group and Stirling Island should be avoided. Care should also be taken when using other locations, as Hakai abounds with traditional use and village sites, and you could inadvertently be disturbing other cultural areas.

The second main beach is Wolf Beach, named for the high number of wolves. It is a popular kayaking beach. A short trail leads from the middle of the beach to Goose Grass Bay. The trail doesn't reach the lodge, and simply ends at the drying mudflat of the bay. It is a pleasant enough jaunt through the woods.

The third beach is smaller, more sheltered and bounded by rocks. The fourth beach, known as North Beach, is the most expansive, with a lot of protection from the outlying Surf Islands. At low tides the sand bank extends to one of the Surf Islands.

Hiking: From North Beach's west end, a trail leads through the forest to a boggy lake and then to West Beach. This trail is actually on private Hakai Beach Resort land. If you continue along West Beach you will find the trail leading to Pruth Bay and Hakai Beach Resort, which is also a private route. Go farther south along West Beach and you will find a rough trail continuing via boardwalk, rope and ladders to the next two beaches along Calvert Island's outer shores. The resort constructed this trail on Hakai conservancy land, and it has since become somewhat established, though it is not currently sanctioned or maintained by the park. The trail from the resort leads north along the shore from the pier, then west around the north side of the resort to West Beach. An interim agreement with the park allows public access to the float and pier from 8 a.m. to 5:30 p.m. daily for use of the trail. At other times the public is asked to land dinghies on the north side of the pier to gain trail access. The resort management reserves the right to deny access, but won't do so unreasonably. Visitors can help by not letting dogs run loose, for instance, or by not pressing noses to windows to see what's inside.

Travel notes: One of the strangest fish in the ocean is the sunfish, also called *Mola mola*. It is easily mistaken as the head of a fish without a body, and grows to weigh more than a ton (907 kg). It is found widely but rarely, and has been sighted in Choked Passage. The sunfish was estimated at 3 m (10 feet) in length and a weight of about 360 kg (800 pounds). Another was spotted by the folks at Hakai Land and Sea near the Goose Group. It was lying near the surface, allowing birds to pluck off the sea lice.

Camping: N51°40.05'/W128°07.15'. Wolf Beach is located almost due south of Sandspit Point. It is a fantastic beach—well sheltered and with beautiful white sand. It is nicely high-backed to escape spring tides.

N51°39.84'/W128°07.75'. The beach immediately west of Wolf Beach is quite a bit narrower and set in a cove of rocks. The beach itself is pleasant, sheltered and high-backed, though not with as much high tide room as Wolf Beach. There is also more driftwood and there are no trails.

N51°39.77'/W128°08.54'. North Beach has the most room for campsites, and the majority are well protected by Surf Islands. It is nicely high-backed, but stones appear along much of the central beach at lower tides. Stick to the west side and you should be fine.

Outer Calvert Island

This is the adventurer's route down the coast, and recommended for expert paddlers and mariners only. The trip from Surf Islands to Clark Point is about 42 km (26 miles) of open water. For kayakers, the obvious advantage is miles of sand beach in absolute seclusion. The most northerly beaches on the island's outer coast are accessible by trail, but after that it is marine access only. A multitude of marine trail sites are indicated on the west coast of Calvert Island. For the best bets look for a beach at Bolivar Islet, a place behind Blackney Island and a small but unimpressive spot at Chic Chic Bay.

Rocky shorelines typify the coast in Kildidt Sound.

See Bella Bella, page 121
See Bella Coola, page 149
See Queens Sound, page 113
See Calvert Island, page 99
Miles
Km
Mont Merritt
903
FISHER CHANNEL
Fog Rocks
KING I.
Kisameet Bay
Kiping I.
De Cosmos Pt.
Hart Group
Canso I.
Merritt Lagoon
301
De Cosmos Lagoon
Kinsman Inlet
Kildidt Lagoon
370
HUNTER ISLAND
BURKE CHANNEL
Kildidt Inlet
Kiltik Cove
Stewart Inlet
Kildidt Narrows
Goodlad Bay
Harlequin Basin
Pattison Group
Cliff I.
Seafire I.
Kiwash I.
Rock Inlet
317
NAMU
Bremner Bay
Crab Cove
Watt Bay
Kiwash Cove
Mosquito Its.
Hanna It.
Sea Otter Inlet
Ontario Pt.
Clare I.
Warrior Cove
Mustang Bay
Target Bay
Namu Range
Rupert I.
Camel I.
Hergest Pt.
Uganda Pt.
Leckie Bay
Tomahawk I.
Serpent Group
Daedalus Pt.
Nalau Passage
FITZ HUGH SOUND
Middleton Pt.
KILDIDT SOUND
Underhill I.
Koeye R.
NALAU I.
Lewall Inlet
Edward Channel
Ward Channel
Turnbull Inlet
STIRLING I.
Bayly Pt.
Planet Group
Goldstream Harbour
Kelpie Pt.
Breaker Group
HAKAI PASSAGE
HECATE I.
Barney Pt.
Whidbey Pt.
Kwakume Inlet

HUNTER ISLAND

With its maze of islands and channels, boaters and paddlers could spend months exploring the waters around Hunter Island. But while there are numerous places to go, many of the channels and island groups suffer the downfall of lacking major attractions. This is particularly true of Nalau Passage and the nearby islands. Add to that a lack of beaches and this area becomes mainly a pass-through point. Sea Otter Inlet is often a wet launch drop-off point for kayakers aboard the *Queen of Chilliwack*, but most attractions tend to lie on the east side of Fitz Hugh Sound outside Hakai's boundaries or around the islands on the west side of Kildidt Sound. A must-see location is Namu with its ruins of the cannery and village.

Kildidt Sound

This is a paddling paradise of island groups, inlets and bluffs. Interesting channels lie between tall, rocky islands, and including this area on your itinerary would not be time wasted. The campsite at the Serpent Group would make the ideal base camp for this region (see page 117). Unfortunately other recreational beaches are difficult to find in this area. When park campsites are finally designated, it is likely a spot in the cove to the east of Watt Bay will be included. Highlights in Kildidt include the tall, bluff-like shorelines and scenic channels that run

Kildidt Sound's sometimes complex shoreline.

between islands such as Clare and Camel. Kildidt Inlet extends deep into Hunter Island, but it is rarely explored given the 8 to 10 knot current at Kildidt Narrows. The passage is suitable for small craft at high water slack only. Sub-tidal rocks lie along both sides of the narrows. High water turns 1 hour and 10 minutes after high tide at Prince Rupert, while low tide turns 1 hour and 25 minutes later.

A number of marine trail campsites are indicated in Kildidt Inlet. Bremner Bay is a protected anchorage and boat haven.

Nalau Passage

The area around Stirling and Nalau islands is a key fishing area, reflected in the high number of nearby fishing lodges. Joe's Salmon Lodge is set in a bay in south Nalau Island and Olie's Lodge is in what's known locally as Barney Bay on the south side of Hakai Passage near Barney Point. Together these and other lodges can feed dozens of sport fishing boats out into the channels around Nalau and Bayly Point.

When Hakai Luxvbalis was first made a park, a beach on Stirling Island on the south side of Edward Channel was one of the park's five established camping areas. Unfortunately the campsite turned out to be a cultural site with the camp placed atop a midden. For that reason it is requested you avoid camping here. Places to consider instead include the rough beaches of Tomahawk Island, Sea Otter Inlet or Goldstream Harbour. If you are travelling through Sea Otter Inlet at or near high tide, take the route to the south between the unnamed island and Hunter Island. This pretty stretch was cleared of rocks by Heiltsuk long ago to make a navigation channel.

Koeye River

Located on the east side of Fitz Hugh Sound, Koeye River (pronounced *kway*) has a rich history. Four native villages were located along its length, with evidence in fish traps, archaeological sites and culturally modified trees. In more recent years the lower river was the site of a limestone quarry (from 1952 to 1976) and ruins, including the dock pilings and tramline rails, can be seen from the waterfront.

In more recent times the south headland was logged and a resort built, but its failure led to a unique opportunity for the Heiltsuk First Nation of Bella Bella. A consortium of philanthropists, including billionaire Warren Buffet, purchased the operation and set it up as a non-profit entity for use by the Heiltsuk. The band has embraced the

Unusual rock formations cap the beach at Koeye River.

opportunity, and with three cabins along the riverfront and a longhouse on the beach, the resort now offers camps for Bella Bella children and youth, healing retreats and eco-holidays for the public.

Rediscovery camps are also held here. They provide an opportunity for aboriginal youth to learn about themselves and their culture. The first rediscovery camp started on Haida Gwaii in the Queen Charlotte Islands in 1978, and since then the concept has spread across several countries as a way to combat substance abuse, delinquency and family troubles. The camps involve wilderness and survival skills, plus an emphasis on traditional knowledge.

The surrounding land is being sought by the Heiltsuk First Nation in land claim negotiations. Fortunately their attitude to visitors like kayakers is highly welcoming, and the beautiful sand beach at the mouth of Koeye River is currently available for recreational use, including camping. The lodge's season is short but a caretaker will likely greet you warmly if the lodge is closed, as will the staff if the season is open.

The lodge is in the process of rebuilding under the new First Nation management, so follow the progress of their programs and schedule at **www.koeyelodge.com** or call **250-957-2567**. You also might want to call to confirm the status of beach camping before setting out.

Koeye River is navigable for a considerable distance, but surf can break along the sandbar at the river's mouth. Transit at higher tides or at times of low swell, or portage along the beach past the sandbar. Also, expect the possibility of moderate swell at the main cove, especially if a westerly is blowing up Hakai Passage. If you do travel up the river, watch for the large meadow that makes for prime grizzly habitat. Both grizzlies and black bears are drawn to the chinook, chum, coho, pink and sockeye salmon that the river supports. Look for the quarry ruins on the riverbank.

Travel notes: On a visit here in June there were no bears in evidence, much to the chagrin of a young woman who travelled from Germany specifically to see them. On a return visit in August, the beach was littered with bear prints. Duly warned, I packed up my food tight at the end of the day in my kayak and pulled it close to the tent. Later, after sundown, I heard a loud whump on the kayak. I figured the only way a kayak could make a whump like that was a bear hitting it, so I grabbed my bear banger—a device to make a loud noise to scare bears away—and went outside. Sure enough a bear was standing with his front paws on my kayak. Reckoning a bear standing on my kayak a few feet away was the ideal time to let a bear banger go, I pulled the trigger. Nothing. Another pull, still no sound. Flicking away I suddenly realized I was defenceless with a bear just a few feet away. The bear, however, gave me a sheepish look, as if to say, "Oh, this is *your* kayak. I suppose you want me off it then. Let's just pretend this didn't happen..." and strolled away.

Place names: In Heiltsuk Koeye means "sitting on water."

Camping: N51°46.43'/W127°52.43'. At the mouth of Koeye River is a beautiful circular beach tucked in behind the headland of Koeye Point. This is contested Heiltsuk land and currently under unofficial Heiltsuk First Nation control, but their attitude is welcoming to visitors. In the off-season the cabins may be available, while rooms might be available at the lodge in season.

Namu

Radiocarbon dating has established almost 10,000 years of habitation at Namu, making it the earliest inhabited site on the B.C. coast. An easily seen reminder of this history is a fish trap at the mouth of Namu River.

European presence began in 1893 when Robert Draney (see Draney Inlet, page 85) established a fish cannery here and in later years, a sawmill. The cannery passed to B.C. Packers Ltd. in 1928 and continued to operate until a fire in 1962 destroyed a large portion of the plant. It was rebuilt and processed fish (instead of canning it) until the late 1980s.

Left deserted and its population gone, the town was sold and packaged as a resort. After a few changes in ownership and plans over the years, Namu now offers a dock and other limited facilities for visitors, including showers, laundry, fuel and dormitory-style accommodation. Plans for the future include adding a store and selling cottages for private residences. Many are currently rented out during the summer.

Meanwhile, the ruins of the cannery and the town continue to deteriorate. Ruins include the old bunkhouse on the waterfront identifiable by the fading "Edgewater" sign (nicknamed the "Namu Hilton"), the recreation centre and the mess hall—all located left to right as seen from the waterfront (the mess hall is the u-shaped building on pilings).

Boardwalks once joined the buildings but they are now deteriorating. The B.C. Ferries' *Queen of Chilliwack* until recently included Namu on its list of destinations, but the worsening condition of the dock forced it off the list of stops.

A trail leads from the town to Namu Lake.

Visiting boaters, including kayakers, can tie up at the dock tucked in behind the north side of the cannery, while a sand beach is suitable for kayaks south of the mess hall ruins (though this is not convenient to the amenities offered at the dock). Other rest areas in the vicinity of Namu Harbour include a lovely clamshell beach on Lapwing Island (N51°51.26'/W127°52.97') and on beaches at Kiwash Island facing Namu (N51°51.76'/W127°53.49' or N51°51.99'/W127°53.39').

The protected anchorage in this area is in Rock Inlet, just to the northeast of Namu, on the north half of the inner basin.

Place names: Namu is Heiltsuk for "place of high winds" or "whirlwind."

Camping: N51°50.65'/W127°52.10'. Kiwash Cove is located just south of Namu, with a wide sand and gravel beach at its head. Although a nice spot, it is unfortunate that many fallen trees take up much of the higher beach, and the uplands vegetation is overgrown. A few sites to escape a spring tide might be found where fallen trees are fewest. Note that the beach dries extensively at lower tide levels.

N51°53.72'/W127°53.07'. Several islets are located north of Namu and south of Edmund Point. They are joined by a variety of crushed shell beaches. Two are of particular interest: a beach to the south ends in a flat area well protected from westerlies, and a wonderful beach of crushed shell to the north rises to a height that would appear safe at almost any tide level. This is a spot for small groups only (I would suggest two tents maximum).

QUEENS SOUND

The waters around Queens Sound are one of the key recreational areas for the central coast. Kayakers from Bella Bella can use Hunter Channel to quickly reach the northwest portion of Hakai Luxvbalis Conservancy Area. The remote Goose Group is one of the most intriguing destinations on the coast, with its exposed shores and wonderful beaches, while intricate waterways can be explored around Spider Anchorage. Queens Sound itself is a large and exposed waterway where winds can whip up or down, and the Goose Group offers little in the way of a breakwater. Entering the sound is the equivalent of entering open ocean conditions, as the wave-battered bluffs of Simonds Group testify. Tidal currents can run as high as 3 knots northwest of Purple Bluff.

Spider Anchorage

This anchorage lies amid a jumble of island groups connected by intricate passages such as Brydon Channel between Hurricane Island and the Kittyhawk Group. Here navigation will be hazardous for many boats but ideal for kayakers. Small picnic sites may be found among the maze of islands, but the beaches at Triquet Island are the standout. Another option is a beach in the Serpent Group in Kildidt Sound. Spider Island has two interesting bays to explore, with the western one backed by a wonderful sand beach. Unfortunately it is clogged with driftwood, leaving no shelter for tents above any reasonable tide level, and the upland is steep and overgrown.

Spider Island was the site of a low-flying early warning radar station during the Second World War. It was part of a chain of such stations along the Pacific coast begun in 1942. This station was in operation by June 1943. (Originally they were called "radio detachments" then "radio units," as the term "radar" did not catch on until 1943.) By August 1945, at the end of the war, the Spider Island

The old Edgewater bunkhouse was known as the Namu Hilton.

station was closed. A wooden boardwalk linked the dock on the east side of the island to the radar station, the location of which is marked on chart 3937 north of Breadner Point with an "ru" to indication ruins. Once easily visible from the water, it has now become almost completely overgrown. So has the trail, which begins near the outflow of the lake's creek and is difficult to find in the brush. To complicate matters, the 30 ha (75 acres) around the east side of

Waves pound the rocks on Spider Island near the old radar station site.

Spider Island at the entrance to the trail is privately owned and may be developed as a fishing resort at some point in the future. If you look for the trail you'll have to push through the bush near the area of the creek to find evidence of the boardwalk.

Place names: This area is a tribute to Second World War aircraft, such as the Supermarine Spitfire, Curtis Kittyhawk and Hawker Hurricane. There is also a nod to the Bristol Blenheim and Hawker Typhoon in the smaller islands.

Camping: N51°47.77'/W128°09.99'. There is a wonderful sand beach on the main group of islands in the Serpent Group, but the campsite is easy to miss. I did. If you approach from the north you will find a sand beach that appears to be intertidal only. Walk past the initial beach area to see the dryland camp up around the corner. Clear sites are located above the beach.

N51°48.50'/W128°14.14'. Triquet Island is blessed with several beautiful beaches. A choice location is in the deep cove on the island's northeast side behind several islets. It is the most expansive of the three beaches on Triquet Island.

N51°48.46'/W128°14.93'. Two wonderful sand beaches on the northwest side of Triquet Island are separated by a rock outcrop. The westernmost beach has several tent pad clearings in the forest behind the beach, as well as an old cedar hut of hobbit-hole-like design.

McNaughton Group

This archipelago is a popular touring area for both boaters and kayakers. Boaters will enjoy the anchorage in the midst of the McNaughton Group while kayakers can take advantage of the sheltered waters. This is a good area for novice kayakers who can take Hunter Channel from Bella Bella, thereby avoiding open water the entire journey. Beaches, unfortunately, are almost non-existent within the archipelago unless you explore the nooks and crannies. One spot is located on the north end at a tidal lagoon. It is a cultural location and should be avoided as a campsite.

Located across Sans Peur Passage, Kinsman Inlet is a long, narrow waterway blocked by a tidal rapid. Evidence of the tidal rapid in the form of foam will drift throughout Sans Peur Passage as far as Hunter Channel if the tide is right. If you do explore inside the inlet, be sure to watch for the stone fishtraps. This inlet has a

Placid waters on the inner channels of the McNaughton Group.

reputation as one of the best areas to see them, though they are abundant throughout this region.

Camping: N51°53.85'/W128°14.06'. The prime camping location in close proximity to the McNaughton Group is to the south of the group just east of Superstition Point. A cove is backed by a fine yellow sand beach with rock and boulders in evidence only at the lowest tide levels. There is good tide clearance on the beach, plus a few clear areas in the upland.

Simonds Group

This rugged and wave-swept set of islands is wonderful to explore but has no beaches. The visual highlight is the line of cliffs at Purple Bluff. (It appears purple in the right light.)

Place names: Lt. General Guy Granville Simonds served with the Canadian forces as commander of the First Canadian Division for the invasion of Sicily in 1943 and later the invasion of Italy. This is just one of many military place name references in this region.

Purple Bluff in the Simonds Group.

Goose Group

Despite its flat topography, the Goose Group is one of the most interesting archipelagos on the coast. Kayakers and boaters alike will probably hone in on the bay formed by Goose, Gosling and Gull islands. The anchorage is surrounded by beaches, and it is possible to walk the beach on Goose Island for miles. Kayakers, though, tend to congregate on Snipe and Gosling islands, which offer magnificent sand. In the right light the waters take on a magical tropical hue.

On the outer shore of Goose Island are tidal inlets around Swan and Duck islands that run shallow at lower tides. Farther north are more beaches, while the top of the island is capped by several cabins formerly used as a Heiltsuk rediscovery camp. That function has now switched primarily to Koeye River, and the cabins on Goose Island are used mostly for community recreation now.

Watch for tide rips around Gosling Rocks.

Camping: N51°55.74'/W128°26.44'. There are many camping options around the Goose Island anchorage. The beach on Goose Island facing the anchorage is long and sandy, but not as clean as the other nearby beaches. It is also considerably more choked with driftwood.

The spit at the north end of Gosling Island.

The choice locations are on tiny Snipe Island or the north end of Gosling Island. On Gosling Island's north point a long spit joins with several outlying islets. The beach will survive most tide levels, but if you need them, there are level mossy areas in a nearby forest clearing above the lower grass berm. The view out across the spit toward the islets and the cove beyond is superb.

Bella Bella

CHAPTER THREE

BELLA BELLA IS ONE OF A KIND ON THE COAST: A COMMUNITY OF ABOUT 1,250 people living in an environment without road access deep within a network of islands and channels. It is an area similar to the hundreds of others along the coast that were abandoned a century or more ago, and yet Bella Bella continues to thrive in its quiet way.

The town has never caught the best of tourism in the area. Most of that drifts toward the resort area of Shearwater, and even the ferry service to Bella Bella misses the town by several miles, landing to the south at McLoughlin Bay. Huge cruise ships pass within several hundred yards of the main dock but none stop, instead continuing their way to Prince Rupert or other ports of call. Shearwater, on the other hand, has a full range of services for visitors.

Still, Bella Bella has its own vibrancy, limited mainly to a few blocks just up from the government wharf. Bella Bella is also the reference point for this region, and the hub for trips that can be as varied as any on the coast. Choices include the protected waters of the archipelagos near Stryker Island, the convoluted channels of Gale Passage or Joassa Channel, the white sands of the McMullin Group, the idyllic and historic waters of Troup Passage or the distant and formidable trips up the northern inlets to mountainous terrain like Ellerslie Falls or Roscoe Inlet.

An appealing aspect of this region is the close proximity of all these features. It doesn't take long from Bella Bella to be deep in mountainous passages or at an exotic coastal location. Reaching these areas is possible by a choice of protected channels, allowing for routes that can be mixed and matched to take advantage of the weather or your whims.

SARAH I.
KLEMTU
Cone I.
SWINDLE I.
Finlayson Channel
DOWAGER I.
Mathieson Channel
Lady Douglas I.
Lake I.
Don Peninsula
Oliver Cove Marine Park
See Fiordland, page 181
Cecilia I.
Ivory I.
Watch I.
MILBANKE SOUND
Seaforth Channel
Yaaklele Lagoon
DUFFERIN I.
ATHLONE I.
Gale Passage
Joassa Channel
HORSFALL I.
Raymond Passage
Cape Mark
Princess Alice I.
Houghton Is.
Stryker I.
Creery Group
Piddington I.
McMullin Group
Tribal Group
124
See Hakai, page 97
Mooto L.
McPherson L.
Miles
Km
141
North Arm
Ellerslie L.
South Arm
Snass L.
Cheenis L.
Ellerslie Bay
Coldwell Peninsula
Emily L.
Emily Bay
Spiller Channel
Bullock Channel
Briggs Inlet
Florence Peninsula
Ripley Bay
Shack Bay
Roscoe Inlet
Clatse Bay
YEO I.
Mount Harington
Clatse IR
Clatse L.
Return Channel
Grief I.
Dearth I.
CHATFIELD I.
Troup Passage
Johnson Channel
Walker L.
Webster L.
Shipping route
CUNNINGHAM I.
Gunboat Passage
Bella Bella
Bella Bella Is.
Shearwater
CAMPBELL I.
DENNY I.
KING I.
Port John
Luke I.
Evans Inlet
Lama Passage
Fisher Channel
Hunter Channel
Codville Lagoon Marine Park
Soulsby Pt
HUNTER I.
131
See Bella Coola, page 149

BARDSWELL GROUP

The Bardswell Group is a major cluster that consists of Athlone, Dufferin, Horsfall and Stryker islands. Many other smaller groups dot the nearby waters. Seaforth Channel can be busy with Inside Passage traffic, while many of the channels around the island groups to the south will see almost none.

If the number of unnamed islands is an indication of the wildness of an area, here you have truly reached the wild coast.

Place names: This was first named the Wright Group in 1872. In 1925 they became the Bardswell Islands, then in 1985 the Bardswell Group. The significance wasn't recorded by Land Information B.C.

Tribal Group

The Tribal Group is just one of a number of archipelagos that lie to the southwest of Campbell Island. Piddington Island is the largest in this area, and it in turn is surrounded by its own islands and bays. The miles of shoreline to explore here in relation to the size of area is considerable. This makes it an ideal kayaking area, although good-quality beaches are rare. A visual highlight is the steep bluffs on the outside of Iroquois Island.

Camping: N52°00.14'/W128°11.50'. Just east of Dodwell Island facing Hunter Channel is an unnamed island with an islet to its south. On the islet is a beautiful crushed shell beach—perhaps the most perfect crushed shell beach on the coast at all tide levels. It is easily missed at higher tides because some fallen logs obscure it. But if you land here you will be rewarded with a magically pretty pocket beach. Some clear tent sites are set in the upland and connected by a trail, but someone has taken the time to create a level bank of shells on the beach above the high tide level.

A stunted tree grows on the outer shore of the Tribal Group.

N52°04.30'/W128°19.24'. If you require a campsite in the immediate area of the Tribal Group, Miles Island

Oliver Cove
Marine Park
DON PENINSULA
Spiller Channel
Tankeah IR
See Fiordland, page 181
Cecilia I.
Rankin Pt.
Susan Rock
Early Passage
Knarled Pt.
Tuno Cr.
Miles
Km
Blair Inlet
Watch I.
Mouat Cove
Berry Inlet
Grief I.
Ivory I.
Balagny Passage
Robb Pt.
Harmston I.
Locke I.
Bush Pt.
Foote Its.
Image I.
MILBANKE SOUND
SEAFORTH CHANNEL
Wootton It.
Graven Pt.
Dearth I.
Cape Swaine
Welch Rock
Denniston Pt.
Idol Pt.
Beazley Is.
Koqui IR
Nose I.
Yaaklele Lagoon
Tidal Rapids
Muir I.
McGown Pt.
Dundivan Inlet
Tidal Rapids
Rait Narrows
296
Hose Pt.
Cheney Pt.
DUFFERIN I.
Mount Gowlland
Mallory Is.
Reginald I.
ATHLONE I.
Lockhart Bay
Townsend Pt.
St. John Harbour
Louisa Cove
Dyer Cove
Joassa Channel
HORSFALL I.
Gale Passage
Wurtele I.
Tidal Rapids
350
Mount Hand
Quinoot Pt.
Raymond Passage
Waskesiu Passage
Cape Mark
Edwards Pt.
Boddy Narrows
Isabel Pt.
Princess Alice I.
Thompson Bay
Potts I.
Hochstader Basin
Kingsley Pt.
Fingal Pt.
Limit I.
Houghton Is.
Louise Channel
Matilda I.
Clarie I.
CAMPBELL I.
STRYKER I.
DeWolf I.
Hibbard Pt.
Gow I.
Peter Bay
Fingal I.
Kingscote Pt.
Codfish Passage
Piddington I.
Redford Pt.
Tuft Is.
Miles I.
Brown Narrows
Creery Islands
McMullin Group
Guano Rks.
Bella Bella
TRIBAL GROUP
Huron I.
Iroquois I.
Athabaskan I.
Danger Pt.
ADMIRAL GROUP
Tide Rip Passage
Brodeur I.
Safe Passage
PRINCE GROUP
Dodwell I.
Goose I.
QUEENS SOUND
Robert I.
Latta I.
See Hakai, page 97

has an unnamed island directly to its east. In the south end of the channel between the two islands is a grit beach with some rocks at high tide. If you land here, look for the low grass shelf just inches above the spring tide level. This is a pretty, quiet and secluded spot.

McMullin Group

This is a seemingly isolated little cluster of islands between Stryker Island and Goose Island, but when viewed from the water it is surprising how all these little island clusters seem to make a bridge of land. Fingal Island is the most remote, while Guano Rocks lives up to its name through the number of seabirds that inhabit it. It is one of the better locations in the area for viewing cormorants.

The McMullin Group itself is well worth the journey, and an overnight visit is recommended. A beautiful sandy area on the east side of the main island makes a good place to pull out. Magical, windblown islets surround the area, making it a stunning place to visit. Look for the prominent eagle's nest on the northeast corner of the main island.

Place names: Colonel McMullin was a provincial police chief. The archipelago was first named the Broken Group in 1929, but that was changed in 1944 to avoid duplication.

Camping: N52°03.62'/W128°24.79'. A fine white sand beach is on the east side of the main island next to a picturesque rock islet. There are makeshift driftwood tables and seats on the high-backed area of the beach. For highest tide levels there is a clear area in the forested upland. Look for the buoy marker to find the path. The beach runs out extensively at lower tide levels. For this reason you might want to consider instead one of the other beaches on the east side of this island. The one directly north of the main beach is inviting.

Stryker Island

Stryker Island is surrounded by narrow passages and island clusters, all of which can run dry at low tides. On the south side, in among a maze of islets, is a cabin used for youth/religion camps. It sits atop a sandy area that is good for a picnic break. Expect moderate tidal currents through the area.

Camping: N52°06.10'/W128°23.32'. On the west side of Stryker Island is a cluster of islands joined by a shallow subtidal sand and rock shelf. On chart 3938 look for an islet marked "48." It is immediately west of a long, thin island. The sand shelf rises to create a good beach between the southeast end of "48" and a tiny islet. On the islet, planks lead from the beach to a clear forested area. The clearing will house several tents.

Athlone Island

As the outer of the major islands in the Bardswell Group, a dramatic and wild shoreline would seem probable. The exposure to the open ocean, though, is offset by places like St. John Harbour. Housed within it is a unique fishing resort created from a former B.C. ferry, *Queen of the Islands*. The lodge begins its season in Caamaño Sound, then moves to St. John Harbour. At nearby Louisa Cove another lodge, West Coast Resorts, is a more traditional hotel on a barge. Together they add considerable traffic to this stretch of the outer coast, and it is common to see several dozen sport fishing boats within sight of Cheney Point.

Yaaklele Lagoon is hidden by islands and ledges that will run dry at low tide. The entrance is blocked by a tidal rapid passable by small boats at high water only.

The south end of the island is quite quiet and secluded in comparison to the west shore. The traffic is less here and there are numerous serene passages and island groups to explore.

Place names: His Excellency the Right Honourable Earl of Athlone was appointed Governor General of Canada in 1940. Prior to 1944 it was Smyth Island.

Camping: N52°09.49'/W128°29.44'. The cove on the southwest side of Athlone Island north of Edwards Point is backed by a nice sand beach with a spindly forest behind it. The beach will survive most tide levels. Surf may be an issue here. Expect light to moderate conditions.

N52°14.12'/W128°24.80'. Just east of Cape Swaine on the north end of Athlone Island is a sheltered cove. Here you'll find one of the cleaner beaches in the area. This is a good location to wait out a run down the outer coast of Athlone.

Sunset spotlights an islet off the sand beach at the McMullin Group.

Heiltsuk cabins

The Heiltsuk First Nation of Bella Bella has built a number of cabins across the region that are used primarily for youth camps and healing retreats. The Heiltsuk have made a wonderful gesture by sharing use of the cabins when available. All they ask in return is that campers help with the upkeep of the cabin and the wood supply. Alternatively, visitors can make a donation to the charitable youth program Qqs Projects, Heiltsuk Hemas Society, Box 786, Waglisla, B.C., V0T 1Z0.

Two of the cabins are located in the Dufferin Group area, one on the north end of Gale Passage and one on the island north of Quinoot Point. Others are at Koeye River, Cockle Bay, Goose Island and Ripley Bay in Roscoe Inlet. They were built over the last decade and are not all regularly maintained, so the more remote ones may not be in prime condition. The Koeye River cabins are associated with the lodge and are more likely to be in use. For more information on the current status on the cabins call the Heiltsuk band office at **250-957-2381**.

Gale Passage

This often narrow and intricate passage runs between Dufferin and Athlone islands. Several tidal rapids make it suitable only for small boats, and travel is recommended only at high tide slack. Expect rapids when the current is running. A Heiltsuk cabin is located on Koqui Indian Reserve just inside the passage. Marine trail sites are also indicated in the passage.

Joassa Channel

Joassa Channel is a narrow, meandering route that can serve as a scenic alternative for busier Raymond Passage. Many obstacles, including rock-choked Rait Narrows, deter most boat traffic. The passage splits to the south at Potts Island. At Quinoot Point a number of islets and rocks choke the route to Thompson Bay, but it will be navigable by kayak at most tide levels—with care. Surprisingly the tidal currents are quite low. The narrowest passageways are best explored at low tides when the many varieties of anemones and other forms of marine life are best viewed. This is a recommended route for a kayak trip through this region.

Camping: N52°10.21'/W128°20.36'. North of the north tip of Potts Island at Quinoot Point is an unnamed island, numbered "56" on chart 3938, with a conspicuous cove on the north end. Inside the cove is a long, rough beach. Behind it, almost hidden in the trees, is a clean and well-built Heiltsuk cabin available for public use. There is also a clear area here for tent camping.

Raymond Passage

This is the wider, clearer, shorter and less scenic route from Seaforth Channel to Queens Sound. Most boats will use this passage instead of Joassa Channel but the amount of marine traffic isn't substantial. Camping opportunities are poor along this stretch.

Place names: Captain Raymond arrived at the Fort McLoughlin trading post in 1834 on his American brig via this channel. The name was given by officers of the Hudson's Bay Company, but it was later changed to Hecate Channel. It was changed back to the original in 1903 to avoid duplication.

Seaforth Channel

Almost all marine traffic travelling the B.C. coast passes along this route, including ferries and cruise ships. It is wide, clear and backed by beaches along most of Dufferin Island. The north shore offers some rugged bluffs and numerous islets and reefs. Westerlies can build through the channel, making for choppy water. The effect can spin off into Return Channel and the south end of Troup Passage.

Place names: Francis Humberston Mackenzie, Baron Seaforth (1754–1815), achieved fame by offering to raise a Highland regiment against Spain for the Nootka Controversy (see *The Wild Coast, Volume 1,* page 194), but the matter was settled before the regiment was needed. Campbell Island is believed to be named after Dr. Samuel Campbell, the assistant surgeon aboard the surveying vessel *Plumper* that surveyed this area 1866–69.

Camping: N52°15.63'/W128°18.52'. There are many beaches along the banks of Watch Island and around Bush Point. Most are lined by rock at lower tides. This one east of Bush Point is exceptionally clear for the area.

N52°16.34'/W128°16.22'. On the east side of Locke Island is a pronounced gravel bar in the midst of intertidal rocks. Some drift logs are set at the high tide level, but there is space to support a camp.

N52°14.15'/W128°20.26'. Gravel beaches extend along a good deal of the north end of Dufferin Island, but this is my choice for a campsite. It is located midway along Dufferin Island's north side at a southward hook in the shore that protects the beach from westerlies. The beach continues west to Koqui Indian Reserve, providing one of the few places in this region to take an extensive stroll along a beach.

Blair Inlet

This inlet begins at Rankin Point and continues deep behind Watch Island. The protected east side is a serene passage with grassy banks; the side toward Rankin Point is exposed, open to westerlies and can be choppy in the entryway. Once in the protection of Ivory Island or the islets off the southeast side of Cecilia Island, the rough conditions quickly drop off.

Ivory Island is a staffed light station. The original was a wooden tower built in 1898. It was replaced by a steel tower in 1957. The original lighthouse was destroyed in a winter storm in 1982. A trail leads from a shed on the north side of the island to the lighthouse. There's a good beach at the shed.

Place names: David Blair was a merchant in Victoria at the time the inlet was surveyed by Captain Pender in 1867.

Camping: N52°17.18'/W128°23.09'. An islet on the southeast side of Cecilia Island has a pleasant sand, gravel and clamshell beach. There is a very nice flat area at the top of the beach that will withstand all tide levels.

Johnson Channel.

See Bella Bella's Northern Inlets, page 141
YEO ISLAND
Yeo Cove
Yeo Island IR
McArthur Pt.
RETURN CHANNEL
Coldwell Pt.
Ettershank Pt.
Rochester I.
Hoonees IR
Nicholson I.
Mount Keyes
1222
900
500
Kokyet IR
Wigham Cove
Donald Pt.
Morehouse Bay
600
Jagers Pt.
Beaumont I.
Troup Narrows
McCroskie Is.
Walker L.
Law Is.
Dearth I.
Raven Cove
CHATFIELD I.
Noon Pt.
Christiansen Pt.
Munsie Pt.
SEAFORTH CHANNEL
Newbie I.
Troup Passage
700
Webster L.
JOHNSON CHANNEL
800
Kintail Pt.
Odin Cove
Sabiston I.
Lang I.
Nevay I.
Kynumpt Harbour
Thorburne I.
Discovery Cove
CUNNINGHAM I.
Dumas Pt.
Norman Morrison Bay
Ormidale Harbour
Ardmillan Bay
Dryad Pt.
Mount Verney
365
Bainbridge Cove
Beales Lagoon
Beales Bay
Forit Bay
Cavin Cove
300
Martins Cove
Saunders I.
Pole I.
Rainbow I.
Meadow I.
GUNBOAT PASSAGE
Magee It.
Cypress I.
Manson Pt.
Shave Pt.
Maria I.
BELLA BELLA (Waglisla)
Whisky Cove
Klitsoatli Harbour
Kunsoot IR
Dingle I.
Hampden Bay
Story Pt.
Old Bella Bella
Atli Pt.
SHEARWATER
McLoughlin Bay
Mount D'Arcy
637
FISHER CHANNEL
Napier Pt.
Archibald Pt.
CAMPBELL I.
LAMA PASSAGE
Alarm Cove
Alert I.
DENNY ISLAND
Williams Range
547
Luke I.
Canal Bight
Brend Pt.
German Pt.
Twilight Pt.
Cliff Bluff
Mouse I.
Beak Pt.
Serpent Pt.
Start Pt.
LAMA PASSAGE
Westminster Pt.
Codville Lagoon MP
HUNTER CHANNEL
Harbourmaster Pt.
Strom Pt.
Kaiete Pt.
Pointer I.
See Bella Coola, page 149
Want I.
End I.
Hart I.
Bob Bay
Lizzie Cove
Fancy Cove
Long Pt.
Jane Cove
Howeet IR
HUNTER I.
The Trap
FITZ HUGH SOUND
Miles
2
Km
2
4
Bella Bella
Mount Merritt
903
See Hakai, page 97

DENNY ISLAND

Bella Bella and Shearwater are the communities in this region. Two major passages carry all the Inside Passage traffic—Lama Passage or Return Channel. Quieter alternatives are Troup Passage and Gunboat Passage. Hunter Channel provides the main passage for traffic to Queens Sound.

Hunter Channel

Joining Lama Passage with Queens Sound, Hunter Channel can have strong currents at the south end, particularly near the islets across from Soulsby Point (the point is off the corner of the regional map for Bella Bella; see the main chapter map to place the point).

Camping: An islet at the south entrance has a wonderful clamshell beach. See the full description on page 123.

Lama Passage

This is a key route between Fitz Hugh Sound and Seaforth Channel. It doglegs at Twilight Point and continues north, with the community of Bella Bella near the north end. Numerous anchorages can be found along the south end at Lizzie Cove and Jane Cove. The passage constricts to a width of 320 m (0.2 miles) between Campbell Island and Saunders Island—an interesting point as so many large cruise ships pass through here. Tidal streams are strongest in the narrows.

Camping: N52°04.51'/W127°59.68'. Serpent Point isn't named on all charts, but it is the northerly point of Hunter Island in the middle of Lama Passage. The site is west of the navigation light located on the point. The beach will disappear at high tides but there is a good camping area up the hill from the east side of the beach.

N52°04.03'/W128°05.97'. A good assortment of gravel beaches of similar quality can be found along the shoreline of Hunter Island, particularly around outer Lizzie Cove. The beach to the west of Westminster Point is among the better, and is conveniently located at the junction of Hunter Channel and Lama Passage.

McLoughlin Bay

Located about 5 km (3 miles) south of Bella Bella, McLoughlin Bay is the B.C. Ferries terminal for Bella Bella. Its distance means visitors cannot stroll through town during ferry layovers as they can at other locations such as Klemtu and Ocean Falls. For those loading or unloading kayaks for transport by the ferry, the beach here is rough and far from ideal; a launch or loading at nearby Shearwater is recommended instead. In the meantime B.C. Ferries is considering building a launch ramp at McLoughlin Bay. A fee would apply. The Heiltsuk are also examining the feasibility of a hotel and bighouse at the bay.

Despite impressions to the contrary, McLoughlin Bay is actually the old community of Bella Bella, not Old Bella Bella on Denny Island. McLoughlin Bay was first settled by Europeans as a Hudson's Bay Company trading post in 1833. It was abandoned in 1843, and later burned. A trading post run by John Clayton replaced the fort and the community of Bella Bella sprung up around it. The land around the trading post was private, though, forcing the community into one corner of the bay. That prompted the chief to move the community to the reserve, and Clayton and his trading post weren't invited to join them. Clayton then moved his store to Denny Island and took the Bella Bella post office name with him. As a result the community of Bella Bella was temporarily usurped of its name on paper but not in practise. Thus Bella Bella took Waglisla for a post office name and the trading post site eventually became known as Old Bella Bella by common usage.

Place names: Dr. John McLoughlin had a remarkable career with the Hudson's Bay Company beginning in the early 1800s. In 1821 he was named chief factor and placed in charge of the Columbia department. He ordered the establishment of both Fort Simpson and Fort McLoughlin. The native name for the original village site is 'Qelc.

Waglisla

Bella Bella (Waglisla) is a thriving waterfront community of 1,250 people. The commercial centre is small, localized and convenient to boaters if they stop at the government wharf on the south end of the town. Water and garbage disposal are available at the dock. Straight up the road from the wharf are a bank, liquor store and well-stocked band grocery store. One block up are a restaurant and a convenience store. The community also has a hall, a band office, three schools—including a high school—a hospital and an airport with regularly scheduled flights. The post office is Waglisla, V0T 1Z0.

The government wharf at Bella Bella.

A crowded commercial dock is located at the north end of the town at Martins Cove. There are also a shipyard and a log-sort station nearby.

Place names: Waglisla is a Heiltsuk word meaning "river on the beach." The name was originally created just for the post office, but evolved to become the community name as well, with both Waglisla and Bella Bella placed on maps.

Old Bella Bella

Old Bella Bella is a former fish company settlement. B.C. Packers closed down its operations here in the late 1970s/early 1980s after about 50 years, and the property has since been handed over to the Heiltsuk First Nation. Old buildings from the cannery are still visible and homes dot the waterfront, but only one is currently inhabited. The rest are decaying and no longer livable. Also located here are a Fisheries and Oceans Canada office, float and rescue centre.

Shearwater

This resort area lies 3.2 km (2 miles) east of Bella Bella in Kliktsoatli Harbour. The hub is Shearwater Marine Resort. Here you can find moorage, a general store, a marine store, accommodation, camping, laundry, showers, a post office, banking, yacht charters and the Fisherman's Bar and Grill. Cottages surround Whisky Cove, and conspicuous on the west shore just north of the resort are the ruins of the old Pacific Canadian Fisheries cannery.

At the entrance to Shearwater is an unnamed islet with a pleasant beach on the west side. A trail from the beach crosses the island.

Shearwater's European history began in the Second World War when the Royal Canadian Air Force chose the harbour as a reconnaissance base. The base was built to accommodate 2,000 soldiers and included amphibious airplanes, hangars, air raid shelters, barracks and bomb storage shelters. After the war the air force base was purchased by several partners to provide marine services for the region. Widsten Marine was a fixture on the coast here for the next 20 years, performing repairs plus running a sawmill and a towing operation. A son of one of the original partners purchased Shearwater in 1967, and it has since grown into a thriving resort where fishing remains the staple attraction.

The eagle tree, Shearwater.

A regular water taxi service runs between Shearwater and Bella Bella.

Rainbow Island

Rainbow Island is one of an interesting cluster of islands that become interconnected at low water by rock ledges. The islands, and Meadow Island in particular, are used as a First Nation cemetery. Trails from the beaches on the south end of Meadow Island crisscross the cemetery. On the east side of the island is a rocky ridge with a large collection of petroglyphs.

Camping: N52°10.69'/W128°04.54'. Rainbow Island has an extended point on the north side that creates a grass-covered spit. The grass is untamed but there are enough flat areas for a large group.

Gunboat Passage

This is a little-used route that connects Seaforth Channel with Fisher Channel. It is scenic but strewn with reefs. Rough beaches run its length, with the best camping possibility on the gravel beach on the south end of the dogleg at Hampden Bay. The tidal stream sets west and is not strong.

Place names: D'Arcy Anthony Denny (Mount D'Arcy and Denny Island) was commander of the gunboat *Forward* that served the B.C. coast 1860–69. The gunboat *Grappler* served here 1860–65 and was at one time commanded by E.H. Verney (Mount Verney). Thomas Cunningham (Cunningham Island) purchased Vancouver Coal Company's general store in 1864. He became chief fruit inspector for B.C. in 1906.

Johnson Channel

Lama Passage is the main route for the Inside Passage, but Johnson Channel offers a little-used alternative. It is also a corridor from Fisher Channel to many of the northern inlets and passages, such as Roscoe Inlet and Bullock Channel. It is a pleasant place to travel, with a mountainous backdrop and some waterfalls on the north end. Remnants of an old cannery, the Walker Lake Cannery, are visible on the east shore at the unnamed creek leading to Walker Lake. The old pilings are conspicuous. Just across the channel is a former native village site. If you pass by Beaumont Island to the north, keep your eyes open for a faint and difficult-to-see petroglyph.

Camping: N52°16.10'/W127°54.38'. The old cannery site is lined with a rocky beach on both sides of the creek. The best access is to the north on a small sandy strip. Clear areas for camping can be found among the forest cover. Some good, clear, level areas under the trees are located just south of the river. Access to that spot is via a rock beach only.

Pilings of an old cannery, Johnson Channel.

Troup Passage

A few fishing or crab boats might use this passage, but otherwise it sees little traffic despite the opportunity to explore the intricate shoreline. The cultural inventory includes a midden, longhouse remains, totem poles, a large intertidal stone fish trap and pictographs. The passage north of the narrows is an incredible place to paddle, with perfectly peaceful waters between a maze of islands and islets. Currents at Troup Narrows run as high as about 2 knots, so it is best but not vital to travel with the current (it floods north, ebbs south). Be sure to watch for pictographs on the cliff wall of the narrows. The south portion of Troup Passage is large, wide and mostly rocky shore. Boats will have a difficult time in the north section. Local knowledge is advised.

Place names: Originally named Deer Passage, it was changed to avoid duplication. It was renamed after a Captain Troup of the Canadian Pacific Railway.

A petroglyph, Troup Narrows.

Camping: N52°17.73'/W127°59.88'. If you explore the north end of Troup Narrows, you will probably find yourself wanting to stay. It lacks any established camping areas, but there are some good, sheltered beaches in among the islets. This particular spot lies between the two main islands. There is a choice of beaches with high, grassy areas. Double-check to make sure they're not intertidal.

N52°17.12'/W127°59.77'. This spot is near the bay to the northeast of the Narrows behind an islet. On one side of the channel is a grassy beach; on the other is a level grassy area on the islet.

N52°13.60'/W128°06.98'. At the south entrance to Troup Passage, behind Sabiston Island, is a nice sand beach with a level upland area. There is a rough cabin in the woods.

Return Channel

This passage links Seaforth Channel with Johnson Channel and some of the inlets to the north. It isn't particularly remarkable for its scenery, though Morehouse Bay might be interesting to explore if you have the time. The beaches tend to be rough along the channel's length. Watch for eddies off Donald Point and turbulence northwest of Jagers Point.

Behind Grief Island on a promontory on Yeo Island was a village known as Kilkitei. A large midden is a reminder of the history. Petroglyphs are cut into a boulder on the beach below the village site (the four coppers can be hard to see). Kilkitei is just one of many village sites in this area. Raven Cove on the south shore of Return Channel was another.

East Seaforth Channel

This area is interesting due to the large vessels, including ferries and cruise ships, entering from Lama Passage. Currents throughout Seaforth Channel are usually variable and weak. Wind will likely be a stronger consideration. Afternoon westerlies can blow down the channel.

Good anchorages can be found at Kynumpt Harbour. The best spot is near Spratt Point at the entrance to Strom Cove. Green Neck, at the head of the harbour, was once cultivated and has returned to forest, though signs of the settlement remain, including pilings. Earlier it was a camp used by the Heiltsuk in the late summer for berry picking.

Dryad Point is home to a lighthouse. The current concrete tower was built in 1919, with the lighthouse first established in 1899. Nice picnic beaches can be found west of the lighthouse.

Weather: Dryad Point tends to be cool, with daytime average summer highs in the teens. The highest average takes place in August, at 19.2°C (66°F). Daily lows are about 12°C (53°F) in July and August. Freezing temperatures are rare even in winter; the lowest average daily low in January is 1.4°C (34.5°F).

Dryad Point receives 2,480 mm (97.6 inches) of rain a year, with most falling in November—322 mm (13 inches). July gets 104 mm (4 inches) and August 133 mm (5.2 inches)—almost the same amount as June, which receives 138 mm (5.4 inches). The rain increases substantially in September, when the average month gets 207 mm (8.1 inches). Expect some rainfall on about 16 or 17 days in July and August, with 18 or so in June and 20 in September. Moderate rainfall of 5 mm (0.2 inches) or more will occur in about 8 days in June, 6 days in July, 8 days in August and 10 or 11 days in September. Heavy rainfall of more than 10 mm (0.4 inches) will occur 4 or 5 days a month from June to August and 7 days in September.

Winds are lowest in the summer months, with averages of 7.4 km/h (4.0 knots) in July and August. Winds reach an average of 8.9 km/h (4.8 knots) in May and 8.0 km/h (4.3 knots) in September, and rise to a high of 14.1 km/h (7.6 knots) in November and December. Prevailing winds are southwest from May to August, south in September and southeast during the winter months.

Camping: N52°12.20'/W128°10.23'. Green Neck at Kynumpt Harbour has a good sand beach. A small camp can be made below the trees above the high tide line. There is flat ground overgrown with blackberries. A trail leads to Norman Morrison Bay.

Ellerslie Falls crashes down several tiers into the lagoon below.

BELLA BELLA'S NORTHERN INLETS

Don Peninsula serves as a massive natural barrier between two very different destinations. Most boaters follow the route to the west into Finlayson Channel, the main thoroughfare for the Inside Passage. A few, though, will take the time to venture into the meandering waterways to the east, the inlets north of Bella Bella. Here visitors will find long, intricate waterways passing through sky-high mountain ranges.

Many visitors consider the scenery of Roscoe Inlet and Ellerslie Bay the best on the coast. It's a hard thing to argue as so few go these routes—not surprising, as the area was uncharted until 1996. A handful of motor cruisers are the primary visitors. The passages are long and campsites few and far between, but it is still an area that can be enjoyable to paddle. The most adventurous could portage to rarely visited Ellerslie Lake to spend time upon its sand beaches viewing the mountainous bluffs.

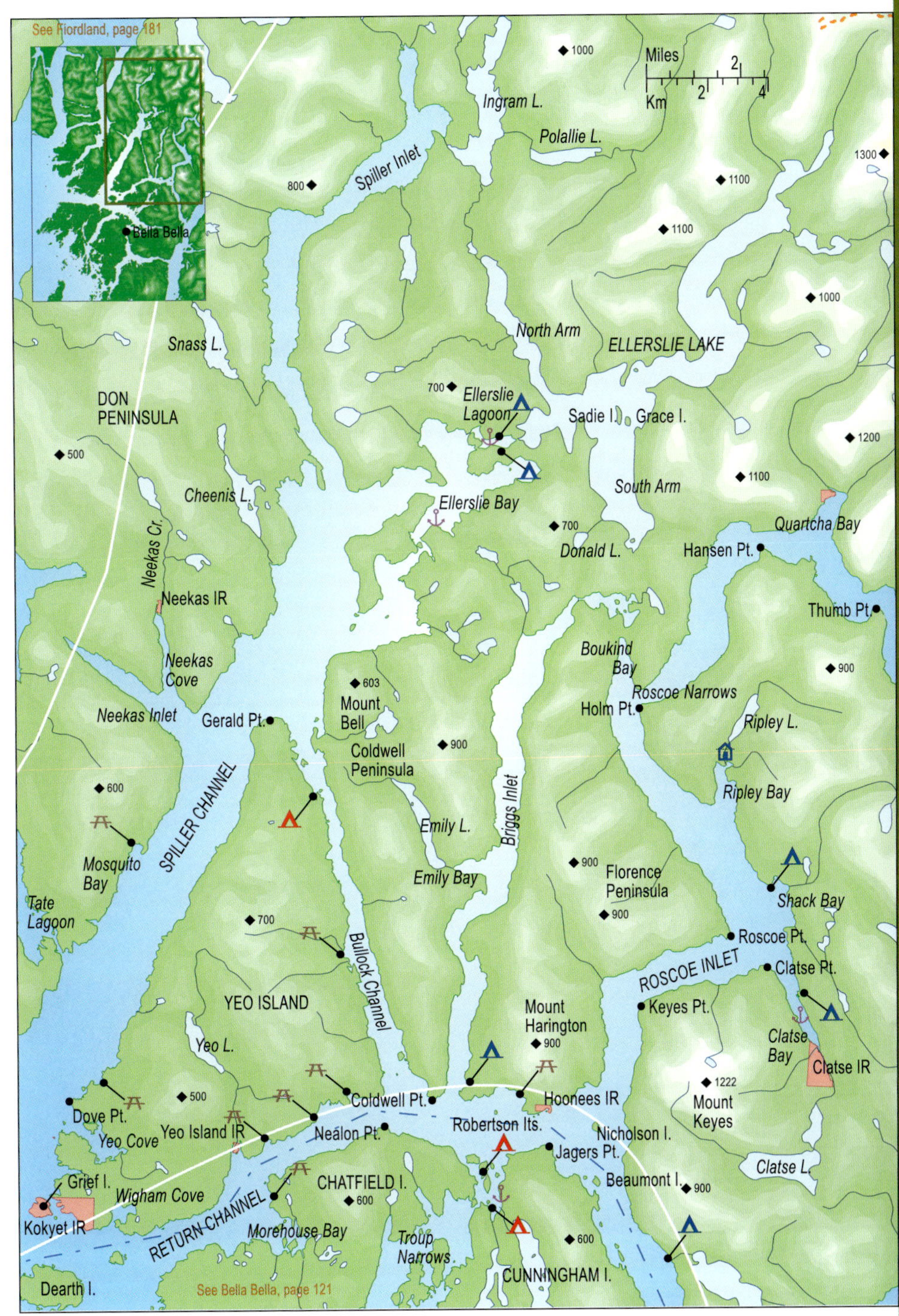

See Fiordland, page 181
Bella Bella
Miles
Km
Ingram L.
Polallie L.
Spiller Inlet
North Arm
ELLERSLIE LAKE
Ellerslie Lagoon
Sadie I.
Grace I.
South Arm
Ellerslie Bay
Donald L.
Hansen Pt.
Quartcha Bay
Thumb Pt.
Snass L.
DON PENINSULA
Cheenis L.
Neekas Cr.
Neekas IR
Neekas Cove
Neekas Inlet
Gerald Pt.
Mount Bell
Coldwell Peninsula
Boukind Bay
Holm Pt.
Roscoe Narrows
Ripley L.
Ripley Bay
Briggs Inlet
Emily L.
Emily Bay
SPILLER CHANNEL
Mosquito Bay
Tate Lagoon
Florence Peninsula
Shack Bay
Roscoe Pt.
Clatse Pt.
ROSCOE INLET
Keyes Pt.
Bullock Channel
YEO ISLAND
Yeo L.
Mount Harington
Clatse Bay
Clatse IR
Dove Pt.
Yeo Cove
Yeo Island IR
Coldwell Pt.
Hoonees IR
Robertson Its.
Nealon Pt.
Nicholson I.
Mount Keyes
Jagers Pt.
Clatse L.
Beaumont I.
Grief I.
Wigham Cove
CHATFIELD I.
Kokyet IR
RETURN CHANNEL
Morehouse Bay
Troup Narrows
CUNNINGHAM I.
Dearth I.
See Bella Bella, page 121

Camping on the boulder headland at Shack Bay.

Roscoe Inlet

Steep, high mountains back this meandering inlet that twists and turns for 42 km (24 miles). Impressive cliffs line the shore of the first two legs until Roscoe Point. From there the shoreline becomes more staid until Roscoe Narrows, after which peaks over 1,200 m (4,000 feet) crash directly to the inlet's shores. The first legs are notorious for westerlies funnelling through and blowing over Shack Bay. This is unfortunate, as Shack Bay makes a scenic area to stop.

Tidal streams are low along the inlet. It can be safely navigated by boat by staying on a mid-channel course.

Expect only rough campsites along most of the inlet. Various bays provide the best likelihood of beaches. A Heiltsuk cabin, available for public use, is located at Ripley Bay. Just west of the mouth of Roscoe Inlet was a winter village located on either side of a point 1.8 km (just over a mile) west of Nicholson Island and Roscoe Rock. Look for a canoe runway and a fish trap. The east side was known as Hwinis (meaning "landslide"), referring to the mountainside scar behind the village, and the west was Tiai'is ("ready," as in to fight). Middens mark both village sites. Today it is the Hoonees Indian Reserve.

Camping: N52°23.30'/W127°51.81'. At the north entrance to Shack Bay is a distinctive jumble of boulders that form an unusual headland. To the east (inside the bay) is a rough beach giving access to the boulder spit. On a closer look you'll see a smooth bedrock platform composes most of the headland, with boulders strewn across it. Clear, level grass patches dot the area. The upper portion sits above the spring tide line. It's an exposed location, but exceedingly pretty.

N52°21.28'/W127°50.91'. Beaches are rough in Clatse Bay, but you'll notice from a distance there's what appears to be a white sand beach on the southeast shore. That's an illusion, as it is actually a bedrock spit. Normally these aren't suitable for camping, but this particular rock ledge is smooth, gently sloping and relatively well protected. It would be possible to pull out on the ledge and camp on the most level portions at the top of the rock. This might be preferable if it is windy at Shack Bay.

Briggs Inlet

Briggs Inlet begins wide and open, then quickly constricts to a winding narrows. Currents will be strong at the narrows, where they can run

5 knots. North of the narrows the tide range is limited to half that of the outside portion of the inlet.

Place names: The earliest charts named this Sisters Inlet, but in 1925 the official name was changed after Thomas S. Briggs, a former agent with the Canadian Pacific Navigation Company.

Camping: N52°19.53'/W128°00.50'. A rock headland near the east entrance has a sheltered and fairly clean grit beach on the south side. This provides access to the rock and boulder headland, which has several grassy areas suitable for tents. It is more sheltered than the headland at Shack Bay in Roscoe Inlet.

Bullock Channel

This is a narrow and sheltered alternative to Spiller Channel for reaching Ellerslie Falls. It is lined with high grass banks, so there are plenty of picnicking options.

Camping: N52°24.84'/W128°04.84'. An islet on the northwest side of the channel connects to Yeo Island at lower tides, creating coves on either side. The shores of both coves are suitable for camping in the grass alongside the forest. Look for high-backed areas at the various points of the coves or on the islet facing Yeo Island.

A view toward Ellerslie Bay from Bullock Channel.

Sunrise over Spiller Channel.

Spiller Channel

Spiller Channel runs northeast from Seaforth Channel to Ellerslie Bay, after which it continues on northward as Spiller Inlet for another 18 km (11 miles). The channel is wide, deep and in many ways unremarkable as it passes alongside Don Peninsula. As is often the case along inner routes, the beaches are generally rough and rocky.

Place names: Richard Spiller was a corporal in the Royal Marines who served aboard the paddle steamer *Beaver* when it surveyed this coast 1863–70. Yeo Island is named after Gerald Yeo, a surgeon on HMS *Ganges* from 1857 to 1860.

Ellerslie Falls

The scenery on the coast doesn't get much better than this. If you time it right you will be whisked through the narrows at the entrance to Ellerslie Lagoon with little trouble. Then you will come down a small channel into the lagoon to face the falls that dominate the eastern side of the lagoon.

It might not be that easy, however. The narrows before the lagoon is prone to strong currents and a tidal falls. *Sailing Directions* claims 5 knots or more; I place emphasis on the "more." The channel has a depth of 0.9 m (3 feet).

A good anchorage is reported in Ellerslie Bay behind a small peninsula on the east side of the north entrance to Bullock Channel. By anchoring there you can dinghy into the lagoon.

A five-minute trail leads alongside the falls in the lagoon to Ellerslie Lake above. To find the trailhead, look for two huge stump, one near the trees and another on its own on the lagoon's bank (N52°31.63'/W127°59.62'). The lake is a beautiful place and could be paddled if you portage along the rough trail (expect it to be a challenge). There are numerous beaches and cliffs along the lake's length of just a little more than 16 km (10 miles).

The Heiltsuk cultural inventory in this area includes middens, pictographs on cliff faces, burial box remains, a fish trap and a canoe skid.

Travel notes: Slack tide for the rapids is a bit of a guessing game. As slack does not coincide with the regular change of tides, it is best to be prepared to spend some time watching and waiting. I arrived near high tide and was pleasantly pulled into the lagoon with a light current. I timed my departure for early the next morning to take advantage of a falling tide down Spiller Channel. When I reached the rapids it was in full bore—a chute with numerous rapids along its length and a drop of about 1.5 to 2.5 m (5 to 8 feet) into Ellerslie Bay. I ran it anyway. I figured if I could stay to the left of the first rapid I would clear the worst. Unfortunately the first rapid was created by two folds of converging water and I was pulled right into the middle. I was pounded by that wave and then several more. I came out the bottom end backwards but upright. It was an adrenaline rush I wouldn't recommend loaded down with gear at 5 a.m. Maybe on another visit a practice run down and a portage back would be a better idea.

Camping: N52°31.57'/W128°00.04'. If you make it into Ellerslie Lagoon, most of the shore is intertidal grass. The grass continues to the tree cover. If you search around a bit, especially on the north shore, you will be able to find flat, open areas for camping in the forest. On the south side, southwest of the trailhead, someone has been building a cabin. During my visit in 2005 it was simply a large

A view of one of the several tiers that make up Ellerslie Falls.

frame made of thin, unplaned logs. It will be interesting to see if it is ever finished.

Ellerslie Lake

If you do venture here, you'll find pockets of sand beach, exposed bedrock cliffs, avalanche tracks and tundra pockets at higher elevations. The easternmost arm is bordered by spectacular rock walls. Expect it to become parkland at some point in the future. It and the area encompassing the falls is one of the key priorities for recreation and tourism in the central coast area, and it is one of the coast's new designated areas (see page 207).

Clayton Falls, North Bentinck Arm.

Bella Coola

CHAPTER FOUR

THERE'S SOMETHING EERIE ABOUT STEPPING INTO A COMMUNITY THAT has been abandoned—about seeing modern office buildings sitting empty, a seven-storey concrete hotel with trees and vines growing in the foyer, or what should have been comfortable, well-built townhouses vacant and collapsing. That rather apocalyptic image is waiting at Ocean Falls at the top of Cousins Inlet. And it's just one of the many historic and somewhat unusual attractions along this stretch of coast.

Vestiges of civilizations past dot the Bella Coola region. Pictographs are etched on cliff faces. Another ghost town lies hidden in the trees behind Port John. And perhaps most historic of all, Alexander Mackenzie crossed North America to touch the Pacific at a rock near Elcho Harbour—the first European to do so.

The wonderful thing about this region is how all these elements make distinct destinations along the length of Dean Channel. At Eucott Bay you can relax in a hot spring; at Cascade Inlet you can marvel at the waterfalls; at Codville Lagoon a beautiful red sand beach at a freshwater lake awaits.

Kayakers are a rarity along this stretch of coast, but it is possible to take advantage of the attractions within a short distance of one another along Dean Channel if attention is paid to wind and current hazards. Passengers on the Discovery Coast Passage ferry will also get an opportunity to see this countryside, with the chance of a side trip up Cascade Inlet if conditions are ideal. The best opportunities to see scenery along Dean Channel are the Wednesday and Friday departures from Bella Coola to Port Hardy.

Because the Bella Coola Valley can be reached by vehicle, this region is one of the more accessible on the coast.

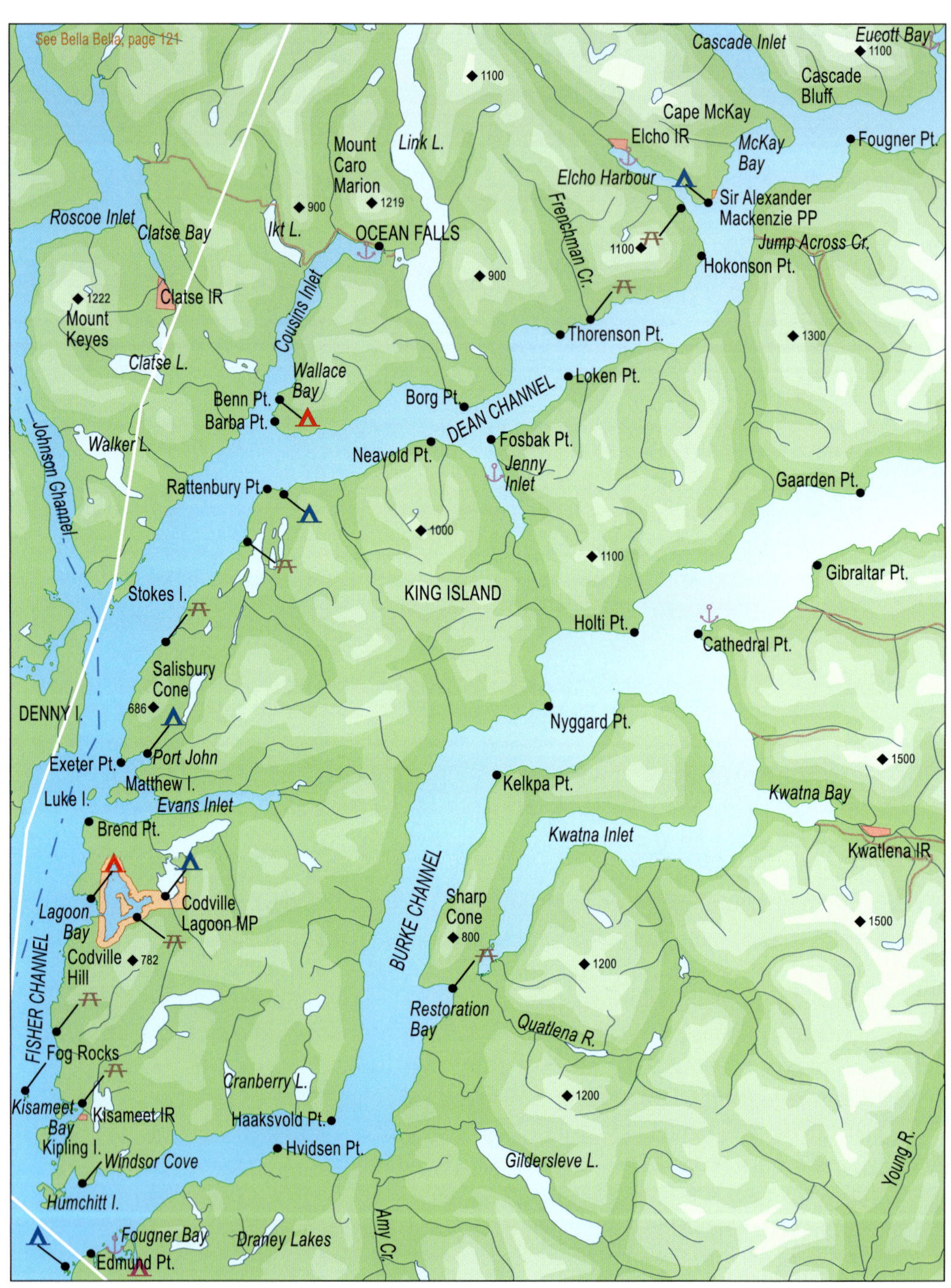
See Bella Bella, page 121
Cascade Inlet
Eucott Bay
1100
Cascade Bluff
Cape McKay
Elcho IR
McKay Bay
Fougner Pt.
Elcho Harbour
Sir Alexander Mackenzie PP
Jump Across Cr.
Hokonson Pt.
Frenchman Cr.
1100
1100
Mount Caro Marion
Link L.
1219
900
Roscoe Inlet
Clatse Bay
Ikt L.
OCEAN FALLS
900
1222
Mount Keyes
Clatse IR
Cousins Inlet
Thorenson Pt.
1300
Clatse L.
Wallace Bay
Loken Pt.
Benn Pt.
Barba Pt.
Borg Pt.
DEAN CHANNEL
Fosbak Pt.
Johnson Channel
Walker L.
Neavold Pt.
Jenny Inlet
Rattenbury Pt.
Gaarden Pt.
1000
1100
Gibraltar Pt.
Stokes I.
KING ISLAND
Holti Pt.
Cathedral Pt.
Salisbury Cone
686
DENNY I.
Nyggard Pt.
Exeter Pt.
Port John
Matthew I.
1500
Luke I.
Evans Inlet
Kelkpa Pt.
Kwatna Bay
Brend Pt.
Kwatna Inlet
Kwatlena IR
BURKE CHANNEL
Sharp Cone
Codville Lagoon MP
Lagoon Bay
1500
800
Codville Hill
782
1200
FISHER CHANNEL
Restoration Bay
Quatlena R.
Fog Rocks
Cranberry L.
1200
Kisameet Bay
Kisameet IR
Haaksvold Pt.
Kipling I.
Hvidsen Pt.
Windsor Cove
Gildersleve L.
Young R.
Humchitt I.
Fougner Bay
Draney Lakes
Amy Cr.
Edmund Pt.

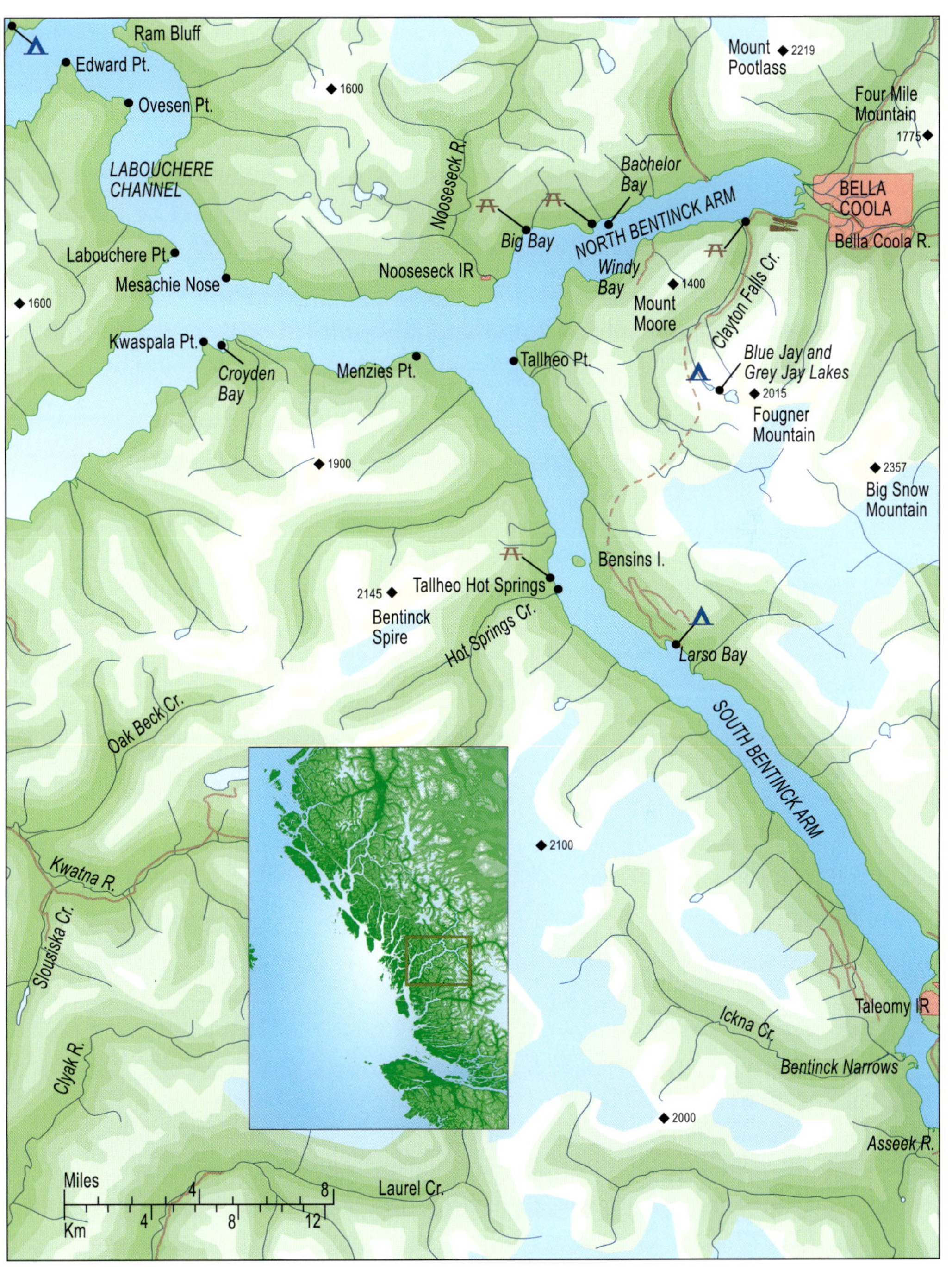
Ram Bluff
Edward Pt.
Ovesen Pt.
1600
LABOUCHERE CHANNEL
Labouchere Pt.
Mesachie Nose
1600
Kwaspala Pt.
Croyden Bay
Menzies Pt.
1900
Nooseseck R.
Nooseseck IR
Big Bay
Bachelor Bay
NORTH BENTINCK ARM
Windy Bay
Mount Moore
1400
Tallheo Pt.
Mount Pootlass
2219
Four Mile Mountain
1775
BELLA COOLA
Bella Coola R.
Clayton Falls Cr.
Blue Jay and Grey Jay Lakes
2015
Fougner Mountain
2357
Big Snow Mountain
Bensins I.
Tallheo Hot Springs
2145
Bentinck Spire
Hot Springs Cr.
Larso Bay
SOUTH BENTINCK ARM
Oak Beck Cr.
Kwatna R.
Slousiska Cr.
Clyak R.
2100
Taleomy IR
Ickna Cr.
Bentinck Narrows
2000
Asseek R.
Laurel Cr.
Miles
4
8
Km
4
8
12

FISHER CHANNEL

Fitz Hugh Sound becomes Fisher Channel where it runs alongside Hunter and Denny islands, after which it transforms into Dean Channel. Tidal currents are rather odd in Fisher Channel, with the flood stream from the north meeting the flood stream from the south about midway between Fog Rocks and the east entrance to Lama Passage. More likely to be a factor when transiting the area are summer winds that can blow up the channel from Fitz Hugh Sound. Like other channels and inlets in the area, the inflow winds can begin early in the day and continue until sundown. Captain Vancouver had a less than favourable impression of this channel, writing, "The evening was very rough, rainy, and unpleasant, and what contributed to render our situation more uncomfortable was the steep, precipices that constituted the shores, not admitting us to land until near midnight."

Travel notes: I found this a great stretch to view both killer whales and humpbacks, seeing them both on several days. At night one passed so close to my camp that its exhalation sounded like an oboe and was loud enough to set my tarp pole humming like a tuning fork (it has never made such a sound before or since).

Overcast skies over Fisher Channel.

Red sand on the beach at Sagar Lake.

Place names: Rev. John Fisher was the vicar of Stowey and a friend of Captain Vancouver. He named the channel in 1793.

Codville Lagoon

Most popular today as an anchorage, Codville Lagoon is a former Heiltsuk defensive site, with evidence of the native occupation remaining in pictographs. A trail runs from the northeast corner of the lagoon to Sagar Lake. The trailhead is at the east end of the lagoon (N52°03.72'/W127°50.21'). The trail is short (20 minutes) but can be muddy. Sagar Lake is blessed with an unusual red sand beach, slightly coarser than regular sand. The lake would make a wonderful camping destination for people who don't mind carrying their gear over the trail. Excellent anchorages can be found in the lagoon.

Place names: On charts dating back to 1874 this was given the simple title of "Lagoon." It was named in 1946 after Mr. Codville, the lightkeeper at Pointer Island from 1899 to 1962. The lighthouse was located off the south entrance to Lama Passage until the 1960s. It was replaced with a navigation beacon.

Low rolling hills surround Codville Lagoon.

Camping: N52°03.64'/W127°52.44'. There are some pleasant sandy beaches along the inside of the lagoon, but they are mostly intertidal. The best beaches are along the south shore (try N52°03.39'/W127°50.69'), but clear areas above high tide are hard to find. A bit rougher but with better tide clearance are the beaches lining Lagoon Bay. My pick is on the north shore. It provides level areas among the smaller rocks with views down Fisher Channel.

Codville Lagoon Marine Park

This small park located on King Island in Fitz Hugh Sound is an all-weather anchorage with an unmaintained 20-minute hiking trail to freshwater Sagar Lake created by the Ocean Falls Yacht Club in years past. The park protects 315 ha (778 acres) of marine area and 440 ha (1,087 acres) of land. It was created in 1965. There are no amenities.

King Island

This island is the backbone of both Dean and Burke channels, dividing the two waterways with peaks as high as 1,600 m (a mile). It is 71 km (44 miles) from tip to tip, and as narrow as 4.5 km (2.8 miles) thanks to Jenny Inlet. Most of the shore is steep and inaccessible.

Place names: Captain Vancouver served as midshipman for Captain James King on the *Discovery*. King was second lieutenant of the *Resolution* on Captain Cook's third voyage in 1776 and was

Mile-high peaks cap the interior of King Island.

promoted upon the death of Captains Cook and Clerke. Vancouver named the island after "the family of my late and highly-esteemed and much lamented friend" during his voyage here in 1793.

DEAN CHANNEL

Running Dean Channel to its conclusion deep in the B.C. interior would involve a voyage of 117 km (72 miles). Most traffic stays between Labouchere and Fisher channels. Dean Channel lacks the rips of Burke Channel, but even so, inflow and outflow winds can be strong, and outflow currents, thanks to the fresh water from the many waterfalls and rivers draining into Dean Channel, can override flood tides. Currents will be most noticeable, anecdotally, in the stretch between Thorenson and Hokonson points. *Sailing Directions* states the maximum streams are 1 to 2 knots, but I suspect 4 to 5 in stretches around these points. An outflow current combined with an outflow wind can make up-channel travel an ordeal. The prevailing wind in the summer, however, will be from the southwest—an inflow—that begins at 10 a.m., reaches its height at mid-afternoon and continues to sundown, when it generally calms.

Unusual shoreline near Cascade Bluff.

There are few rest opportunities between Cousins Inlet and Elcho Harbour. Northwest of Elcho Harbour the bedrock shoreline shows interesting hues and patterns.

Travel notes: The prevailing wind may be from the southwest, but I never had that luxury on my trip up Dean Channel in June. Eventually the outflow wind beat me back. Leaving Eucott Bay I needed to make just the 3.2 km (2 miles) eastward to Edward Point to reach Labouchere Channel. But a strong northeasterly was blowing that morning and I ended up within about 100 yards/metres of the point but unable to make headway. The wind knocked me to a dead standstill and I found myself simply treading water while paddling hard. When I finally gave up and turned around I was blown all the way back to Elcho Harbour, the first safe pullout. The entire trip up the channel was a tough one. At Thorenson Point I pulled out for two hours to await the tide change to gain some much-needed assistance. It never came. My best advice is travel from Bella Coola in the early summer before the inflow winds settle in, and in later summer try the route that I tried in June. Later in the summer inflows are more likely and the current from freshet will have lessened.

Port John

Evans Inlet is a deep channel with several islands at its mouth. Branching off to the north is Port John, where pleasant cliff-lined mountains border the way to a wide beach and a river. Along the river, if you venture into the bush, you'll find ruins of an old community. Many buildings have collapsed; others that remain show the simplicity of the cedar construction.

Remnants of the community at Port John.

Predating the community is the First Nations use of the area. A large cliff at the bay shows what is considered the largest and best display of pictographs on the coast. A multitude of drawings can be found along the base and two more panels high on the cliff. Another archaeological feature in the area is a burial cave.

Camping: N52°07.42'/W127°50.57'. The beach is extensive at Port John, but portions can become rocky and rough at lower levels. The best and clearest stretch is to the north. If you search behind the trees you'll find a clear, flat area in the forest for use at spring tides.

Homes nestle along the shoreline in the approach to Ocean Falls along Cousins Inlet.

Cousins Inlet

Cousins Inlet runs north about 10 km (6 miles) to face Martin Valley, the residential side of Ocean Falls, then turns eastward to the Ocean Falls dam. On a clear day the approach will be an impressive one as Martin Valley comes into sight. At Wallace Bay an extensive beach is backed by cabins dating to the heyday of Ocean Falls. Some are abandoned but a few are still in use. At the beach south of Benn Point look for petroglyphs. Faces are cut into the granite on the north side of the beach. At Wallace Bay another petroglyph can be found on a boulder.

The dock for Ocean Falls is near the dam; what remains of the pulp mill is to the south of the dam.

Camping: N52°14.69'/W127°45.35'. Strategically located across Dean Channel from the mouth of Cousins Inlet is a group of islets in the cove just east of Rattenbury Point. On the south end an islet has a pleasant crushed shell beach. The middle islet is best suited for camping. If spring tides preclude using the beach, there are clearings in the uplands. Look for a hidden path leading up to a great tent clearing on the west side. A wooden chair overgrown with moss must hail from the earlier days of Ocean Falls.

N52°17.09'/W127°45.58'. Inside Cousins Inlet south of Wallace Bay is a beach on the south side of the point. It is crushed shell at the high tide level. An alternative is in Wallace Bay by one of the abandoned cabins.

Ocean Falls

Once an impressive waterfall fell from Link Lake to Cousins Inlet, and a native village, Liak, was located at the base. That all changed

A waterfall leads down to the power plant and pulp mill site at Ocean Falls.

in 1901 when a lease was granted to build a power station for the Bella Coola Pulp and Paper Company. By 1966 the mill was being run by Crown Zellerbach, and six paper machines were producing newsprint, tissue and specialty papers.

Due to high production costs the mill closed in 1980, and the town that once boasted a population of 4,000 dwindled away. But it never died completely. The prospect of oceanfront property at a bargain price made it an ideal location for retirees, fishermen, former mill workers and a few other hardy souls. About 50 people live year-round at Ocean Falls today, plus about three times as many seasonal residents. The dam continues to provide electricity for Ocean Falls, Shearwater and Bella Bella through the Central Coast Power Corporation (CCPC). The blue building on the water is the CCPC workshop, while the power plant is at the base of the falls. A fish hatchery provides more employment, and a steady flow of visiting vessels during the summer has prompted a few tourist-oriented ventures. Most notable among them is a gourmet restaurant in the former church with the wonderful name The Holy Grill.

A lodge near the dock provides accommodation, food, laundry and showers. A store keeping limited hours is located at Martin

Sir Alexander Mackenzie Provincial Park

When Mackenzie arrived here he etched his achievement in paint made of vermilion and bear grease on the rock at the north entrance to Elcho Harbour. It was later inscribed into the stone by a survey party, but even that is beginning to fade. At the top of the point a cairn marks Mackenzie's achievement. The 5 ha (12.35 acres) at the point is protected as parkland.

The park is the possible end to a journey along the Alexander Mackenzie Heritage Grease Trail, which extends through Kluskoil and Tweedsmuir provincial parks, though the last portion to this rock must be travelled by boat, just as Mackenzie did.

Valley, the residential side of Ocean Falls. Fresh veggies, berries and flowers can be found at Audrie's Plants. A bank and post office (V0T 1P0) are also located here. The post office is open weekdays for limited hours (generally 11 a.m. to 4 p.m.).

You can walk to the causeway of the dam but can no longer cross it due to a fence. A trail leads up the Martin River, which is frequented by wolves. Probably the best walk, though, is through the abandoned downtown core. The large, seven-storey, concrete structure was once a thriving hotel with an annex built to accommodate the overflow of customers.

Camping is offered near the dock, but the site is essentially a collection of empty lots.

Beyond Ocean Falls is 28-km (17-mile) Link Lake. Once three separate lakes, the links are now joined as a result of the dam. It is famous for its cutthroat trout and empty cabins. It would be possible (but not easy) to portage a canoe or kayak to the bay above the dam.

Travel notes: If the north coast is renowned for its grizzlies and Princess Royal Island for its spirit bears, Ocean Falls is the land of the majestic and noble porcupine. Eva Prine of the Holy Grill says when she saw her first porcupine at Ocean Falls it was so large she thought it was a bear cub. The loop at the base of the porcupine's quill was used by local First Nations for jewelry, but at the risk of handling the barbs, which are notoriously sharp. The best place to see Ocean Falls' porcupines is apparently by the post office at dusk.

Elcho Harbour

Elcho Harbour was surveyed in May 1793 by Captain Vancouver, who missed Alexander Mackenzie by just two months. Mackenzie would complete the first crossing of North America north of Mexico

Typical forest along the Grease Trail.

here on July 22, 1793. Elcho Harbour is a narrow inlet extending northwest 4.6 km (3 miles) from Dean Channel. It is believed Mackenzie Rock was once a fortified village site of four houses held by the Heiltsuk. The Heiltsuk still held this point at the time of Mackenzie's visit and their hostile welcome was the reason Mackenzie turned back before reaching the open ocean.

A misfortune in Elcho Harbour's history was a landslide in 1922 that destroyed a logging camp and killed five employees.

Expect some nice waterfalls in the harbour if it has rained recently.

Hiking the Grease Trail

Alexander Mackenzie ensured his place in history by reaching the B.C. coast, but the route he took had been travelled many times before. It was part of a network of trails used by First Nations for travel and trade, the primary item being oolichan grease. The small fish was dried and rendered into valuable fat.

Searching for the Northwest Passage, Mackenzie and his crew of nine left Fort Chipewyan in the fall of 1792. They wintered at Fort Fork near the Peace River and eventually canoed down the Fraser River, switching to an overland route on the advice of their native guides. They started near the mouth of Blackwater River west of Quesnel, continuing into what is now Tweedsmuir Park and on into the Bella Coola Valley. Locals escorted them on the last leg down Dean Channel.

The Alexander Mackenzie Heritage Grease Trail preserves that route, beginning at Blackwater River and continuing 450 km (280 miles) to his inscription at Sir Alexander Mackenzie Provincial Park. The whole trip can be completed in an epic hike or it can be broken into smaller portions. Day hikes are possible near the Lower Blackwater Bridge, the Euchiniko River Loop Trails and the Nazko Valley. A hike in Bella Coola is the 5-km (3-mile) Valley Loop Trail, starting at Burnt Bridge Creek.

Cascade Inlet.

Camping: N52°22.66'/W127°28.35'. One of the best camping areas along Dean Channel is just to the west of the cairn. There you'll find a crushed shell beach backed by a forested area clear of undergrowth. Flat areas are at a premium unless you hike up to the level grassy area near the cairn.

Cascade Inlet

This long, narrow inlet heads almost straight into the B.C. interior for 26 km (16 miles). Peaks over 1,600 m (1 mile) tall press down on the inlet. And if you are fortunate enough to be here shortly after a period of rain you will encounter one of the most impressive collections of waterfalls on the coast.

B.C. Ferries' *Queen of Chilliwack* passes here on its Friday route, and if conditions are right—little cloud cover and the prospect of waterfalls—the ferry will take an hour-long diversion into the inlet.

Place names: Captain Vancouver entered the inlet in June 1793. His journal reads: "These cascades were extremely grand, and by much the largest and most tremendous of any we had ever beheld. The impetuosity with which these waters descended produced a strong current of air that reached nearly to the opposite side of the channel, though it was perfectly calm in every other direction." The reason for the name he chose speaks for itself.

The hot spring at Eucott Bay.

Eucott Bay

This bay has a fairly narrow entrance, after which it turns northward into what is almost a circular lagoon. On the northwest side of the bay are some old pilings. Behind the pilings is a wonderful little hot spring (N52°27.31'/W127°18.75').

The hot spring empties into a natural pool enhanced with some concrete to make a tub large enough for a group. The water reaches the pool through a pipe that can be manipulated to control the water temperature by an ingeniously simple method. A stick pinches the passage of water. Pull out the stick and more water will come out to heat the pool. Push the stick back and the water constricts, slowing the pace of heating the pool. A bathtub is set up next to the pool for those who want to scrub away their grime. The old bathtub notwithstanding, this is a wonderfully scenic spot that is preferable to some of the other more developed hot springs, even if it is uncovered.

Eucott Bay is a key anchorage for the area—well protected, though northerlies can blow down the surrounding mountainside and through the bay in certain conditions. In other conditions howling winds outside can leave the bay without a ripple.

Camping: N52°72.37'/W127°18.73'. Eucott Bay is surrounded by a gently sloping, grassy shoreline. The grass continues well above the high tide line in most areas, particularly near the hot spring. A developed site with a fire pit lies directly north of the hot spring. For more privacy and a spot within walking distance of the spring, look for the jumble of boulders just north of the spring. There are flat, clear areas in front of and around the boulders.

Labouchere Channel

This passage runs about 12 km (7 miles) north-south between Dean and Burke channels. Inflow and outflow winds in Dean and Burke channels diminish rapidly here. After a rainfall waterfalls line this route. Both the east and west shores are bordered with 1,600-km (mile-high) peaks. Tidal streams are weak.

Place names: The Hudson's Bay Company paddle steamer *Labouchere* travelled here 1859 to 1866. It hit a reef and sank on a voyage from San Francisco to Victoria. Two people drowned. Henry Labouchere was secretary of state for the colonies from 1855 to 1858.

BURKE CHANNEL

This channel runs 73 km (45 miles) between Fisher Channel and Labouchere Channel along the southeastern extent of King Island. It is the fastest route for boats travelling between Bella Coola and Fisher Channel. For paddlers it is among the most challenging routes on the coast, notoriously difficult for its turbulence and lack of suitable camping spots. It should be considered an adventurer's route only. It is stunningly beautiful, though, and its steep, snow-capped mountains make up for having fewer landmarks than Dean Channel.

Anchorages dot the channel; key locations are Fougner Bay and a nook just east of Cathedral Point midway along the channel. Both are boat havens.

The rarity of campsites is problematic. For paddlers with favourable winds and currents it would be possible to travel the 55 km (34 miles) from Big Bay in North Bentinck Arm to Restoration Bay, the best cobble beach and only recreational beach along the entire Channel. The bay is a traditional use area and was once a village site.

Several factors add considerably to the challenge of running this channel. One is the probability of wind, which usually begins mid-morning and continues through the day. On warm summer days it will blow up Fitz Hugh Sound and funnel through Burke Channel, following the turns of the channel. (Winter has a different problem; "Squamish" winds are gale-force winds that funnel in the other direction.) Another factor is the ebb current, which can run at all tides. Turbulence and rips often appear at the turns in the channel, particularly Haacksvold and Kelpa points. These rips can be strong enough to thwart travel by punts, the local workboats designed to go just about anywhere. Currents are strongest from Edmund Point to Restoration Bay. They can be weak northward toward Bella Coola.

Restoration Bay is where Captain Vancouver stopped with the *Chatham* and *Discovery* in May 1793 for repairs that included fixing a leak in the bow, repairing the launch, replacing several spars, caulking and mending sails.

Travel notes: Two humpbacks have taken up residence in the waters between Edmund and Haaksvold points, and can be seen here regularly.

Place names: Edmund Burke was a famed parliamentary orator, remembered for his speech advocating conciliation with the insurgent American colonies. Captain Vancouver named Restoration Bay during his trip here on May 29, 1793. His visit coincided with the 133rd anniversary of the restoration of King Charles II.

Kwatna Inlet

This inlet curves for 26 km (16 miles) alongside Burke Channel. The ecological highlight is Kwatna Bay, where Kwatna River creates a large tidal flat that serves as rearing habitat for juvenile salmon and a feeding area for both waterfowl and grizzly bear. The area was logged in the 1950s, and log handling reserves, camps, forestry roads and an airfield are all part of the landscape. In the 19th century several winter villages were shared by the Heiltsuk and Nuxalk at the mouth of the river at what is now the Kwatlena Indian Reserve. It was abandoned by the early 1920s.

The inlet ends in Quatlena River, another major coastal estuary most popular with sports fishermen for the summer steelhead run. Red-breasted merganser, western grebe, great blue heron and trumpeter swan are known to winter here.

South Bentinck Arm

This inlet meanders 45 km (28 miles) southeast into the B.C. interior. Some of the peaks to the east are the highest to be encountered near the coast, with Snowside Mountain soaring to 2,966 m (9,731 feet).

This area is unique for the coast in that some of the features are accessible by road. If you turn left onto the active logging road after the ferry terminal at Bella Coola you will head up some steep and

North Bentinck Arm.

treacherous stretches to an alpine lake known as M. Gurr Lake. A hiking trail loops the lake. Beyond M. Gurr Lake is the campground at Blue Jay and Grey Jay lakes where there are boardwalk trails over peat bogs and a view of South Bentinck Arm. After more logging roads you will reach Big Cedar Tree Picnic Site that has one of the largest western red cedars in B.C. A picnic area is located at the estuary. Camping is possible here. The route involves active logging roads. For road conditions call **250-982-2000**.

The Big Cedar Tree Picnic Site is also accessible by boat.

Another key feature of this inlet is Tallheo Hot Springs (N52°12.39'/W126°56.28') 12 km (7.5 miles) south of Talheo Point. A beach to the north provides a landing opportunity for the oceanfront pools. This is a popular location in the summer on what was once a native village site. Three longhouses were located here. Traditional use continues with a sweat lodge.

Three major estuaries are located in South Bentinck Arm. Asseek, Ickna and Taleomey rivers are key locations for waterfowl and habitat for juvenile salmon.

The arm is prone to north winds during the summer that can begin at about 10 a.m. and carry on throughout the day. South of the narrows at Taleomy Indian Reserve strong wind is rare. Taleomy is the site of a former Haisla village abandoned in the 1920s in favour of Bella Coola.

Place names: William Henry Cavendish Bentinck was the Duke of Portland. The inlets were named by Captain Vancouver in 1793.

North Bentinck Arm

If you start your vacation with a launch from Bella Coola, you will be starting from just about the most outstanding mountain scenery on the coast. Peaks about 2,400 m (1.2 miles) high line the Bella Coola Valley and extend to lesser but still impressive heights down the sides of North Bentinck Arm. The Bella Coola River empties into the arm, creating an ecologically healthy wetland. Juvenile pink, chum, coho, chinook and cutthroat use the estuary, as do a high number of waterfowl.

The prevailing summer wind is southwest, and can begin in mid-morning and continue all day.

Look for beaches at Big Bay and Bachelor Bay as a way to break up a run to Eucott Hot Springs. A public dock, marina and the B.C. Ferry terminal for Bella Coola are all located near the head of the inlet on the south shore. Facilities are available 2 km (just over a mile) along the road in town.

Across from the harbour on the north end of the inlet is Tallheo Cannery, a 1900s cannery village restored and now operating as a historic site with accommodation in the 1920s bunkhouse. Meals are available, as well as air and water tours. Pickup is available from the government wharf. Call **250-982-2344** or visit **www.centralcoastbc.com/tallheocannery**.

Bella Coola

This full-service community of about 2,300 is located just behind the Bella Coola River estuary at the bottom of the Bella Coola Valley. This was originally Q'umk'uts, where a number of longhouses stood, beckoning visitors to pot-latches and feasts with carved human figures that moved by strings. Q'umk'uts was just one of a number of Nuxalk communities in the area.

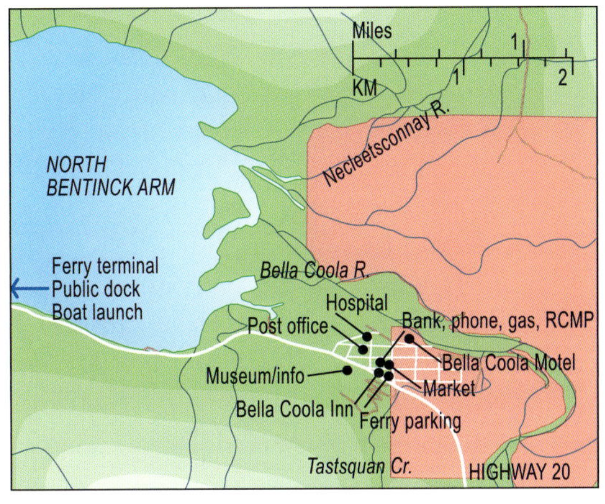

Bella Coola is on the ferry route during the summer weeks only. After the first weekend in September and before June the only access is by road—a difficult and winding one (see page 53 for details).

A pleasant place to visit is Clayton Falls, located on the logging road just past the ferry terminal. Here you'll find trails, picnic sites, a rough beach area and a boardwalk trail to a viewing platform of the falls behind a hydro power station. At Thorsen Creek on the east side of Bella Coola a collection of 40 petroglyphs lies hidden in the woods. Guided tours are available. Call the regional tourism office at **1-800-663-5885** for details.

Weather: Summertime temperatures in Bella Coola are typical of the B.C. coast, reaching into the low 20s°C (70s°F) through July and August, and only mildly cooler in June and September, with average daytime highs of 19.5°C (67°F) and 18.1°C (65°F) respectively. Temperatures will drop to about 11°C (52°F) at the coolest points of the night or morning in July and August. Average lows in June are 9.3°C (49°F), while September drops to 8°C (46°F) on average. Temperatures rarely, if ever, go above 24°C (75°F) at any time during the year.

Cold outflow winds from the Bella Coola Valley give the community the distinction of daily average temperatures below freezing for January and December—a rare occurrence on the coast. Temperatures will remain below freezing all day for about nine days in January and eight days in December.

That can mean snow—about 16 cm (6.3 inches) a year. Otherwise Bella Coola is blessed with very little precipitation, or a modest average of 1,652 mm (65 inches) a year. The wettest months are January, October, November and December, which each get about 230 mm (9 inches) of rain. May, June, July and August will see anywhere from 53 mm (2.0 inches) to 64 mm (2.5 inches). The most rain in one day was August 23, 1895, when 233.7 cm (9.2 inches) fell in 24 hours—so don't necessarily expect dry weather just because it's August.

If you are here during July or August, expect about 14 days of that month to have some amount of precipitation. In most cases it will be minimal. On about 4 days expect 5 mm (0.2 inches) or more of rain. Only 1 to 2 days of each month will get a good soaking of 10 mm (0.4 inches) or more.

The government wharf at Bella Coola.

Winds generally average well below 10 km/h (5.4 knots) throughout the year, with lowest winds in October at an average of 5.6 km/h (3 knots). Winds tend to be higher in the summer, with the highest in June and July—about 11 km/h (5.9 knots) both months. The prevailing wind is westerly March through October, then easterly for the rest of the year except December, which favours a northeast wind.

Place names: The area was first recorded as "bel-kula," then officially the Bellakula River in 1914. In 1924 the name was changed to Bella Coola River to reflect an 1875 map by G.M. Dawson. (Other spellings were Bill Whoalla by Captain Venables and Balla Koula by John Pawson, both in 1862.) Alexander Mackenzie referred to the village as "Pascall's Village" when he arrived here in 1793. The name Bella Coola was thought to come from the "bella coola wind"—the cold wind that blew down the valley in winter. However, the theory that Bella Coola is simply a tribe name—Billqula—given to the Dean Channel and Bentinck Arm residents by the Kwakiutl is now the most widely accepted.

A hint of clearing skies over Swindle Island, Finlayson Channel.

PART TWO

Spirit Bear

SPIRIT BEAR IS A LAND OF CONTRASTS: STEEP, MOUNTAINOUS PASSAGES or remote coastal island clusters with unusual characteristics such as wetlands. One feature brings this diverse region together. It is the land of the kermode bear, the rare white bear of the rainforest that is found in greater numbers on Princess Royal Island than anywhere else.

The name for this region is an invention, but it aptly serves to divide Princess Royal Island from the rest of the North Coast. Fiordland, meanwhile, is the name for the provincial park that links two beautiful and historic waters: Mussel and Kynoch inlets.

The Inside Passage transits this region via Finlayson and Princess Royal channels. Venture to the east and you enter the scenery of Fiordland. Venture to the west and you enter Laredo Sound, the gateway to the spirit bear sanctuary of Laredo Inlet and the remote island groups to the north, such as the Estevan Group.

The key here is to linger. Too many visitors rush through via the Inside Passage. As pretty as Princess Royal Channel is, capturing the beauty and variety of this area requires a more thorough look.

GETTING HERE

By road

There is no road access to this region.

By ferry

The Discovery Coast Passage offered by B.C. Ferries stops at Klemtu on Sunday afternoon. The trip originates from Port Hardy on Saturdays at 9 p.m., meaning a night aboard the *Queen of Chilliwack*.

See The Northern Channels, page 265
FARRANT I.
GRIBBELL I.
BANKS I.
PITT I.
Cridge Passage
Fin I.
Lewis Passage
McKay Reach
NEPEAN SOUND
Otter Channel
Squally Channel
GIL ISLAND
Whale Channel
TRUTCH I.
ESTEVAN SOUND
CAMPANIA I.
Ashdown I.
ESTEVAN GROUP
CAMPANIA SOUND
Dewdney I.
Glide Is.
Dewdney and Glide Islands Ecological Reserve
Chapple Inlet
CAAMAÑO SOUND
Emily Carr Inlet
Surf Inlet
Racey Inlet
Rennison I.
Anderson Is.
Helmcken Inlet
Laredo Channel
Gander I.
Moore/McKenney/Whitmore Islands Ecological Reserve
Beauchemin Channel
ARISTAZABAL I.
Clifford Bay
Byers/Harvey/Conroy/Sinnett Islands Ecological Reserve
Weeteeam Bay
6 LAREDO
HECATE STRAIT
10
Kilometres

SPIRIT BEAR

See Kitimat, page 243
Whidbey Reach
Egeria Reach
Kowesas R.
Fraser Reach
PRINCESS ROYAL CHANNEL
Scow Bay
Klekane Inlet
Whalen L.
Work I.
BUTEDALE
Marmor
Peak
Aaltanhash Inlet
PRINCESS
Khutze Inlet
Khutze R.
Kitlope L.
ROYAL
Canoona IR
KITLOPE
HERITAGE
CONSERVANCY
ISLAND
Kitasoo
Spirit Bear
Designated Area
Graham Reach
Yule L.
Swanson Bay
Green Inlet Marine Park
Carter L.
Mussel Inlet
Laredo Inlet
Tolmie Channel
FIORDLAND
RECREATION
AREA
Sheep Passage
POOLEY I.
Kynoch Inlet
Culpepper Lagoon
SARAH I.
Finlayson Channel
RODERICK I.
Griffin Passage
Mathieson Channel
See Bella Bella, page 121
LAREDO
SOUND
Meyers Passage
KLEMTU
Spiller Inlet
Kitasu
Bay
SWINDLE I.
Jackson Passage
Ellerslie L.
Ellerslie Bay
SUSAN I.
Oscar Passage
DOWAGER I.
DON PENINSULA
PRICE
ISLAND
Rudolph Bay
Bullock Channel
Briggs Inlet
Spiller Channel
Yeo I.
MILBANKE
SOUND
Oliver Cove
Marine Park
McInnis I.
Day Pt.
Return Channel
5 FIORDLAND
Seaforth Channel
Chatfield I.
Miles
10

A group heads out from Milne Island for a day trip.

From Klemtu foot passengers can enjoy the many services offered by Klemtu Tourism, including accommodation, guided tours and water taxi service. Kayakers can unload their boats here or request a wet launch at some point along the route. Most often those requests are for locations along the central coast, not near Klemtu.

By air

Regularly scheduled flights are available to Klemtu. For latest service information visit **www.klemtutourism.com** or call Klemtu Tourism at **1-877-644-2346**. In 2006 service was provided by Pacific Coastal Airlines. For information visit **www.pacific-coastal.com** or call **1-800-663-2872**.

By boat

Most boaters visiting this region do so as part of an Inside Passage trip. The most popular route is up Finlayson Channel to Princess Royal Channel. Boat havens/anchorages along this route are located at Port Blackney/Oliver Cove, the coves at Nowish Island, Rescue Bay, Bottleneck Inlet, Goat Cove, Horsefly Cove and Green Spit (Khutze Inlet). For those wishing for a diversion through Fiordland, anchorages are at James Bay, Culpepper Lagoon, Kynoch Inlet, Windy Bay, David Bay, Poison Cove and Oatwish Bay. For those choosing the

Outer Passage, boat havens can be found at Cann Inlet, Alston Cove, Smithers Island, Carne Bay (Racey Inlet), Chapple Inlet, both Ethelda Bay and Devlin Bay in the Estevan Group, Cameron Cove (Whale Channel) and Hawk Bay (Fin Island).

By kayak

You have a choice of launching from Klemtu by using the *Queen of Chilliwack*, taking a water taxi to a destination of your choice (from Klemtu or by arriving from points farther afield) or paddling in from another region. From the south, possible points of entry are Port Hardy, Bella Bella (by ferry connection) or Bella Coola. From the north it would be Prince Rupert. Obviously, some of these areas would involve a major expedition well beyond the boundaries of Spirit Bear.

Having completed almost all the Spirit Bear kayaking routes (hatched lines on the map I cannot completely vouch for), I can say the paddling conditions for the most part were idyllic, though the rain and cloud cover were heavy in this region. Given the weather statistics for Boat Bluff, it's not surprising. The highlights were

Campania Island and Fiordland. Though visually stunning, wet weather and low cloud cover allowed me only a glimpse of the full splendour of Princess Royal Channel.

I will definitely return to visit Campania Island, the Estevan Group, Laredo Inlet, Princess Royal Channel and Fiordland. Areas I'm ambivalent about after having visited are Gil Island, Aristazabal Island and Finlayson Channel. While scenic, they didn't compare to Campania or Fiordland. But then again, few areas do.

RECOMMENDED KAYAKING TRIPS

The recommended minimum time: Due to the lack of road access, most people will be looking at a considerable ordeal just to get here. The quickest option is by plane, and a kayak rental service at Klemtu means you could leave Vancouver and be on the water at Klemtu the same day. This is a costly option, of course, but in conjunction with a water taxi from Klemtu you could quickly get to places that would take days to reach any other way.

The most popular option is ferry. The Discovery Coast Passage ferry leaves Port Hardy Saturday night and arrives in Klemtu Sunday afternoon. (Note the return journey goes through Bella Coola, which means you won't get back to Port Hardy until Monday night. An option to save time is to take your car on the ferry and drive back via Bella Coola.)

A simpler alternative would involve an arrival by ferry at Klemtu and a departure at Bella Bella/Shearwater. This would certainly make your arrival times and departures more flexible. You could arrive at Klemtu on Sunday, and instead of returning to Klemtu, head down Finlayson Channel and Seaforth Channel to the ferry connection. With a Sunday arrival in Klemtu you could conceivably leave Shearwater Wednesday afternoon, though a Friday departure would allow a more reasonable itinerary.

Another option is a water taxi from Bella Bella, Kitimat or Prince Rupert to your chosen destination. This is an expensive but fast way to a location such as Campania Island. It also reduces or eliminates the reliance on ferry schedules.

Trip recommendations are for time spent on the water and do not include travel time.

- *If you have four days*: If you are arriving at Klemtu on Sunday and leaving Bella Bella (Shearwater) on Wednesday, this is a possible agenda. A relaxed itinerary could be Rescue Bay (via Jackson Passage), Dallas Island or Cockle Bay and Kynumpt Harbour. An alternative route, though a bit more demanding, is heading to the beach at Pidwell Reef on Swindle Island, a day trip into Higgins Passage and then a run to the ferry terminal with a stop at any of the camps along the way back.
- *If you have six days*: This works if you arrive at Klemtu on Sunday and leave Bella Bella on Friday. Veteran paddlers could explore Fiordland in that time (though it would be rushed). An itinerary could be Wallace Bight, Mathieson Narrows, a day exploring Fiordland, Rescue Bay, Blair Inlet and Bella Bella.
- *If you have a week*: This is the minimum length of a trip if you wish to arrive and leave by ferry at Klemtu. Most visitors will do the traditional route, exploring Laredo Sound and Laredo Inlet either by Meyers Passage or a combination of both Meyers and Higgins passages. It's a shame that the Campania and Estevan islands cannot be reached by most people in a week, but a trip up Laredo Channel to Baker Point would be a worthwhile adjunct to any trip involving Laredo Sound. An itinerary might be Sarah Island, Milne Island, Baker Point (or Emily Carr Inlet), then a return via Higgins Passage. An exploration of Fiordland is also possible. An option is Wallace Bight, Sheep Passage, a day exploring Mussel Inlet to end at Mathieson Narrows, a day exploring Kynoch Inlet to end on Mathieson Channel, then Rescue Bay and back to Klemtu.
- *The ideal trip:* Take two to three weeks to circumnavigate Princess Royal Island. A clockwise itinerary would be Pidwell Reef, Higgins Passage to Wilby Point, Milne Island, a day or two up Laredo Inlet and back, Emily Carr Inlet, an option of a side trip up Surf Inlet, Campania Island (with maybe a day to hike and explore), a day or two exploring the Estevan Group, Otter Channel to Fin Island, McKay Reach, Butedale, Flat Point, Sheep Passage, Mussel Inlet, Kynoch Inlet, Rescue Bay, then back to Klemtu. This would allow visits to both the remote outer islands and some of the best mountain scenery in Princess Royal Channel and Fiordland.

GEOLOGY AND ECOLOGY

The geography of this region begins on the coast with large glaciers on the snow-capped mountains of Fiordland. The coastal temperate rainforest is composed of western red cedar, Sitka spruce, yellow-cedar, mountain hemlock and amabilis fir. Cutting through these mountain forests are saltwater channels. Many of the resulting watersheds create valuable grizzly and salmon ecosystems, such as those at Barnard Harbour on Whale Passage and Khutze Inlet off Princess Royal Channel. The islands toward the outer coast feature the predator-prey relationship of wolves and deer and in many cases extensive wetlands, such as those on Dewdney Island and the bogs of nearby Campania Island. Isolated areas of forest on limestone can be found at Emily Carr Inlet and Aristazabal Inlet in a muskeg plain. Rich karst features of sinkholes, underground streams and caves can be found in these areas.

The rare species to be found here are western grebe, Brandt's cormorant, common murre, Keen's long-eared myotis, Canada anemone, lesser saltmarsh sedge, short-beaked sedge, coast mountain draba and smooth willowherb.

The kermode bear is the symbol of this region. The government offers two estimates. One is that of the 135 bears on Princess Royal Island, about 5 to 15 are white-coated (*The Central Coast Protected Area Strategy Report* appendix information on Revised Study Areas Descriptions). Another is that 400 bears live on Princess Royal Island, and about 40 are white-coats (*The Central Coast Land and Coastal Resource Management Plan Socio-Economic and Environmental Base Case: Final Report*). Either way they are a rare occurrence and are rarely seen, with their main range roughly a triangle running from Princess Royal Island north to Prince Rupert and then east to Hazelton in the B.C. interior. The highest concentrations tend to be around Terrace and Princess Royal Island.

The bear's scientific name is *Ursus americanus kermodei*. It is simply a black bear with a recessive gene that makes it white, not black. It is not an albino.

A Tsimshian legend tells that the Creator, Raven, made every 10th bear of Princess Royal Island white as a reminder of when the land was covered with snow and ice.

FIRST NATIONS OVERVIEW

Mussel Inlet, Fiordland.

The Land of the Spirit Bear is also the land of the Kitasoo/Xai'xais. Two distinct tribal groups came together to reside at just one location: Klemtu off Finlayson Channel. The rest of their traditional land is currently uninhabited. The two groups were the Kitasoo of Kitasu Bay and the Xai'xais (pronounced *hice-hice*) of Kynoch Inlet. They first used Klemtu as a trade campsite and then for trading directly with steamships for cord-wood fuel. Today the Kitasoo/Xai'xais number about 460, or about double the population of 20 years ago. Their traditional lands encompass more than 100 cultural sites, including middens, fish traps, culturally modified trees and village sites. Abundant resources and mild weather allowed them to stay in semi-permanent settlements. A strong matriarchal culture developed along four clan lines: raven, wolf, eagle and killer whale. The crests represent lineages that possessed special privileges, such as sites for fishing and the use of certain dances or ceremonial masks.

See Laredo, page 209
Brew I.
1000
Green Lagoon
Baffle Pt.
Green Inlet MP
Green Inlet
Lomax L.
Tolmie Pt.
Hewitt I.
202
Carter L.
Hiekish Narrows
Finlayson Head
Carter Bay
Bloomfield L.
PRINCESS ROYAL ISLAND
Tolmie Channel
SARAH I.
Kid Bay
Goat Cove
Sheep Passage
Lime Pt.
Mount Learmonth
1019
Cougar Bay
Ditmars Pt.
844
Denton Pt.
Wallace Bight
Skilak IR
Waterfall Pt.
Bottleneck Inlet
Split Head
Watson Bay
Bancroft Pt.
Roderick Cove
Alexander Inlet
Meyers Passage
Boat Bluff
Jane I.
FINLAYSON CHANNEL
RODERICK I.
Griffin Passage
Mary Cove
Roderick L.
Counsel Pt.
KLEMTU
Cone I.
Charles Head
800
Freeman Pt.
Klemtu Passage
700
Hird Pt.
SWINDLE I.
Jackson Passage
Jackson Narrows MP
Nowish I.
SUSAN I.
Nowish Inlet
Hyne Range
Rescue Bay
700
Higgins Passage
Swindle Pt.
Legace Pt.
Oscar Passage
Bulley Bay
Mount Jane
723
Jorkins Pt.
Factor Its.
PRICE I.
Suzette Bay
Keith Pt.
DOWAGER I.
Dallas I.
Moss Passage
Cockle Bay
MILBANKE SOUND
Salal I.
Lake I.
Lady Douglas I.
Perceval Narrows
Oliver Cove MP
Cecilia I.
196
Reid Passage
Ivory I.
Seaforth Channel
Miles 2 4
Km 2 4 6
Cape Swaine
DUFFERIN I.
1400
Kitlope Heritage Conservancy
1100
Lizette Cr.
Oatswish Bay
Thomas It.
Mussel R.
1200
Poison Cove
McAlpin Cr.
Mussel Inlet
David Bay
Crosson Pt.
Heathorn Bay
Bolin Bay
Mathieson Narrows
FIORDLAND RECREATION AREA
Lessum Cr.
Windy Bay
Garvey Pt.
1100
Desbrisay Bay
POOLEY I.
Kynoch Inlet
Kynoch Pt.
James Bay
Near Cr.
1000
Mooto L.
Western L.
See Bella Bella, page 121
MATHIESON CHANNEL
McPherson L.
Ingram L.
Polallie L.
Spiller Inlet
Snass L.
DON PENINSULA
Cheenis L.
Ellerslie Bay
Salmon Bay
Carmichael Pt.
Arthur I.
Gerald Pt.
De Freitas Its.
Spiller Channel
Tom Bay
YEO I.
701
Lake Mountain
Tate Lagoon
Grief I.
Dearth I.

Fiordland

CHAPTER FIVE

MY INTRODUCTION TO FIORDLAND CAME THROUGH A FEW PAGES IN AN old marine park guide. The landscape pictured was stunning, and it became a goal to paddle this area one day. But there was the nagging doubt—fiords are steep and inhospitable. Would it be possible?

I had visions of having to spend a night hunkered down in the cockpit of my kayak—a better choice than sleeping in an estuary home to numerous grizzlies. Facing the prospect of travelling long, steep channels, I thought I might even have to hitch a ride on a passing yacht.

In the end my fears were unfounded, and I discovered Fiordland makes a wonderful place to explore by both boat and kayak. While camping locations are rare, they do exist, and the scenery is definitely among the most sensational on the coast.

Most visitors tend to pass up the opportunity to visit Fiordland, instead sticking to Finlayson Channel and heading as fast as possible into Princess Royal Channel. This isn't necessarily a bad thing. Princess Royal Channel is without doubt a beautiful area, with impressive mountain scenery, breathtaking waterfalls and even the old ruins of Butedale to explore.

Historic Klemtu, the last Kitasoo/Xai'xais community on the coast and the only community in this region, has an active tourism program with guided tours leading into areas difficult to explore and to cultural attractions easily overlooked.

Outside of Klemtu most other evidence of human occupation is historic, and all of it is slowly being reclaimed by the forest, whether it is the skeleton of a century-old beached ship at Carter Bay or the ruins of a pulp mill at Swanson Bay. It seems long, steep, waterfall-filled passages and glacier-chiselled mountains are the only attractions that last in this part of the world.

Mathieson Channel looking north through Mathieson Narrows.

MATHIESON CHANNEL

This channel is the gateway to Fiordland, leading northward toward the park boundary in ever higher elevations. The peaks aren't necessarily as tall as some areas of the coast but the glaciated cliffs and numerous waterfalls are stunning.

Mathieson Channel runs about 58 km (36 miles) alongside Don Peninsula. The south end is complicated by Perceval Narrows, but the north end is wide, steep-sloped and free of hazards. The mountain backdrop is not particularly high until nearing Kynoch Inlet. The tide floods north, but tidal currents are likely to be a small second consideration to the inflow-outflow winds, which tend to funnel along the channel. (On an afternoon when nearby Ivory Island was reporting calm winds, Mathieson Channel was churning up whitecaps near Mathieson Narrows.)

Camping: N52°34.26'/W128°14.05'. Tucked in behind Hird Point is a relatively clean and wide beach.

N52°37.58'/W128°11.08'. Located in an indentation in the east shore of Mathieson Channel is a series of three beaches facing north. The northeasternmost of the three, the largest and cleanest, has the most potential as a campsite.

N52°41.04'/W128°12.77'. Set on the south end of James Bay, this is a clean beach that appears to offer good camping potential. The detraction may be that in 2005 James Bay was being used as a logging camp, with active logging in the hills behind the bay.

Perceval Narrows

Mathieson Channel begins at the southern tip of Lady Douglas Island, where it quickly constricts into Perceval Narrows, just 160 m wide (525 feet) at its narrowest. A popular way to approach the narrows is from the east side of Cecilia Island (Reid Passage). One reason is the swell and weather from Milbanke Sound can hit the southwest end of Lady Douglas Island hard, causing nasty seas and a harsh chop. Reid Passage also offers the sanctuary of the anchorage at Oliver Cove.

Currents through Perceval Narrows can run at 5 knots. Currents will be strong from the south end of Lake Island to Cockle Bay. Expect some rips and standing waves. Add the possibility that swell will filter into the narrows. Slack periods are one hour before the tide change at Prince Rupert.

The beach at Cockle Bay makes an ideal picnic spot. Camping is also an option here. A Heiltsuk cabin, available for public use, is located behind the beach. If you wish to avoid the narrows altogether, the outside of Lady Douglas Island makes a wonderful area to explore. If there is a moderate swell you will get a fantastic show of waves pounding the rock bluffs until about Keith Point, where the exposure is reduced.

Oliver Cove Marine Park

Oliver Cove is a boat haven on the north end of Reid Passage. Its charm lies in the old-growth western hemlock, amabilis fir and western redcedar forest to be found on the shore. The best place to see it is from the trail that runs alongside Oliver Creek. There is a beach area on the south end of the cove, but it would make for poor camping. The beach is rough and the uplands overgrown.

Established in 1992, this small park contains just 74 ha (183 acres)—26 ha (64 acres) of marine and 48 ha (119 acres) of land. It and Port Blackney, a boat haven directly to the north, provide strategic all-weather anchorages for the Inside Passage. There are no amenities.

Moss Passage

Considering this passage constricts to just a few hundred metres/yards at Sloop Narrows, strong currents might be expected here. That's not the case. Currents can run several knots (and as high as 4 knots at spring tides) but the waters are generally placid. The low shoreline is not particularly interesting, though, and the beaches tend to be rough. Much better beaches can be found just outside the west

Looking toward Dowager Island from Dallas Island.

entrance. Note that the passage between Salal and Lady Douglas islands runs dry at low tide.

Camping: N52°22.10'/W128°28.29'. Off the northeast corner of Dallas Island is a wonderful clamshell beach in among a maze of reefs. The beach can be used on most tides, and a rough camp has been built on a clearing just inside the forest. It is a Kayak Bill signature campsite with a driftwood-and-tarp shelter. Other nice beaches line the southwest corner of Dowager Island.

Oscar Passage

This passage is rarely used as a travel corridor, but for those wanting to head into Mathieson Channel while avoiding Perceval Narrows, it is certainly a very picturesque way to travel. The steep cliff faces of Hyne Range lie to the north. There are no beaches until Bulley Bay, after which rocky options extend to the junction with Mathieson Channel. The current floods east and ebbs west.

Jackson Passage

This is considered the scenic option for travel through the Inside Passage, and boats are regularly anchored in Refuge Cove on the east

Rescue Bay, Jackson Passage.

Kayak Bill

Every so often, hidden at the back of beaches in out-of-the-way places you may discover a camp with a driftwood windbreak, a tarp cover and sturdy planks for a bed. These are invariably the camps of Kayak Bill, a recluse who travelled the coast, wintering in areas like Goose Island and Harvey Island—places too wild and remote for most people even in the summer.

One such camp is on Dallas Island. Most others are far more secluded.

Kayak Bill was an adventurer whose legendary status is reflected in the October 2005 issue of *Sea Kayaker* magazine. He died on Goose Island at some point in 2004 after years of living off the land. He was also an artist, and two of his paintings can be seen at Hakai Sea and Land (see page 103). His mode of travel was a double Frontiersman kayak. Though Bill may be gone from the coast, his camps remain.

side. Currents are generally low at not more than a few knots through Jackson Narrows. The main hazards are the S-curve, which limits visibility, along with rocks and drying reefs. It is recommended for small boats at high-water slack.

Camping: N52°30.80'/W128°17.16'. There is no camping within Jackson Narrows Marine Park, but Rescue Bay offers a number of rough beaches. The cleanest is a cobble and grit beach at the south end of the bay. At highest tides, cover can be found in the uplands. A rough trail leads into a small clearing in the bush.

Waterfall at Lessum Creek, Kynoch Inlet.

Kynoch Inlet

Set within the protection of Fiordland Provincial Park, this inlet is a scenic highlight of the B.C. coast. Sheer granite rock cliffs, the impressive mountainous skyline and the waterfall at Lessum Creek are breathtaking. Anchorages can be found at Desbrisay Bay and Culpepper Lagoon (see the Spirit Bear map on page 173 to locate the lagoon). This is the traditional home of the Xai'xais, and Klemtu Tourism offers cultural tours that include visits to village sites and pictographs.

Jackson Narrows Marine Park
Established in 1992, this is another in a series of small marine parks, at 71 ha (175 acres), that dot this portion of the coast. Most recreation—that is, camping and anchoring—takes place outside the park in Rescue Bay. There are no amenities.

Place names: Petty officer John Arthur Culpepper was killed in action August 21, 1944, aboard HMCS *Alberni*.

Mathieson Narrows

This can be a challenging location when flood or ebb tidal currents combine with wind waves from Mathieson Channel, creating rips and standing waves. Anecdotally I can tell you the east side seemed relatively serene and afforded a calm crossing, while the water

Mussel Inlet.

Heavy cloud cover, Fiordland, Mathieson Channel.

churned and curdled on the west side. However, conditions are apt to differ. Slack tide can be waited out in Heathorn Bay southeast of the narrows.

Camping: N52°50.39'/W128°08.22'. Just to the east of Mathieson Narrows is Heathorn Bay, with a pleasant cobble beach on the west end. Waves on the beach can be low to moderate when a southerly is blowing up Mathieson Channel.

Mussel Inlet

This is the more northerly of the two arms of Fiordland Recreation Area. Mussel Inlet extends 14 km (9 miles) north and west into Oatswish Bay and Poison Cove. The inlet has its place in history for the poisoning of Captain George Vancouver's crew with tainted mussels. It shares many of the features of Kynoch Inlet with its rugged granite peaks. Scenic highlights are the waterfalls at McAlpin and Lizette creeks. The major estuary for the inlet is Mussel River. The most secure anchorage is in David Bay, with other options at Oatswish Bay, Poison Cove and the head of Mussel Inlet.

Place names: Captain Vancouver named the inlet June 17, 1793, in association with the death of John Carter. The mussels that killed Carter were collected here. See Carter Bay, page 191.

Sheep Passage

This scenic passage into Fiordland runs for 20 km (12 miles) along the north end of Pooley Island. A highlight is a waterfall on the north shore near Windy Bay. Impressive cliffs line much of the north side of the passage. The passage floods east.

Camping: N52°46.87'/W128°16.48'. This interesting grit and cobble beach offers the best camping option in the area. A bar of barnacled grit and rock becomes exposed off the beach at low tides and can create an unfortunate portage. Otherwise the beach is wide and appealing in an area where beaches are rare.

Glaciated cliffs, Sheep Passage.

Griffin Passage

This route between Pooley and Roderick islands is for the adventurous only—for those who want to brave waters rarely travelled. The challenge is a series of narrows over the course of the 26 km (16 miles), and both boats and paddlers will have a difficult time here. Tidal rapids at the midpoint on either side of an islet add to the adventure. Expect the possibility of having to wait out one or even several tides. Note that the scenery is low rolling hills, especially on the north end, and it has been heavily logged. The shoreline, protected from ocean storms, has nondescript forest growing to the high tide line. Don't pass up Fiordland for this route unless you're determined to conquer the challenge.

Fiordland Recreation Area

Encompassing 6,645 ha (25.6 square miles) of marine area, including Kynoch and Mussel inlets, and 84,355 ha (325.7 square miles) of land, Fiordland is remarkable for its sheer granite cliffs and multitude of waterfalls, making it one of the best examples of fiords carved by glaciers on the B.C. coast. It is an area limited almost exclusively to marine recreation. The steep valleys are thick with growth, making hiking difficult. This is also black bear and grizzly country, especially in the estuaries where salmon spawn. Estuaries are the most accessible land areas, but camping within the park is not advised by B.C. Parks. Fine camping locations can be found outside the estuaries or on the park periphery.

It was made a recreation area in 1987.

The *Ohio* at rest, Carter Bay.

Carter Bay

Lying just off the beach at the head of the bay is the wreck of the *Ohio*, with its rusting bow jutting above the waterline. The vessel's demise dates back to 1909 when it hit an uncharted rock off the southwest corner of Hiekish Narrows (now Ohio Rock). With the steamship about to sink, the captain made the decision to cross Finlayson Channel and beach the ship in Carter Bay. The decision helped avoid any loss of life.

Carter Creek can be navigated for a short distance to a waterfall. There is an anchorage here.

Place names: John Carter, a crew member with Captain Vancouver, was buried at this bay in 1793. He died at age 24 from eating contaminated mussels gathered from what Vancouver named Poison Cove in Mussel Inlet. Vancouver wrote, "He pulled his oar until the boat landed, but when he arose to go on shore he fell down, and never more got up, but by the assistance of his companions."

Camping: N52°49.97'/W128°23.55'. Of all the potential camping sites in the Heikish Narrows area, Carter Bay has the most attractive beach. The sand, grit and cobble extends behind the wreck of the *Ohio*. The grit develops into an offshore bar at low tides.

FINLAYSON CHANNEL

The tide in Finlayson Channel floods north, and it will be stronger here than in Tolmie Channel. Oddly enough the reverse is true on ebb tides, when the current in Tolmie Channel is stronger. The narrow portions of Finlayson Channel have currents of up to 3 knots, while wider sections will have currents of a knot at worst. Hiekish Narrows can have a maximum flood current of 4 knots and a southerly ebb of 4.5 knots. Most currents will be considerably less.

North of Oscar Passage there is much to explore. Nowish Inlet extends deep into Susan Island, but strong currents at the entrance ensure it is rarely visited. The archipelago and surrounding coves have only rough or rock beaches. Two boat havens are located around Nowish Island. One is tucked into the cove on the southwest side. The other is on the opposite side in Nowish Cove. The southwest anchorage is used to avoid tidal currents in Nowish Narrows. Look for a petroglyph on the island.

Finlayson Channel.

The scenic highlight of the channel is Waterfall Point on Sarah Island. Across the channel are numerous bays and bights; Wallace Bight is probably the most interesting to explore due to the convoluted shore, including a lagoon joined by a tidal rapid. Kid Bay and Goat Cove are home to a large fish farm that dominates the shoreline. An anchorage can be found in Goat Cove.

Place names: Roderick Finlayson was an employee of the Hudson's Bay Company at Fort Simpson in 1842. He moved to what would become Victoria in 1843 and was a founding citizen of that city.

Camping: N52°44.57'/W128°25.44'. A very pretty spot can be found in the cove to the north of Wallace Bight. At first glance it appears to be just another rocky beach. But tuck in behind the islet on the north side of the cove and you will see a sand beach—one of the few places with sand in this region. A few rocks dot the beach. A sandy bar connects to the islet at low tide. Spring tide protection can be found under a welcoming, old fir tree. Its branches allow space for tents on the upper portions of the sand and rock beach. Extra opportunities are located atop the berm in the pleasant forest area. An early attempt to domesticate the area can be seen in an old bench and fire pit. This is a wonderful place in an area where good campsites are few.

Tolmie Channel

At the south entrance to Tolmie Channel, Boat Bluff, Jane Island and Cone Island form a bit of a line south of Sarah Island. This is a difficult place to navigate, as boats and ships alike enter Tolmie Channel north or south of Jane Island, and sightlines are not good. Kayaks will probably want to keep close to the west shore. Northbound vessels are encouraged to travel Sarah Passage (see map page 196). Southbound vessels are asked to keep to the west of Jane Island and use Jane Passage, which makes Jane Island a natural navigation barrier. Unfortunately, not all boats follow this advice, which can be hazardous.

Tidal streams are odd in Tolmie Channel, with a south-heading ebb tide stronger here than Finlayson Channel. It also lasts longer, running 1 hour and 30 minutes after the same ebb current has stopped in Finlayson Channel. Expect currents up to 3 knots in narrow portions and no more than 1 knot in wider portions. Tidal currents flood northwest in Sarah Passage and ebb southeast.

At Split Head, Tolmie Passage widens to appear more like a sound where it connects with Meyers Passage, Alexander Inlet and Cougar Bay. The remainder of the channel is straight and narrow.

The Boat Bluff lighthouse, a manned light station, dominates the south end of Sarah Island. A light station was first built here in 1897. The original tower is gone, but an extensive array of buildings on the hillside support the current skeletal beacon.

Place names: William Fraser Tolmie was a medical officer for the Hudson's Bay Company. In 1833 he served at Fort McLoughlin (Bella Bella) and eventually moved to Victoria to serve in the legislative assembly. Sarah was the wife of Roderick Finlayson.

Weather: In the shelter of Finlayson Channel at Boat Bluff, temperatures tend to be warmer and winds lower than many other coastal locations. It is also much wetter. The Boat Bluff lighthouse records average daytime summer highs in the neighbourhood of 19°C (66°F), with average summertime lows of 11°C (52°F). Expect some measure of rain on 16 to 17 days even during the summer months, with 8 to 10 days with moderate rain of more than 5 mm (0.2 inches). Summer months will also typically see 5 to 7 days of heavier rain of more than 10 mm (0.4 inches). This is substantially more than many other areas of the coast. The total: a staggering 5,029 mm (198 inches) of precipitation per year. There are no dry months, just months that are less wet. The driest is July, which receives 166 mm (6.5 inches). Every other month receives more than 200 mm (8 inches); the wettest months are November and December, when close to 700 mm (27.5 inches) will fall each month. That's almost an inch a day, every day. The one-day record is 256.9 mm (10.1 inches) set November 12, 1992. That's scuba gear weather.

Camping: N52°41.47'/W128°32.56'. North of Split Head, Sarah Island widens slightly, creating a cove on the west side offset by an islet. A navigation light is just offshore. Behind the islet is a nice beach with established clear areas in the upland forest.

SWINDLE ISLAND

The small native community of Klemtu is tucked into the east shore of Swindle Island. Two passages, Higgins and Meyers, provide gateways to Laredo Sound, where many recreational opportunities lie—and the chance, however remote, to spy a spirit bear.

Milbanke Sound

This is a moody stretch of water, where westerlies can stir up the waters when Finlayson Channel is in relative calm. The dividing line is just north of Jorkins Point. Should conditions be unacceptable, there are two storm channels just north of the point that could be used as emergency haulouts. Otherwise the shore tends to be steep bedrock between the beach at Pidwell Reef and Klemtu.

Tidal currents in Milbanke Sound divide in the middle of the sound, with a portion running to Seaforth Channel and two-thirds heading up Finlayson Channel. Currents rarely exceed 1 knot.

The sound was first surveyed in a sketch by Captain Charles Duncan of the *Princess Royal* in 1788. Captain Vancouver used a copy when he entered here June 20, 1793, recognizing it from the drawing.

Place names: Admiral Mark Milbanke had a colourful career beginning with forged papers that allowed him to enter the navy at age 18. He was named captain in 1748 and commanded the *Guernsey* until 1763. He served on the *Princess Royal* 1777–78 and was Commander-in-Chief of Newfoundland 1790–92. He was named admiral in 1793. Captain Duncan named the sound in 1788.

Fishing boats travel in tandem north through Milbanke Sound.

Camping: N52°27.15'/W128°33.92'. Pidwell Reefs provide a partial breakwater for the wonderful sand beach tucked in to Swindle Island just to the north of the reefs. There was no upland shelter in a 2005 visit.

Price Island

Price Island's rough and reef-strewn shoreline tends to keep most visitors away. The west shore is pocked with rocks and is often windblown from the westerlies gusting through Laredo Sound. The east side of the island is relatively featureless. McInnes Island off the south end provides weather updates for the area. The light station was established in 1921. Two marine trail campsites are indicated on the west shore of Price Island, but would be fair-weather stops only, given the open water and number of reefs to navigate.

Weather: The exposure of the McInnes Island light station makes it one of the cooler places to be during the summer, with average highs of under 17°C (63°F) in July and August. Weather rarely goes below freezing, with daytime lows of 2°C to 3°C (36°F to 37°F) in December, January and February. Rain is likely about 15 days a month in summer, with moderate rainfall of more than 5 mm (0.2 inches) 6 to 8 days a month and heavier rainfall of more than 10 mm (0.4 inches) 3 or 4 days a month during the summer. The total annual precipitation is 2,595 mm (102 inches). That's about half what nearby Boat

Monk Bay
Dallain Pt.
Hague Pt.
Mansell Pt.
Laidlaw Is.
Croft I.
Hastings I.
Waser Pt.
Thistle Passage
PRINCESS ROYAL ISLAND
Alexander Inlet
McRae Cove
Jorgensen Harbour
Split Head
Errigal Pt.
Boat Bluff
Pering Pt.
Sarah Passage
Jane I.
Jane Passage
Aitken Is.
Milne I.
Hartnell Pt.
Meyers Passage
Meyers Narrows
Saunders Pt.
Wingate Pt.
Draper Its.
Trout Bay
KLEMTU
Cone I.
Finlayson Channel
See Laredo, page 209
800
Bell Peak
Klemtu Passage
Wilby Pt.
Jamieson Pt.
SWINDLE I.
Kitasu Bay
Cann Inlet
Freeman Pt.
Abrams I.
Marvin Is.
Osment Inlet
Parsons Anchorage
Larkin Pt.
600
Higgins Lagoon
Kitasu Hill
746
Grant Anchorage
Higgins Passage
Mount Sarah
746
Kipp It.
Lohbrunner I.
Swindle Pt.
Jaffrey Rock
Goo-ewe IR
PRICE ISLAND
Pidwell Reef
Jorkins Pt.
Rudolph Bay
LAREDO SOUND
200
Jocelyn Hills
MILBANKE SOUND
Dowager I.
Dallas I.
Moss Passage
Langford Cove
Salal I.
Miles
Km
2
4
2
4
6
Muir Cove
McInnes I.

Bluff experiences. July is the driest month at 100 mm (4 inches), and expect in the neighbourhood of 135 mm (5.3 inches) during June and August. The amount of rain increases substantially in September and peaks in November when 336 mm (13.3 inches) will fall.

Wind drops to an average of 12.9 km/h (7 knots) in August, while the average is slightly higher in June and July—15 km/h (8 knots) and 13.5 km/h (7.3 knots) respectively.

Place names: Captain John Adolphus Pope Price commanded the 21-gun HMS *Scout* on the Pacific coast 1858–68. His career ended as commodore of the flagship *Princess Charlotte* in Hong Kong in 1869.

Higgins Passage

This waterway is unusual for the coast. The shoreline is low-banked and highly convoluted, with islets, reefs, coves and even a lagoon. The passage is almost completely blocked by Lohbrunner Island, which raises the spectre of strong currents, except that the tide splits just to the northwest of Lohbrunner. That means the current can be dead still just where you would expect it to be worst. Oddly, *Sailing Directions* states tidal streams north of Lohbrunner Island can reach 5 knots. Anecdotally I can tell you I encountered only calm waters during two crossings not timed for slack tide, and given the tidal split, strong currents would seem unlikely.

Numerous beaches can be found in Higgins Passage; some of those are long and impressive, particularly west of Lohbrunner Island.

The meandering channels make great exploration by small boat or kayak. Crabbing is particularly good here as well. Be sure to keep an eye open for the Kitasoo Xai'xais watchman pole. A Kitasoo community was once located on the south shore here and at Grant Anchorage, and the carved pole symbolizes the continuing occupation of these lands by the Kitasoo Xai'xais as well as their custodial role over the lands. Cultural tours from Klemtu are offered for this area.

The passage also contains a mystery: the structural remains of a house at Grant Anchorage. Two charred wooden boards and other badly decayed boards indicate a prehistoric home. Studies have found that Grant Anchorage had been occupied for about 3,500 years until it was abandoned in 1865.

A white-cobble rock beach at Kipp Islet at the west entrance to Higgins Passage.

The islands to the west entrance of the passage are a considerable jumble, and many become joined at lower tides. A good smattering of reefs adds to the maze. The beaches at the bays to the north may look inviting, but they are invariably rock. Also, don't be fooled by the islands with the white cobble-rock beaches, as appealing as they might appear from a distance. The beaches are steep and the rocks difficult to walk on.

The west entrance can be a difficult area to transit for boaters and kayakers alike, as the swell from Laredo Sound crashes onto the outer islets and reefs. Be prepared for open ocean conditions on the outside of Kipp Islet.

Camping: N52°28.53'/W128°45.40'. Given the historic nature of Grant Anchorage, it should be avoided as a campsite. The beach to the west of Lohbrunner is a good option, but the best beach in this area is probably the one right at the west entrance to Higgins Passage on the south shore. The beach is fairly clean and there appears to be good space in the forest. It's unfortunate that a bushy tree had fallen sideways here, blocking probably the best spots and views.

Meyers Passage

Meyers Passage is used more often than Higgins Passage as a way across Swindle Island, but it has stronger tidal currents, which flood east from Laredo Sound at as much as 3 knots. Low water is 1 hour, 20 minutes before low water in Prince Rupert, while high tide is 1 hour, 15 minutes prior. Westerlies can blow down the western leg, making for tough paddling.

At the narrowest portion of the narrows, keep an eye open for a petroglyph cut into the intertidal bedrock.

Camping: N52°35.91'/W128°34.99'. On the south side of the turn is a beach of grit and small stones that stand out for their white colour. Behind the beach is an established campsite. It is spacious and quite pretty.

N52°38.94'/W128°33.98'. Set 3.3 km (2 miles) south of Split Head is a small islet that protects a grit, stone and clamshell beach. It is high-backed, creating a pretty possibility for a small group to camp on the beach.

Klemtu

Klemtu is a fairly modern settlement, founded in 1870 by Tsimshian and Xai'xais families to provide wood and supplies for the growing steamer trade plying the Inside Passage. The Kitasoo originally came from Kitasu Bay, while the Xai'xais came from Kynoch Inlet. The population has doubled to 460 over the last two decades.

Klemtu was first known as China Hat, named for the shape of Cone Island when viewed from the south. A major employer for many years was a salmon cannery that operated from 1927 to 1968.

Sheltered by Trout Bay, Klemtu is a pretty little community split between the north and sound ends of the bay. On the north end, on the outer edge of the bay, is a band-run fish plant (formerly the historic cannery) and the government dock, where gas and water can be obtained. East of that is a barge acting as a breakwater and a community dock with close access to the visitor centre, band store and cafeteria. A laundromat is available next to the visitor centre; the centre is open infrequently. (A number to call may be posted on the door and a phone is available at the band store.)

A steep hill behind the bay separates the north and south ends of the community. A boardwalk was once the only link, but now a road runs alongside. The south end of the bay is the main residential and

A carved pole, Klemtu.

commercial centre of Klemtu, dominated by a highly visible and central church. A store is located just east of the church and the post office is just west of the church. The postal code is V0T 1L0. A beach for kayaks or dinghies on the south end of the bay is convenient to the downtown.

On Sunday afternoons the *Queen of Chilliwack* makes its weekly stop in Klemtu, and the community gathers to have lunch on board. It is the only time B.C. Ferries allows non-paying members of the public aboard.

A major landmark is the longhouse on the south point at the entrance to the bay. Guided tours are available.

Despite its possibly sleepy nature if you visit at times other than Sunday afternoon, Klemtu has a vibrant tourism program, from walking tours of the village to kayak rentals and outfitting, complete with the option of transport to your destination of choice.

Possible accommodation includes bed and breakfast packages, camping or use of the Floathouse Inn. Amenities in the floathouse include showers, a kitchen, three bedrooms, two sitting rooms and a television. If you have spent a week or two on the water and are returning by ferry, this may be the ideal way to spend the final night.

Klemtu also has a Coastal Hut program with bunkhouse-style cabins at strategic locations. These are available for rent. Given the nature of weather in this region, such cabins could reduce the hardship of multiple days of foul conditions.

Klemtu offers a selection of four ecotours. One is a grizzly bear-viewing excursion to Fiordland. Another is a culture and nature trip of Neeso Wakwis—a phrase meaning "our lands" in Kitasoo. A third option is Spirit Bear Quest, an outing to track and view the elusive white kermode bear. And lastly, a guided kayaking tour of the historic waters of Kitasoo/Xai'xais is available. More information on all these services is provided at **www.klemtutourism.com**, or call **1-877-644-2346**.

If you are just visiting Klemtu during the ferry stop, be sure to take a look at the carved poles and the many historic plaques that dot the village. A trail to the nearby lake may also be of interest.

Travel notes: My visit to Klemtu coincided with the end of my first month on the water—and the end of my supplies. Before I left I mailed food and fuel for the second month under my name to general delivery at Klemtu. The packages were waiting when I arrived.

Place names: Klemtu means "blocked passage" in Tsimshian. The Tsimshian version of the spelling is Klemdulxk.

Princess Royal Channel in cloud cover.

PRINCESS ROYAL CHANNEL

Princess Royal Channel runs 61 km (38 miles) to Whale Channel in four sections: Graham Reach to the south, then Butedale and Malcolm passages at Work Island, Fraser Reach to the north and finally McKay Reach along the north end of Princess Royal Island. The channel is wide and deep enough for ship traffic, and is well into its second century as the main route for vessels transiting the B.C. coast. It is surrounded on both sides by mountains that are sliced by numerous waterfalls, making this channel a highlight of the Inside Passage for many travellers. Inlets with anchorages dot the east shore, while the ruins of Butedale can be found on the west. Despite a history to the contrary, appropriate camping locations can also be found at strategic points, making it a good place to paddle as well. The channel is wide, with good sightlines along most of the length, so ship traffic should not be a hazard.

Tidal streams enter the channel from both the north and south and meet in Graham Reach near Aaltanhash Inlet.

Green Inlet

This pretty inlet curves for about 8 km (5 miles) into the mainland, where a narrows is formed by Baffle Point. Beyond is Green Lagoon, an area rarely visited due in part to the rapids at the narrows. Most boats will simply head into Horsefly Cove, a popular anchorage protected by Green Inlet Marine Park. A cannery was once located to the south of Horsefly Cove. Pilings and other ruins are still visible. The foreshore at the cannery site is a gently sloping grit beach interspersed with a great many rocks; that, combined with its shallow nature and tall intertidal grasses, makes it less than ideal for a stop, but there are many flat spots above the high tide line for camping if necessary. It is not as pretty or as convenient as Flat Point, though, to the north. The shoreline of Horsefly Cove is rock, so recreational opportunities are limited.

Green Inlet Marine Park

This small marine park was created in 1992 to protect Horsefly Cove, a boat haven and key all-weather anchorage for boats cruising the Inside Passage. It protects 18 ha (44 acres) of marine area and 19 ha (47 acres) of land that is generally inaccessible from the shore. There are no facilities.

Swanson Bay

This small bay is notable for being the site of the first pulp mill in British Columbia back in 1908. Ruins of the old Whalen Pulp and Paper buildings are still visible, including a conspicuous chimney that reaches up above the trees. Good anchorage in the bay and beaches at the head allow exploration of the ruins, which include an old concrete structure. It was a large operation, powered by a 450-kW plant built in 1909. It closed in 1934. In the early years limestone was mined for the mill from two quarries on the east shore of Princess Royal Island 11 km (6.8 miles) south of Swanson Bay.

Place names: From 1843 until 1870, Captain John Swanson of the Hudson's Bay Company commanded many of the most famous vessels on the coast, including *Cadboro, Vancouver, Beaver, Labouchere, Otter* and *Enterprise*.

Camping: N53°00.91'/W128°30.51'. There are several sandy beaches at the head of Swanson Bay. The best beach with good high tide potential is to the north of the old pilings. Another rougher beach is at the south side of the bay's mouth.

Mist in the trees, Princess Royal Channel.

N52°58.88'/W128°30.72'. Named for its low topography, Flat Point has numerous beaches scattered along its length, and camping is possible along most of them thanks to many level upland areas. The main beach north of the point is cobble and stone, with excellent upland tent sites about midway along the beach. This is probably the best-established campsite along Princess Royal Channel and worth working into an itinerary.

Khutze Inlet

Khutze Inlet extends about 10 km (6 miles) from Princess Royal Channel and has a rugged and dramatic shoreline that has, unfortunately, been extensively logged. Past activity includes an active mine in the 1930s complete with a railway system. Prior to that it was part of the 19th-century territory of the Xai'xais. A fishing station on the south shore of the anchorage was abandoned in 1870 for Klemtu. A village site and fish trap are located within the Khutze River estuary.

The Khutze River is a major salmon river, which in turn makes the estuary valuable for grizzly and waterfowl. Nearby is a waterfall and an undeveloped hot spring. The inlet is under consideration for protected status. Green Spit is considered an emergency anchorage.

Across from the inlet is Canoona River, surrounded by reserve land. It is a low-lying area but a wide and impressive waterfall drops directly into the channel. The visible concrete structure is a fish ladder. It is considered the most important fish habitat in the Kitasoo/Xai'xais area. This is a good place to view bears on the open grassy banks or fishing for salmon next to the river. Local knowledge says a spirit bear makes the Canoona its home and it can often be seen at the falls easily visible from the channel. The north bank was once a Kitasoo/Xai'xais fishing station, unique as a village site for its lack of beach access.

Place names: Khutze Inlet first appears on charts in 1870, but the significance isn't known. Canoona River was first named Anchor River and Indian River, and often went by the spelling Kanuna.

Aaltanhash Inlet

This inlet meanders for about 8 km (5 miles), ending at Head Creek, which drains Dome Lake. Aaltanhash River leads northward from the inlet's head. Nearby unnamed peaks soar as high as 1,486 m (4,875 feet). This was a traditional hunting and fishing area and in pioneer times was a steamer landing. The inlet can be used as an anchorage, and a beach across from the inlet can be used for camping (N53°06.94'/W128°35.94').

Klekane Inlet

This inlet dips just under 8 km (5 miles) north into the B.C. mainland. Work Island creates a navigation barrier just outside the inlet, with Malcolm Passage to the north. Marmot Cove, at the mouth of the inlet, provides shelter and a few beaches for kayakers. A little-known feature is an undeveloped geothermal hot spring at the head of the inlet (N53°14.83'/W128°41.00'). The hot spring issues 264 L (58 gallons) a minute from a crevice. The water is over 45°C (113°F) so will be too hot for direct skin contact.

Camping: N53°08.78'/W128°37.59'. There are a few nice beaches on Princess Royal Channel just south of Redcliff Point on both sides of a river. Continue north around a rock bluff and a magnificent beach opens. This is a potentially wonderful camping area.

N53°10.19'/W128°37.69'. An islet shelters Marmot Cove on the south entrance to Klekane Inlet. Grassy banks surround the cove, but a bar of crushed shell has developed along the narrow channel behind the islet, creating a steep, circular beach that extends well above the maximum high tide levels. A flat portion on top could be cleared of its scrubby vegetation, or you could stamp out a level area for your tent on the sloping beach.

Butedale

This is the famous former fish-packing plant with its highly visible ruins as you first turn into the cove. More impressive will be Butedale Falls, which cascades down tiers of granite into the cove. Use caution when approaching the falls as the current from the waterfall tends to be strong.

Many of the buildings of Butedale remain relatively intact, including the rendering plant complete with equipment. Others have been stripped over the years for the valuable copper pipe and wood (it's said a few homes near Kitimat sport framing courtesy of Butedale buildings). While most have been left to languish and many have collapsed or are badly tilting, a few others have been resurrected. Butedale is run by a year-round caretaker who has fixed up the cookhouse for his residence and offers showers, ice, ice cream and pop. The dock is maintained and a moorage fee applies. One of the old cottages has been renovated and is available as dorm-style accommodation for a nominal fee. The comfortable and dry accommodation includes a kitchen, a flushing toilet and a wood-burning stove. Wood for the fire is supplied. The caretaker has also rigged electricity using the old power station. With the turbine still being turned by the waters of Butedale Creek as it enters the falls, a car generator is used to power buildings.

Butedale Falls.

A trail leads from the ruins up to Butedale Lake. It is a muddy route that ends with views of the log-choked south end of the lake.

Fraser Reach

A waterfall 3 km (2 miles) northwest of Work Island on Princess Royal Island remains strong even in dry weather and consequently is a good landmark. The roar can be used as a guide during fog. Elephant Head Mountain is a prominent cliff that, when viewed from the water, resembles the namesake head of an elephant. A particularly striking area is the falls near Elephant Head Point.

About 10 km (6 miles) northwest of Butedale is a helicopter logging camp for operations in the interior of Princess Royal Island. While not normally a highlight, this does present a rare opportunity to see helicopter logging in action.

Newly protected areas

The province of British Columbia has been working on a comprehensive land use strategy for the central coast since 1993, and in 2004 it took a significant step forward by protecting candidate protection areas—possible future parkland—from logging by declaring "designated" areas. The June 30, 2004, order bars logging, mining and road building in 86 key areas of the B.C. coast. Some of these areas are the southern end of Calvert Island not already protected by Hakai Luxvbalis Conservation Area, Koeye River, the south portion of King Island, Khutze Inlet and significant portions of Princess Royal Island, as well as Ellerslie Lake and surrounding area.

What it doesn't include, though, are areas now available for resource development, including Gunboat Passage, Blunden Harbour and Home Bay. These were removed from the original study area in 1997.

The current designated status is considered short-term protection and expires May 23, 2006. When complete, the Central Coast Land and Resource Management Plan is expected to provide long-term protection, including park status, for many of these designated areas.

A white sand beach at Campania Island.

Laredo

CHAPTER SIX

COMMERCIAL AND INDUSTRIAL TRAFFIC WILL PROBABLY ALWAYS FAVOUR the Inside Passage through Princess Royal Channel, but an increasing number of recreational boaters are taking the alternative route through Laredo Channel. A small number of kayakers have discovered Laredo Sound, Campania Island and the Estevan Group as highly rewarding kayaking destinations.

One popular route begins at Klemtu and follows Meyers Passage to explore Laredo Inlet, which is newly protected by the Kitasoo Spirit Bear designated area. It is a fairly sheltered location with camping opportunities spread among the islets and on sandy spots at Kitasu Bay.

From there the options depend on how far and how remote you want to travel. And it doesn't get more remote than many of the outlying island groups, which are as much as 17 km (11 miles) from the outer edge of Aristazabal Island. Three clusters of the most far-flung outlying islands are protected as ecological reserves (not that they would see too many visitors even without this protection).

Campania Island is my favourite island on the B.C. coast. Its striking mountain range, sparsely forested slopes, potential for hiking, superb beaches, convoluted and interesting shoreline—all make it simply an exceptional place to explore.

If you visit Campania, the Estevan Group is a natural adjunct. It is a complex maze of islands and passages worthy of at least a day or two in a tour of this area. It is a mix of serene inner passages and an outer shoreline as rugged as any on the coast.

Gil Island and its waterways are most famous as fishing destinations. Those who venture slightly south will discover the beauty

See The Northern Channels, page 265
Farrant I.
GRIBBELL ISLAND
See Kitimat, page 243
McKay Reach
PITT ISLAND
Cridge Passage
NEREAN SOUND
FIN I.
Home Bay
See Fiordland, page 181
Lewis Passage
FRASER REACH
BANKS I.
Whalen L.
Otter Channel
Whale Channel
River Bight
Shipping route
Otter Passage
GIL ISLAND
Cornwall Inlet
Squally Channel
Weinberg Inlet
Drake Inlet
Deer L.
TRUTCH I.
Betteridge Inlet
Taylor Bight
Langley Passage
ESTEVAN SOUND
CAMPANIA ISLAND
Bear L.
Prior I.
Barnard Harbour
Ashdown I.
Barnard I.
Anchor L.
Oswald Bay
Lotbiniere I.
Cougar L.
ESTEVAN GROUP
Dewdney I.
Hickey Is.
CAMPANIA SOUND
Glide Is.
Chapple Inlet
224
Dewdney and Glide Islands Ecological Reserve
Dupont I.
Duckers Is.
PRINCESS ROYAL ISLAND
Surf Inlet
Emily Carr Inlet
CAAMAÑO SOUND
Racey Inlet
Rennison I.
Ulric Pt.
Pine L.
Kitasoo Spirit Bear Protection Area
Baker Pt.
Evinrude Inlet
Anderson Is.
Tuzo I.
LAREDO CHANNEL
Commando Inlet
Helmcken L.
Knight Range
Isnor Rock
Helmcken Inlet
Borrowman Bay
Laredo Inlet
Kent Inlet
Moore/McKenney/Whitmore Islands Ecological Reserve
Gander I.
Kettle Inlet
Ramsbotham Is.
Trahey Inlet
McKenney Is.
Moore Is.
Beauchemin Channel
Monk Bay
Jessop I.
ARISTAZABAL ISLAND
Laidlaw Is.
Aitken Is.
Milne I.
Clifford Bay
Normansell Is.
LAREDO SOUND
HECATE STRAIT
Byers/Harvey/Conroy/Sinnett Islands Ecological Reserve
Kitasu Bay
Weeteeam Bay
213
Harvey Is.
Arriaga Is.
SWINDLE I.
Thistleton Is.
Higgins Passage
PRICE I.
Munro I.
217
Miles
4
8
Km
4
8
12
See Fiordland, page 181

Entrance to Bay of Plenty, Laredo Inlet.

of Emily Carr Inlet and Surf Inlet, a passage that cuts deep into Princess Royal Island and has a historic mining camp at its head.

LAREDO INLET

A long fight to protect this inlet, best known as key habitat for the Spirit Bear, or kermode bear, was partially won in 2004. The result is a substantial portion of Princess Royal Island—96,458 ha (372 square miles)—is now protected as the Kitasoo Spirit Bear designated area. While its future as a park is still in question, it does hand the Kitasoo/Xai'xais some measure of control over the future management of the area.

As it stands, the inlet and surrounding islands remain open to recreational use. That is limited due to the slim number of places where the shore is accessible. Steep, heavily forested slopes mean few opportunities to leave the water. Places like Pocock Island have jagged shores backed by sheer precipices. The boat haven for the inlet is at Alston Cove, while both Fifer Cove and Bay of Plenty are also used as anchorages. Beaches are rare and generally rough throughout the inlet. You won't be able to circumnavigate Pocock Island, as the north end is permanently connected to Princess Royal Island by a strip of land. But the mountains here are truly majestic, making it an extremely worthwhile place to visit.

Camping: N52°48.63'/W128°46.36'. The established camping location is Bay of Plenty. My choice, though, is Weld Cove just to the south. It is strategically located midway up the inlet and has some very nice beaches on the south side behind an islet. It also helps avoid camping at a major (and sensitive) estuary.

At Wilby Point looking into Kitasu Bay.

Kitasu Bay

If your adventure involves using Higgins Passage to enter or exit Laredo Sound, you will have to cross the open stretch between Larkin Point and Wilby Point. It is rugged coastline with many outlying reefs. Laredo Sound is prone to open-ocean wind and swell. Southerlies can be particularly nasty here, and westerlies can blast down Laredo Channel. Once north of Wilby Point it is possible to duck into the cover of Kitasu Bay, the namesake territory and traditional home of the Kitasoo.

At Wilby Point an expansive beach allows landings between ribs of bedrock reefs that jut well out past the point at lower tides. Boaters may want to head to the boat haven at Cann Inlet. Not yet fully charted, the inlet offers land access and water, as well as an impressive waterfall.

A cabin, part of the Kitasoo Coastal Hut rental program, is located on Marvin Islands.

Place names: Acting Sergeant Major George Cann of the detachment of Royal Engineers served in B.C. from 1858 to 1863.

Camping: N52°33.48'/W128°48.76'. The shoreline southeast of Wilby Point on the beach facing Kitasu Bay is easily accessible between rock ribs that extend northward. Camping is possible on the beach. Kids will have fun with the treehouse above the beach.

See Aristazabal Island, page 215
See Fiordland, page 181

The campsite at Milne Island.

N52°31.77'/W128°44.57'. A sand beach joins the Marvin Islands at lower tides. The Kitasoo/Xai'xais cabin is located here.

Aitken and Laidlaw islands

Milne Island is a major staging ground for kayak visits to Laredo Inlet. The collection of islands outside the inlet also makes a good place to explore, but it is unfortunate there are so few beaches along the black granite shore. The clamshell beach in the midst of the Laidlaw Islands group is a good place to stop for a picnic. Watch for the conspicuous eagle nest on the central west side of Hastings Island. Thistle Passage is unremarkable except for the anchorage near the south end.

Place names: Aitken Islands were first labelled South Bay Islands on 1892 charts, but the name was changed in 1926 to honour Major George Griffith Aitken, the chief geographer for B.C. at the time. He served in both world wars. Rear Admiral George Fowler Hastings was commander-in-chief of the Pacific Station for the Royal Navy from 1866 to 1869. His flagship was the 20-gun *Zealous*.

Camping: N52°36.79'/W128°46.23'. The main campsite for this region is on the northeast corner of Milne Island next to a partially connected islet. The rock beach leads to a sandy level area that sits at or slightly above the spring tide line. Developed areas for several tents are set back in the woods. Note the beach is highly uninviting rock, but the little cove it sits in is well protected.

Travel notes: There is a sand strip covered by rocks along the beach at Milne Island where a small stream drains onto the beach. If everyone who stayed here moved a rock or two aside during their visit, it wouldn't be long before a strip of sand beach was exposed for easier landings and launches.

ARISTAZABAL ISLAND

Laredo Channel can be transited quickly, as it is only 34 km (21 miles) from Tildesley Point to Ulric Point. There are, however, hundreds of miles of coastland along the way; Surf Inlet is the longest and arguably the most scenic, with historic features to explore. The outer coast of Aristazabal is rife with islands and dangerous reefs.

Place names: Lt. Commander Jacinto Caamaño named this island during his voyage here on August 30, 1792, on the Spanish corvette *Aranzazu*. Gabriel de Aristazábal, comandante de la armada, was one of the most notable Spanish naval officers of the day. Vancouver misspelled it on his chart: "Aristizable."

Laredo Channel

This wide and varied stretch of water begins with some rugged and rocky shore at Dallain Point on the eastern entrance off Princess Royal Island. Kent Inlet is blocked by Philip Narrows, and all four of the inlets along this stretch—those being Kent Inlet, Helmcken Inlet, Commando Inlet and Evinrude Inlet—should be watched for strong tidal currents.

The tide in Laredo Channel divides mid-channel between Ulric and McPhee points. Ebb turns 1 hour after high water at Prince Rupert, while at Ramsbotham Islands it turns 2 hours after Prince Rupert high water. Flood tide turns 4 hours before high water at Prince Rupert at Ulric Point and 6 hours before at Ramsbotham Islands. If you miss out on the math, don't worry too much. The currents are variable, with a maximum of 1 knot at Ulric Point, 0.5 knots in the centre and eastern side of the channel and 2 knots near Ramsbotham Islands.

A view toward Rennison Island.

Around Ramsbotham Islands are various reefs, islands and small coves to keep the shoreline interesting. Behind Ramsbotham on Aristazabal Island is a limestone/marble outcrop that runs southeast for 1.8 km (1.1 miles). It has a mining history dating back to 1952 when over 10,000 tonnes (11,000 tons) were quarried. Reserves are still estimated at 72 million tonnes (79 million tons), and the current plan by owners Orinda Investments and North Pacific Stone is to mine it as a high-brightness filter for plastics, paper and paints.

Northwest of Shotbolt Point the number of beaches increases dramatically until Baker Point, which boasts one of the longest continuous sand beaches on the north B.C. coast. North of Baker Point the beaches continue sporadically until Ulric Point, but many stretches are rocky or choked with intertidal rocks and reefs.

Place names: Perhaps not surprisingly, Baker Point was first known as Sandspit Point, but it was changed to avoid confusion with the point on Calvert Island. James Baker was a contractor who moved to Victoria in 1867. At age 70 he took part in a 1924 city reunion. The point was named in 1926.

CAAMAÑO SOUND
Duckers Is.
Chapple Inlet
Adams Bay
SURF INLET
Emily Carr Inlet
Mallandaine Pt.
Sagar Is.
Bryant Pt.
Johnstone Pt.
Racey Inlet
Carne Bay
Archie L.
McPhee Pt.
Wale I.
Beauchemin Channel
Rennison I.
Ulric Pt.
PRINCESS ROYAL ISLAND
Nob Hill
Baker Pt.
Tuzo Is.
Evinrude Inlet
700
Mount Parizeau
Hawkins Pt.
Commando Inlet
291
Anderson Is.
Hicks I.
Knight Range
Helmcken Inlet
772
Mount Irving
Smithers I.
Trickey Is.
Borrowman Bay
Shotbolt Pt.
300
Mount Gillespie
LAREDO CHANNEL
Wriglesworth Pt.
Louis Is.
Willis Passage
Kent Inlet
Philip Narrows
Gander I.
Ramsbotham Is.
Kettle Inlet
Kinmakanksk IR
Trenaman I.
Moore Is.
Moore/McKenney/Whitmore Islands Ecological Reserve
Fernie Pt.
Whitmore Is.
ARISTAZABAL ISLAND
Wright Passage
Beauchemin Channel
332
Clifford Bay
Mount Johnston
Woodcock Is.
Tildesley Pt.
Benney Its.
Byers Is.
Bowden Is.
Sinnett Is.
Normansell Is.
Byers/Harvey/Conroy/Sinnett Islands Ecological Reserve
Conroy I.
Harvey Is.
Arriaga Is.
Weeteeam Bay
HECATE STRAIT
LAREDO SOUND
Thistleton Is.
Rogerson Rock
Lombard Pt.
Prior Passage
Munro I.
Miles
4
Km
4
8

Camping: N52°46.11'/W129°10.18'. South of Baker Point is a cove with a beach on the south side. The advantage here is protection from southerlies.

N52°48.17'/W129°12.89'. Baker Point is a sand spit with a beach of sand, pebbles and grit on both sides of the point. The beach is high-backed for most tide levels, and level spots can be found in the upland, though a clearing isn't established yet.

Travel notes: During my visit wolf tracks dotted the beach, a family of otters played in the water off Baker Point and there were almost no bugs despite a hot and nearly windless August day. With wonderful views up and down the coast and miles of beach to wander, this was a great camping location.

Emily Carr Inlet

Inlets, bays and small islands characterize the area around Emily Carr Inlet. So does limestone and the associated karst features—a change from the granite on the coast. This in turn has attracted a plant community that prefers alkaline soil and creates unusual features, such as an old-growth forest on limestone bedrock. This is a popular dive location, and the caves could be popular with spelunkers too.

The archaeological inventory for the area includes a village site, a plank house, a petroform (an image made out of rock formations), a canoe skid (rocks moved aside to accommodate canoes on a beach) and a shed.

A boat haven is located at Carne Bay in Racey Inlet to the south of Emily Carr Inlet. Anchoring is possible in Emily Carr Inlet, but rocks are a problem, and numerous groundings have taken place here.

Place names: Emily Carr, 1871–1945, was an accomplished painter and writer who was inspired by the beauty of the B.C. coast. Her paintings of First Nations culture began with a trip to Ucluelet in 1898. First Nations subjects dominated her art until 1929, after which she concentrated on B.C. landscapes. Her paintings were known for their bold brush strokes. In 1941 she received the Governor General's Literary Award for *Klee Wyck*, stories of her First Nations encounters.

Camping: N52°54.06'/W129°09.00'. The Sager Islands have a couple of rough beach areas worth examining. The best is on the northeast

Rock bluff at Emily Carr Inlet.

side of the southernmost of the islands. The wide stone beach where it is connected to an islet gives access to a very pretty island worth exploring.

Surf Inlet

Travelling Surf Inlet to its head is a 21.5-km (13.4-mile) journey that ends in an abandoned powerhouse and dam, both remnants of an old mining operation. The waterfall from Bear Lake, the dam and the buildings associated with the mining operation are all worth seeing.

The mine ran from 1915 to 1926, and again from 1935 to 1941. During that time it extracted nearly 1 million tonnes (1.1 million tons) of rock averaging 13 g (0.5 ounces) of gold per tonne (2,200 pounds) and created nearly 15.2 km (10 miles) of tunnels. A 270-tonne (298-ton) mill was in operation by 1917. It operated under a variety of names, the last and longest being Surf Inlet Consolidated Gold Mines Ltd.

The mining history may not be over. Testing, drilling and sampling have taken place in recent years, and two claims for the area are still in good standing. Another 15 claims are held in this area. Logging is also active near the head of the inlet, with a number of newly constructed roads. Access to the mine and dam isn't easy as there is no beach.

Mountain scenery in Surf Inlet.

Camping: N53°01.39'/W128°54.49'. Camping is possible at a rock beach next to two rivers on the south side of the inlet's head. Flat level areas can be found above the spring tide level on the vegetated beach. Just be sure to watch out for overgrown drainage ruts. Another good camping opportunity is in Adams Bay, at the halfway point of the inlet.

Anderson Islands

Beauchemin Channel separates the northwest shore of Aristazabal Island from Rennison Island, a large island—7 km (4.4 miles) end to end—surrounded by many reefs and islets. South of Rennison are Anderson Islands, a complex group that has a few sheltered areas but tends to be exposed to open ocean conditions. It is a good place to explore on a calm day, but expect fish lodge traffic and the possibility of commercial trawlers, especially east of Rennison Island. Tidal streams are low in the area, reaching a maximum of 1.5 knots on a northern flood through Beauchemin Channel; a southern ebb will be 0.5 knots at the highest.

The Anderson Islands.

Camping: N52°47.34'/W129°21.12'. On the northeast end of the largest of the Anderson Islands is a narrow but long strip of fine white sand between rock outcrops. This is a good base for exploring the area, as it can be reached without having to transit open water. A cabin is set in the uplands.

Outer Aristazabal Island

This is a long, exposed stretch with the possibility of good protection in places like Borrowman Bay and Weeteeam Bay. The difficulty is the length. It is about 46 km (30 miles) from tip to tip, after which a crossing of Laredo Sound is still necessary on the south end. It is achievable but is for experienced and adventurous travellers only. It is also not necessarily an isolated wilderness experience. North King Lodge is based out of Borrowman Bay, and its charter fishing boats can dot the waters here.

Most of the outer islands west of Aristazabal across Beauchemin Channel are protected as ecological reserves. The exception is Gander Island, which is a Kitasoo/Xai'Xais reserve.

The outer ecological reserves

Two ecological reserves protect the mass of small islands off the west shore of Aristazabal Island. The southern of the two is Byers/Harvey/Conroy/Sinnett Islands Ecological Reserve. The northern is Moore/McKenney/Whitmore Islands Ecological Reserve. The northern islands are host to seabird colonies, rare plants and coastal muskeg. The southern group is a rare site for peregrine falcon nesting in trees, other seabirds and for seal pupping. It is also the only known location tufted puffins breed on the mainland coast.

Moore Islands form a lagoon where eight petroglyphs of faces can be found carved into the intertidal bedrock and boulders. A fishing camp was once located here.

The Moore Islands group is home to fork-tailed storm-petrels nesting on the smaller islands and Leach's storm-petrels that nest on both the small islets and on Moore Island headlands. Other species found here are Cassin's auklets, tufted puffins, pigeon guillemot, black oystercatcher and other assorted species. But it is mainly a nesting site for rhinoceros auklets, with 40,000 pairs nesting here.

The Byers group was established in 1981 and the Moore Island reserve in 1971. The total protected land is 498 ha (1,230 acres). The Byers reserve also protects 11,780 ha (45.4 square miles) of marine foreshore. The reserves are closed to the public.

CAMPANIA ISLAND

Campania Island represents a region where three channels can be used to explore the Outside Passage. Both Squally Channel and Whale Channel are ways to head back to the Inside Passage (Grenville Channel). Estevan Sound is the most direct route if you want to travel north through Nepean Sound and Principe Channel—the continuation of the Outside Passage to Prince Rupert.

Whale Channel

This is a popular fishing area. A number of resorts dot various bays. There are three in Barnard Harbour alone, on barges along the east shore. A boat haven/anchorage is located in Cameron Cove in Barnard Harbour. The harbour is considered ecologically exceptional, with high concentrations of black bears and eagles. River Bight is also known for the high number of black bears that forage there in the spring and fall. Salmon and waterfowl occur here in high numbers.

Cornwall Inlet extends 13 km (8 miles) into Princess Royal Island in two arms off River Bight. The entrance is blocked by Clement Rapids, which is known for its large overfall and rough water. Use caution when approaching on a flood tide.

Stunning scenery on Campania Island.

Gil Island is not particularly scenic, and be warned that the area around Transit Point and Swirl Point at the north entrance to Whale Channel can have turbulent waters and rebound waves on the rocks—a bad combination. Conditions can get ugly here. Currents can run as high as 4 knots in Casanave Passage on the west side of Ashdown Island.

Currents in Whale Channel, on the other hand, are highly variable, occasionally running in different directions at the same time. It sets almost continuously south in the centre and along the west shore, with a maximum of 2 knots. Currents along the east shore, by contrast, are only 0.5 knots.

Place names: Francis Jones Barnard (Barnard Harbour) founded Barnard's Cariboo Express. His stagecoaches became the main form of gold rush transportation in the 1860s on the Cariboo wagon road. He later served in the House of Commons. Barnard Island and Barnard Creek are named after his sons, Lieutenant-Governor Sir Frank Barnard and Senator George Barnard.

Camping: N53°16.29'/W129°04.57'. Home Bay is backed by a sand beach that dries extensively at low tide. This is a pretty spot.

Squally Channel

Any waterway with a name like Squally should be approached with a careful eye on the wind forecasts. This channel can live up to its name, as squalls wash down from Campania Island's mountains, but with proper precautions it is as manageable as any other. The most exposed area tends to be near Otter Passage, where westerlies can blow along the north end into the passage.

Squally Channel runs between Gil and Campania islands. Gil Island has only a few features of note along this stretch. MacDonald Bay has a narrow opening that widens into a sandy beach. To the south are some islets and a convoluted shore to explore around Fish Bay.

Gil Island is low, rolling and heavily forested, with none of the drama of other islands in the area. Contrast that to Campania Island, a long island of mountain ranges interspersed with lowlands. The peaks are particularly distinct. Steep and heavily sculpted, they

A view down Squally Channel.

Sundown at Fin Island facing Gil Island.

have a rare characteristic: very little tree cover. Only the lowest portion of the island is fully treed. The rest is dominated by bald bluffs and alpine-like meadows perfect for veteran hikers. If you can break through the thick lower vegetation and scramble up a bluff, you'll be treated to a wonderful view over the nearby countryside. Expert hikers could spend days here, exploring the bluffs with a combination of hiking and climbing.

Camping: N53°14.39'/W129°29.33'. This site is off the southeast end of Pitt Island at Cherry Islets. Amid the cluster, best approached from the north, is a high-backed clamshell beach.

N53°06.55'/W129°19.06'. Set behind an islet on the southwest side of Gil Island, facing southward, is a clean clamshell beach with a good high bank that would make a well-sheltered location.

N53°06.31'/W129°18.05'. This is the best wide beach in the area of southwest Gil Island behind Skinner Islands. It has wonderful views south to Laredo Channel, but at the possible expense of exposure to southerlies.

N53°04.93'/W129°22.88'. Set along central Campania Island, this beach has rock at the lowest tides, but clamshell at the high tide line. Someone has cleared a tent pad in the bush along the upland bank that will serve to escape spring tides.

Fin Island

Cridge and Lewis passages form two sides of the triangle that is Fin Island. The oddest thing about this area is seeing cruise ships make the turn into narrow and twisting Lewis Passage.

Fishing resorts keep this area buzzing with charter fishing boats. A resort is located in Hawk Bay, as is a boat haven/anchorage. Curlew Bay is also used as an anchorage. Across from Curlew Bay on Gil Island is Fisherman Cove. Captain Vancouver anchored here in 1793.

Place names: *Curlew* was a launch of the surveying vessel *Wm. J. Stewart*. Fisherman Cove was named by Captain Vancouver "from our success in procuring fish, which in these regions were a very scarce commodity."

Camping: N53°17.11'/W129°19.56'. At the northwest entrance to Curlew Bay is an islet connected to Fin Bay by a clamshell bar. The beach is high-backed with space for a tent or two. Another clamshell beach suitable for camping is located on the north end of Howard Islet south of Curlew Bay (N53°16.45'/W129°18.67').

Otter Channel

This channel separates Pitt and Campania islands and is prone to rough water as weather funnels down the channel and mixes with tidal currents. Spring tides will run 1.5 knots with the flood running east constantly on neap tides. Spring tides ebb west 6 hours before and 1 hour after high water at Prince Rupert.

The worst of the harsh seas at Otter Channel will quickly fall away once in the relative cover of either Nepean or Estevan sounds.

Camping: N53°13.24'/W129°31.55'. This beach is within a deep, sheltered bay on Pitt Island on the north side of Otter Channel. It is the cleanest of the many nearby beaches and strategically located for a run up Nepean Sound. The drawback is the amount of driftwood at the high tide level.

Estevan Sound

Estevan Sound lies between the Estevan Group and the west shores of Campania Island. The northwest shore of Campania Island, dotted with small inlets and island/reef clusters, is a recreational wonderland for kayakers. Extensive white sand beaches line the shore south of McMicking Inlet. An impressive mountain range topped by Mount Pender provides a fabulous backdrop. It is possible to hike Mount Pender if you reach a clear ridge and follow it around the south side; a topographic map would be helpful for locating the ridges. Thick tree cover grows at the shoreline; one of the easiest ways to break through to a clear bluff is by following a drying riverbed. For your efforts you will have unobstructed views, walks through stunted, bonsai-like trees and a chance to see peat bogs.

Place names: Second Lieutenant Estevan Jose Martinez of the corvette *Santiago* created a near war with Great Britain by seizing British merchant vessels in 1789 in Nootka Sound. The sound was named in 1774 by Lt. Commander Juan Perez. Martinez was Perez's second in command. Arthur Jewsbury (1878–1969) was a carpenter aboard the survey vessel *Wm. J. Stewart* in 1943. His skilled work included the Empress Hotel and the legislative building in Victoria.

Camping: N52°58.32'/W129°22.03'. This stretch of sand beach is in a bit of a bay on the very southwest corner of Campania Island. Some rocks are evident at lower tides.

The wreck of a recreational boat in the reefs around the Estevan Group is a reminder to be cautious.

N53°02.70'/W129°26.65'. This is the main recreational beach on Campania Island, with a sprawling, white sand beach. A stream makes its way down the north end of the beach.

N53°03.03'/W129°26.90'. Closer to McMicking Inlet and the cover of Jewsbury Peninsula and its outlying islets is this fine white sand beach. It is my choice for the best in the area, with interesting, wave-smoothed, bedrock outcroppings dotting the beach. It is a very pretty location.

Sunrise over Estevan Sound from the Estevan Group looking toward Campania Island.

Estevan Group

This is a fairly attractive archipelago for its many meandering channels. Note, however, that many run dry at low tide. Langley Passage is the main route and is navigable under almost all conditions. The passage's west entrance is surrounded by reefs, rocks and small islands and can be a confusing place to travel, plus swell can break on the outer rocks and islets. Veteran paddlers will especially enjoy this area. The circuit from Langley Passage to Oswald Bay is ideal, as another passage leads from Oswald Bay to shelter north of Dewdney Island. The catch is the passage from Oswald Bay runs shallow at tides lower than a 5.8-m (19-foot) Prince Rupert tide. During my passage through on August 9, the afternoon tide was 5.9 m (19.4 feet) and I barely made it over an extensive sand flat. Otherwise you're looking at what could be a lengthy portage or a paddle around Dewdney Island. The waterfront can be confusing on the outer coast and the various entryways into the passages difficult to find as they are narrow and the shoreline is convoluted.

Trutch Island is topped by a distinctive antenna on Musgrave Peaks. The antenna was a part of a Cold War missile early warning system. The old radar station has houses, a helipad and a dock. It is now leased out to a shellfish farm operation in Ethelda Bay. A fly-in fishing resort is also located in Langley Passage.

There is good exploring in the area south of Lotbinière Island. Boaters will take a warning from the wreck of a recreational boat

Late afternoon fog over Dewdney Island from Lotbinière Island.

that lies partially submerged in a rock-strewn channel north of Hickey Island. Rocks block many of the passages here, and the exposed rock ribs can be extensive at lower tides. The passage west of Lotbinière dries completely at lower tides. A wonderful white sand beach is located on the islet outside of the channel. Unfortunately, for someone looking for a campsite, it is included within the Dewdney and Glide Islands Ecological Reserve. Instead, look for shelter on the northeast end of Lotbinière.

Otter Passage, between the Estevan Group and Banks Island, can have strong tidal currents—as high as 6 knots—and is exposed to open ocean conditions, particularly westerlies. Low water in Otter Passage turns 40 minutes before slack at Prince Rupert and high water 1 hour and 45 minutes prior. Slack tide is 11 minutes. This is a route for experienced mariners and paddlers only. Most of the ebb stream from Nepean Sound must exit through Otter Passage, creating a turbulent sea with breaking waves where the current meets the ocean swell.

South of the Estevan Group the current floods northeast in Caamaño Sound at a maximum flood of 1.7 knots. The ebb current sets southwest and is stronger than the flood current.

Travel notes: On a trip along the outside of the Estevan Group a thick fog blew in that ran parallel to the shore. In a cove I was in sunshine; paddling farther out to go around a headland, I was back in thick fog. There is something eerie about waves pounding on reefs when you can't see more than a few feet. It made this route extremely challenging because charts are only useful when you can see the places they indicate. I was highly relieved to find the passage at Oswald Bay. A GPS chart would have been ideal at this point. Unfortunately mine succumbed to saltwater early in the trip. Remember to field test your electronic dry cases before going on a long trip, and never trust an electronic product that claims to be waterproof.

Flat topography typifies Dewdney Island, shown in the distance.

Camping: N53°01.68'/W129°38.27'. Oswald Bay is backed by a fabulous sand beach. It is extensive, but broken by lines of rocks and shallow sand bars. When you pick a spot, make sure you won't be caught behind a distant shallow bar at lower tides. The portion of beach closest to the entrance to the passage appears clearest.

N53°03.33'/W129°34.41'. A north-facing beach at the entrance to Langley Passage on Prior Island provides the best possible camping beach in the area.

Dewdney and Glide Islands Ecological Reserve: This reserve was created in 1971 to protect seabird colonies, rare plants and examples of coastal muskeg. Dewdney Island contains extensive bogs and fens that are home to beavers. The outer forest provides a fringe of cover for the interior wetlands. The reserve includes 3,845 ha (14.8 square miles) of Dewdney Island and the nearby islands, rocks and islets. Birds that breed here include the sandhill crane and Cassin's auklet nesting on Glide Island. Rare plants include Gmelin's sedge, bog rush, Calder's lovage, bog adder's-mouth orchid and Queen Charlotte butterweed. The reserve is closed to the public.

Rock beach, wind waves and mountains—typical Douglas Channel scenery.

PART THREE

The North Coast

THIS SECTION OF THE BOOK COVERS THE 190 KM (118 MILES) FROM THE south end of Pitt Island to the Alaskan border. Two channels, Grenville and Principe, run for 88 km (55 miles) on either side of Pitt Island. They form the northern leg of both the Inside and Outside passages along the B.C. coast.

A multitude of island groups continue north of Pitt Island, forming enough of a barrier that Captain Vancouver felt himself trapped in Chatham Sound. Today's routes allow the city of Prince Rupert to play a key role as a deep-sea port connecting Asia with North America.

South of Prince Rupert is Skeena River, one of the largest watersheds on the west coast of North America. To the north of the city, Portland Inlet also extends deep into the mainland (and out of the coverage offered by this book). Farther north is Alaska, and a whole new wild coast waiting to be explored.

GETTING HERE

By road

Prince Rupert is accessible by car, but distance is a factor. It is 1,502 km (933 miles) from Vancouver—about double the distance by air of 756 km (470 miles). That means about 24 hours of driving, or 2 long days behind the wheel. The good news is the highway is generally good (without any difficult sections like the highway to Bella Coola).

ALASKA (U.S.)
9 PRINCE RUPERT 287
Wales I.
Portland Inlet
Kwinamass Peak
DIXON ENTRANCE
Zayas I.
Dundas I.
Khutzeymateen Grizzly Sanctuary
Work Channel
Khyex Tower
Dunira I.
Lax Kw'alaams
Melville I.
Metlakatla
PRINCE RUPERT
CHATHAM SOUND
Port Edward
Skeena River
Stephens I.
Smith I.
Edye Passage
Porcher I.
Kennedy I.
PACIFIC OCEAN
Oona River
Kitkatla Inlet
Ogden Channel
Goschen I.
Kitkatla
Dolphin I.
Grenville Channel
Petrel Channel
McCauley I.
PITT I.
Klewnuggit Marine Park
Principe Channel
Anger I.
BANKS I.
HECATE STRAIT
NEPEAN SOUND
10
Kilometres
8 THE NORTHERN CHANNELS 226

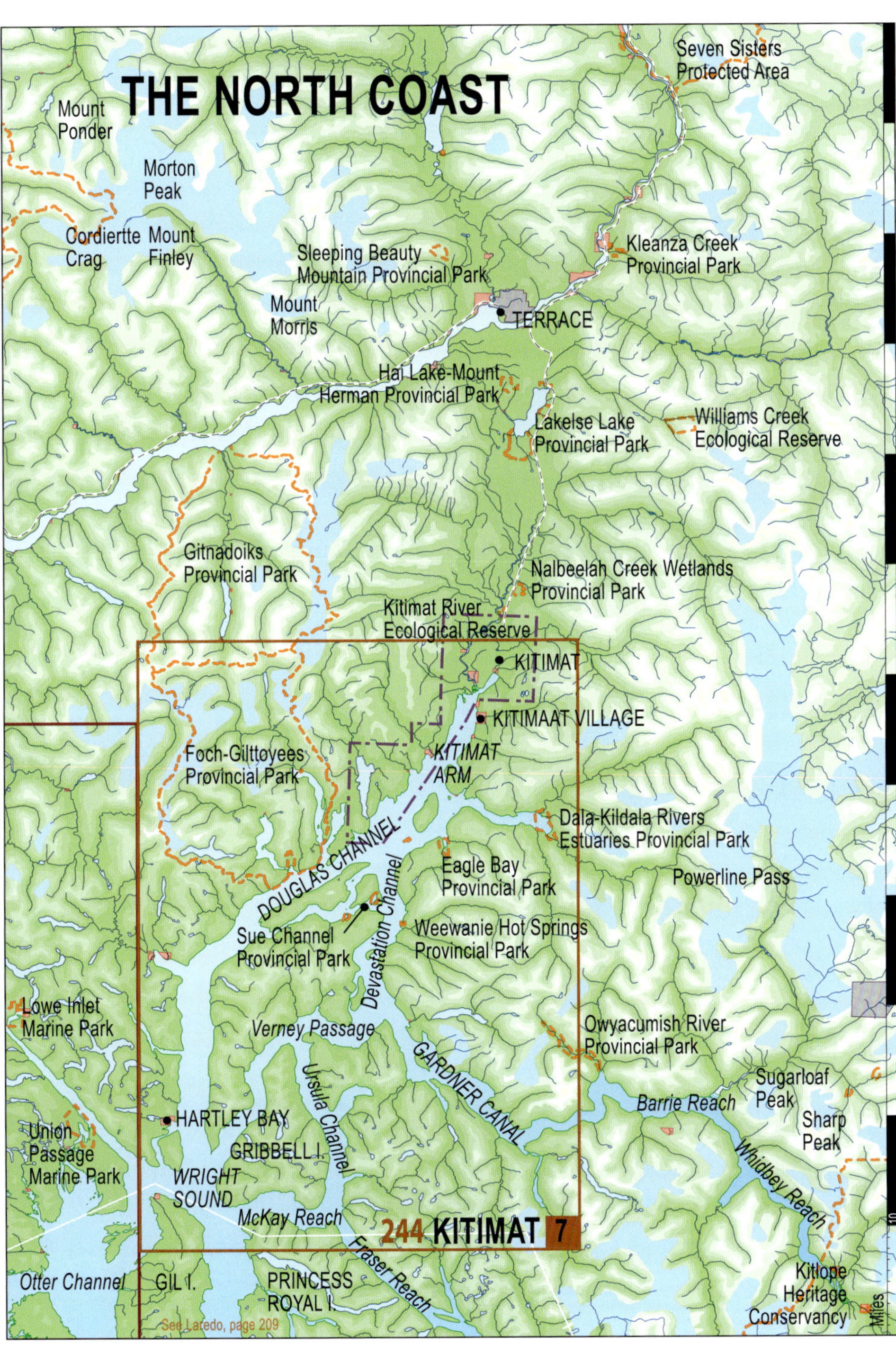
THE NORTH COAST
Seven Sisters Protected Area
Mount Ponder
Morton Peak
Cordiertte Crag
Mount Finley
Sleeping Beauty Mountain Provincial Park
Kleanza Creek Provincial Park
Mount Morris
TERRACE
Hai Lake-Mount Herman Provincial Park
Lakelse Lake Provincial Park
Williams Creek Ecological Reserve
Gitnadoiks Provincial Park
Nalbeelah Creek Wetlands Provincial Park
Kitimat River Ecological Reserve
KITIMAT
KITIMAAT VILLAGE
Foch-Gilttoyees Provincial Park
KITIMAT ARM
Dala-Kildala Rivers Estuaries Provincial Park
DOUGLAS CHANNEL
Eagle Bay Provincial Park
Powerline Pass
Sue Channel Provincial Park
Devastation Channel
Weewanie Hot Springs Provincial Park
Lowe Inlet Marine Park
Verney Passage
Owyacumish River Provincial Park
GARDNER CANAL
Sugarloaf Peak
Barrie Reach
Sharp Peak
HARTLEY BAY
Ursula Channel
Union Passage Marine Park
GRIBBELL I.
Whidbey Reach
WRIGHT SOUND
McKay Reach
244 KITIMAT 7
Fraser Reach
Kitlope Heritage Conservancy
Otter Channel
GIL I.
PRINCESS ROYAL I.
See Laredo, page 209
10
Miles

The *Queen of the North* in south Grenville Channel not far from where it now lies in the waters of Wright Sound.

By train

An option available to or from Prince Rupert is Via Rail's *Skeena* passenger service to Jasper. The 2-day rail journey covers 1,160 km (720 miles). From Jasper it is possible to link with the *Canadian* for rail travel to Vancouver. In combination with the B.C. Ferries Inside Passage route and bus service to Port Hardy it would be possible to do a circuit through British Columbia, including Vancouver Island, Prince Rupert and Jasper, entirely on public transit. Visit **www.viarail.ca** or call **1-888-842-7245**.

By ferry

Considering the distance of the drive to Prince Rupert, B.C. Ferries' Inside Passage service from Port Hardy is a viable alternative. It is also a way to see the coastal scenery from the comfort of a ship without having to take a cruise. It is a popular option during the summer and reservations are required. Call **1-888-223-3779** or visit **www.bcferries.com**.

The Inside Passage service suffered a major setback with the March 22, 2006 sinking of the *Queen of the North*. The vessel hit Gil

Island during a run from Prince Rupert and sank in about an hour. Two of the 101 passengers and crew were believed to have perished in the accident. As of the publication of this book the service was in limbo. Check **www.bcferries.com** for updates.

During winter the Inside Passage schedule shifts to include ports of call left unserviced when the *Queen of Chilliwack* ends its season on the Discovery Coast Passage route. Stops at McLoughlin Bay, Shearwater, Ocean Falls and Klemtu are added to the northbound run to Prince Rupert on most trips, and there are stops at Ocean Falls and McLoughlin Bay on most (but not all) southbound trips. Itineraries differ over the course of the winter, however, and poor weather can also affect schedules and stops.

The winter schedule, in effect from mid-September to the beginning of June, does not include Bella Coola. At no time does the Inside Passage route have wet launch capabilities for kayaks.

Prince Rupert is a hub for other ferry services. B.C. Ferries maintains a route to Queen Charlotte Islands from Prince Rupert, while an old B.C. Ferries vessel is now being operated by the Lax Kw'alaams band under the name *Spirit of Lax Kw'alaams*. It runs several times a week and can carry up to 15 vehicles from Prince Rupert to the head of Tuck Inlet. From there vehicles can drive to Lax Kw'alaams. For a current schedule contact the band at **250-625-3293**.

Under a recent agreement a ferry is also running twice per week from Prince Rupert to Hartley Bay. The 3½-hour trip operates every Monday and Thursday in a schedule that shifts to Friday and Sunday on alternating weeks.

By air

Prince Rupert is surrounded by hilly terrain, forcing the local airport to be located on Digby Island. That means using a passenger ferry service to get to the airport from the city. For airport ferry times contact Digby Island Ferry at **250-624-1027**.

Regularly scheduled flights are available to and from Prince Rupert and Vancouver. As well, Prince Rupert is a hub for regional flights, including Queen Charlotte Islands and floatplane service to Kitkatla and Lax Kw'alaams. Scenic tours of areas such as Khutzeymateen are available. As service providers and schedules are apt to change, contact Prince Rupert Visitor Information at **1-800-667-1994**.

By boat

For those transiting the region, boat havens dot the area. For the Inside Passage, look for established boat havens/anchorages at Lowe Inlet, Klewnuggit Inlet, Kumealon Island and Kelp Passage Anchorage (Lewis Island).

For the Outside Passage, boat havens/anchorages are located at Curtis Inlet and Ire Inlet (Pitt Island, near Anger Island), Colby Bay (Banks Island), Newcombe Harbour and Captain Cove (Pitt Island, Petrel Channel).

For Chatham Sound and nearby islands, anchorages are at Spicer Island and Brundige Inlet at Dundas Island.

For boat havens/anchorages around Portland Inlet, look to Winter Inlet (Pearse Island), Zumtela Bay and Legace Bay (Work Channel).

Other key anchorages not considered boat havens include Freeman Passage (Porcher Island), Qlawdzeet Anchorage (Stephens Island), Edith Harbour (Dundas Island) and Manzanita Cove (Wales Island, Portland Inlet).

By kayak

There are some wonderful choices for paddlers who wish to make the north coast a holiday destination, with mostly short hops from attraction to attraction.

Those transiting the coast will have the choice of the Inside or Outside Passage—Grenville Channel or Principe Channel. Both are rewarding, though I would give the nod to Grenville for its astounding scenery. Principe Channel has a more complex shoreline, but the scenery is not as remarkable.

Having completed the vast majority of the suggested routes (the hatched lines on the map are the ones I have not completed entirely), I can say the toughest portion of this region was Douglas Channel against inflow winds. A close second for difficulty was paddling up Principe Channel. A stiff northwest wind had me working hard all the way up the 75 km (47 miles) of Banks Island. By contrast, heading down Grenville Channel was a pleasure thanks to the same type of northwesterly.

Highlights for me were outer Dundas Island; the campsites on small islands like Proctor, Lucy and Rachel; the outer shores of Porcher and Goschen islands; the sand beaches on north Banks

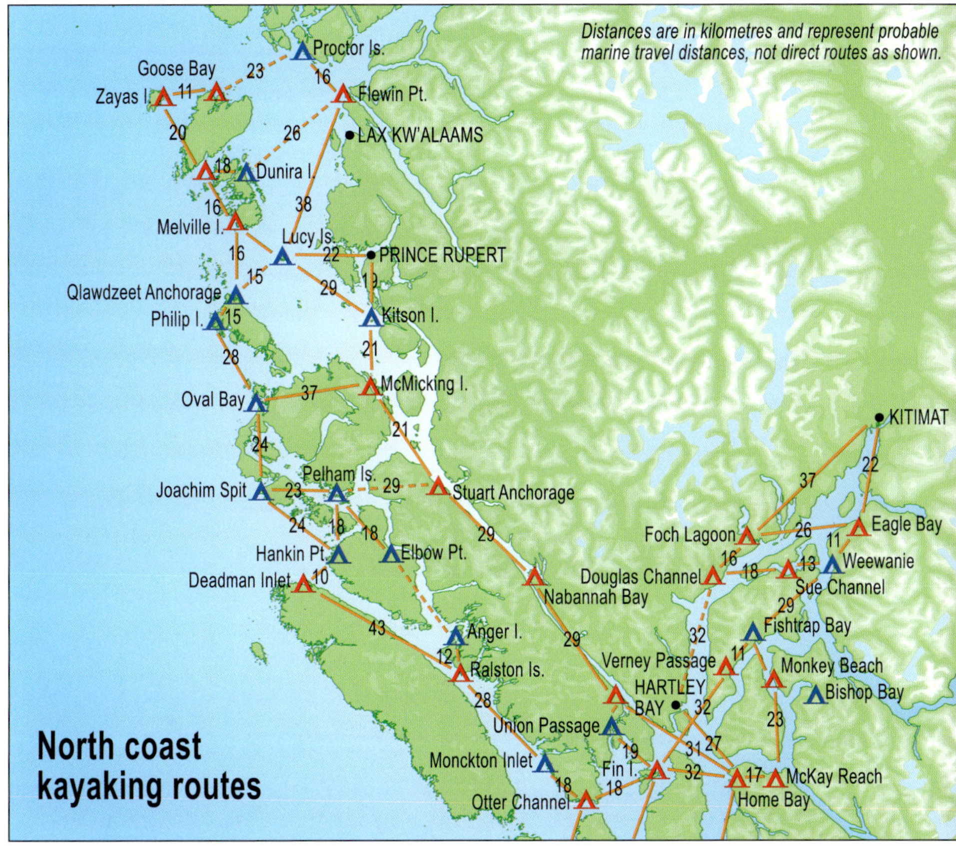

Island and the scenery in Grenville Channel and Verney Passage. I would revisit any area of this coast in a heartbeat except for Kitkatla Inlet and both Principe and Petrel channels. I did not find the scenery varied enough to warrant the distance. My number-one priority for returning here is Gardner Canal and the opportunity to paddle the full extent to the Kitlope Heritage Conservancy. This is surprising, as I normally prefer open ocean to inlets, but such is the charm of the Kitimat area.

Launches: Launching is possible in Prince Rupert at Rushbrook, located at the end of George Hills Way. An option for launching outside Prince Rupert Harbour is Port Edward's Porpoise Harbour boat launch. From Highway 16, take the turnoff before Prince Rupert along Skeena Drive. The launch is located just after Royal Drive.

RECOMMENDED KAYAKING TRIPS

- *If you have a day*: From Prince Rupert explore Venn Passage. From Kitimat try and get as far as Jesse Falls before returning.

- *If you have a weekend*: From Kitimat, consider making it as far as Foch Lagoon (or Eagle Bay if that's not possible). From Prince Rupert, an overnight trip to Lucy Islands is highly recommended. Kitson Island or Rachel Islands are alternatives.

- *If you have three days*: From Kitimat, consider paddling to Weewanie Hot Springs and using the middle day to explore Devastation Channel. From Prince Rupert you still don't have the time to get to the most interesting areas. Consider a loop of Lucy and Rachel islands for a relaxing trip. For those who don't mind the miles, a trip around Stephens Island is recommended.

- *If you have five days*: From Prince Rupert it would be possible to reach the attractions of Porcher Island. Consider Lucy Islands, Philip Island, Oval Bay, Rachel Islands and back. From Kitimat, consider a loop around Maitland Island with an agenda of Foch Lagoon, Sue Channel, Weewanie Hot Springs and back.

- *If you have a week*: From Prince Rupert the agenda with the widest range of attractions would be a trip to Porcher Island, then a run up Dundas Island and a return via Lax Kw'alaams. The traditional holiday is simply spending more time around Porcher Island, perhaps getting as far as north Banks Island (recommended). From Kitimat, a trip to Hartley Bay is a possibility. An itinerary could be Weewanie Hot Springs, Fishtrap Bay, Hartley Bay, Douglas Channel, Foch Lagoon and back to Kitimat. A more relaxed agenda would be to paddle possibly as far as Bishop Bay Hot Springs and back.

- *The ideal trip*: A run up or down the coast would be wonderful. From Prince Rupert consider rounding the outside of Porcher Island with stops at Oval Bay and Joachim Spit before reaching Grenville Channel via Ogden Channel. Enjoy the mountain scenery of Grenville Channel with a stop at Hartley Bay before heading up Verney Passage or Ursula Passage. The latter would allow a stop at Bishop Bay Hot Springs. Consider an itinerary of Bishop Bay, Europa and Weewanie—three hot springs back to back over three nights. Then continue north to end at Kitimat. A bus to Prince Rupert could close the loop, as could a water taxi. If that is too much of a transportation hurdle, two weeks spent exploring around Prince Rupert or Kitimat would not be time wasted. Consider a trip from Kitimat to Campania Island (covered in the Spirit Bear section). A trip to Kitlope down Gardner Canal would also be an interesting holiday.

GEOLOGY AND ECOLOGY

The north B.C. coast is mainly cedar and Western hemlock temperate rainforest, like much of the coast, but only about half the land base is forested. The remainder is high-elevation alpine terrain or muskeg.

The topography of the north coast is heavily glaciated, evident in the exposed bedrock that typifies the Coast Mountains. Prince Rupert receives about 250 cm (98 inches) of precipitation a year, with a moderate temperature driven by north Pacific low-pressure systems through most of the year. Rain intensifies farther inland where elevations reach as high as 3,000 m (9,800 feet). Typical for the north coast are long fiords, fiord lakes, lagoons and tidal rapids. A few areas of limestone can be found here as well, creating a karst geology where caves are common.

Most of the north coast is bordered by Hecate Strait, a submarine valley that narrows sharply in the north. The deepest parts hug the mainland shore. To the south it can reach 300 m (164 fathoms); to the north it reaches depths of only 50 m (27 fathoms). North of Hecate Strait is Dixon Entrance, a deep trough that lies between the Queen Charlotte Islands and the Alaskan Panhandle. Fresh water from the Skeena and Nass rivers aid water circulation, and Dixon Entrance forms a key migratory corridor for salmon.

The north coast experiences one of the world's largest tidal ranges, creating a diverse intertidal zone that is important for shorebirds and migratory birds of the Pacific flyway. Flood plains, estuaries, tidal marshes and freshwater wetlands are common.

Peat bogs and fens, often referred to as muskeg, are a common feature here, accompanied by low, scrubby bog forests.

Over half the world's remaining unlogged coastal temperate rainforest is on the west coast of North America, from California to Alaska. Due to the mountainous terrain logging is difficult in the north coast, contributing to a slim network of logging roads in the region. Only about 15 per cent of the north coast forests are considered suitable for logging, which also helps protect the forests.

Salmon is central to many aspects of the food chain here, and there are about 167 known salmon streams in the north coast region. Thirty-two other species of fish, 248 bird species and 62 species of mammals—from bats to whales—inhabit the area.

Vulnerable (blue-listed) species found here are grizzly bear, fisher, wolverine, northern goshawk, peregrine falcon, great blue heron, short-eared owl, gyrfalcon, sandhill crane, surf scoter and pine grosbeak. Only one species of sea lion is found here: the Steller sea lion. Rare species include marbled murrelet, horned puffin, Cassin's auklet, pelagic cormorant, tufted puffin, ancient murrelet and rhinoceros auklet. The north coast remains an exceptional place to view whales; humpbacks are common year-round.

FIRST NATIONS OVERVIEW

The north coast is the land of the Tsimshian, a word meaning "going into the river of the mists." The Tsimshian are divided along four linguistic groups: the Nisga'a of the Nass River, the Gitskan of the upper Skeena River, the Coast Tsimshian of the lower Skeena and the outer coast and the Southern Tsimshian, who extended as far south as Klemtu. The Tsimshian traditional territory covers about 3.4 million ha (13,000 square miles) of northwestern B.C.

The Coast Tsimshian's southern neighbours are the Kitasoo of Klemtu; to the west are the Haida, to the east is Kitselas and Kitsumkaum territory and to the north are the Tlingit of Alaska. The Coast Tsimshian were hunters of halibut, seals, sea lions and sea otters, and like the other Tsimshian groups that favoured land mammals, also took advantage of the annual bounty of the salmon runs. The abundance of resources contributed to an area more densely populated than anywhere else north of Mexico. Today the Tsimshian communities are Lax Kw'alaams, Metlakatla, Kitkatla and Hartley Bay.

The Tsimshian culture was rich in artwork, including intricately carved houseposts, but most evidence has been reclaimed by the forest. One in Git'k'a'ta, an old village near Hartley Bay, is used for cultural purposes. Metlakatla has recreated a longhouse for its cultural tours of the petroglyphs and village sites at Pike Island. The few reminders still visible are petroglyphs and pictographs, stone fish traps, middens and culturally modified trees.

Kitimat

CHAPTER SEVEN

WHEN I SHOWED UP AT MOON BAY MARINA IN KITIMAT 38 DAYS INTO the kayaking trip, I was somewhat of an oddity—not just because I was coming out of 13 days of rain in a row and looked the part, but because I was travelling by kayak.

Two days later as I chatted with marina owner Don Pearson, recreational fishing boaters came and went, but no kayaks. Don told me there was once a place in town that rented kayaks, but that was a few years ago. There were no tours based out of Kitimat and just as few visitors planning their own tours from here. Other than a few kayaking enthusiasts in town, fishermen owned the nearby channels.

Somehow Kitimat and its nearby waterways have missed the kayaking radar. Maybe it's the distance, even though a ferry trip isn't needed. More likely it is because the word simply hasn't gotten out yet. But when it does, Kitimat will undoubtedly evolve into a world-class kayaking destination. It has some of the best mountain scenery on the B.C. coast. It has the highest concentration of kermode bears (south Gribbell Island). And a string of hot springs are just a day's paddle apart, making it possibly the only place on earth where you can end each day of a three-day paddle at a different hot spring.

It's also one of the few car-accessible locations on the B.C. coast, meaning you can drive here and launch without being held up by a ferry schedule.

In all it makes for one of the most appealing destinations on the coast, with the added advantage that it has yet to be discovered—though I suspect in a few years those who fish out of Kitimat will be wondering where all the kayaks suddenly came from.

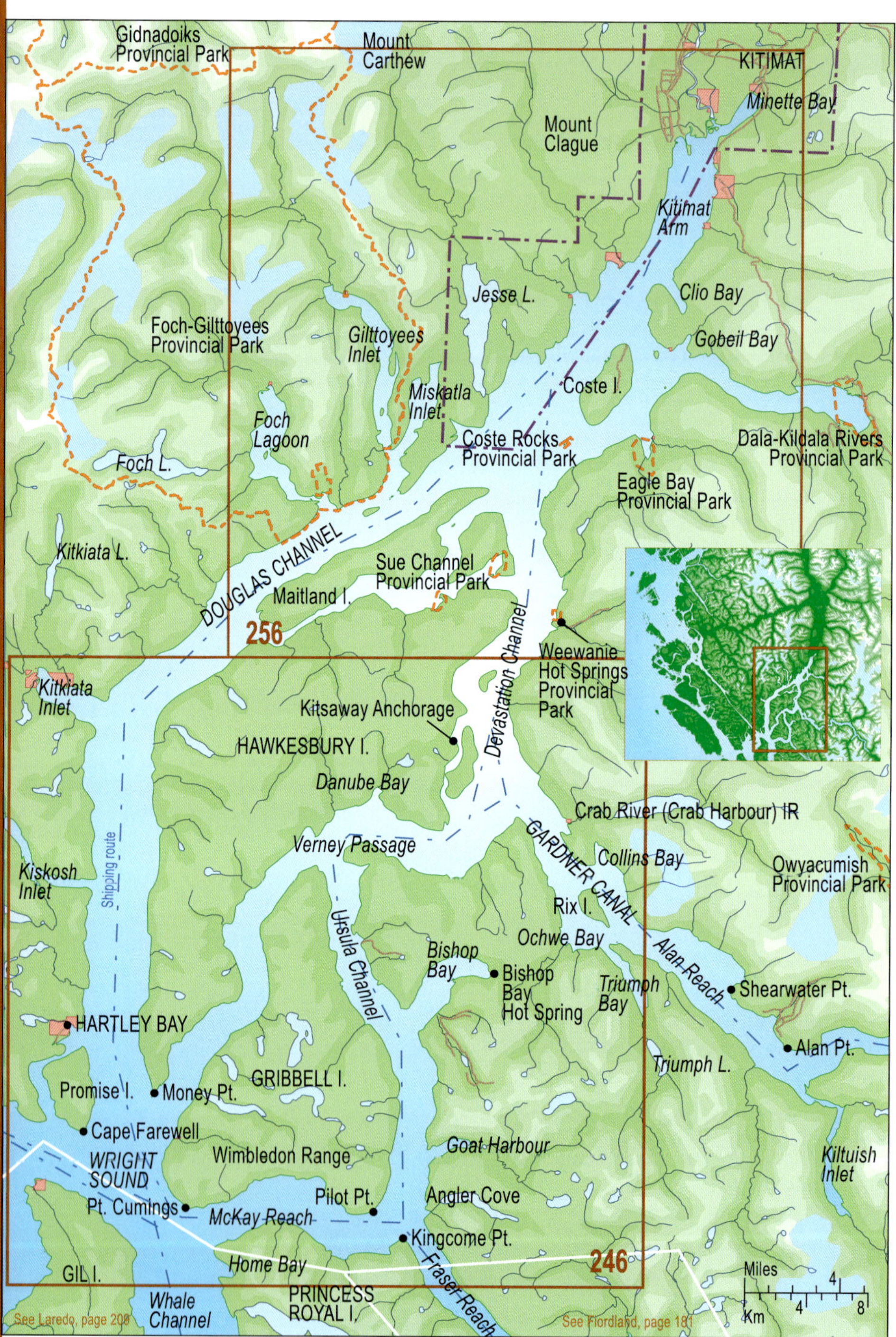

See Laredo, page 208
See Fiordland, page 181

THE VERNEY PASSAGE REGION

This beautiful region has one difficulty for kayakers: few beaches with protected upland clearings. The saving grace comes from the Haisla, who have made trappers' cabins available to the public (see page 249). Otherwise these channels are beautiful, clear and accessible, and well worth the time to navigate, by boat or by paddle.

Tidal currents are complex through this entire region. The good news is that currents are generally low.

McKay Reach

This is the northernmost leg of Princess Royal Channel, and the beauty of the rest of the channel continues here. This waterway connects Fraser Reach with Wright Sound, the southern entry to Grenville Channel. Steep, rounded mountains with sheer cliff faces descend to a wonderful assortment of small coves with cascading waterfalls. The Wimbledon Range is the backdrop on Gribbell Island, which is known for having the highest percentage of white-coated bears among the resident population. Some estimates place them at one-third of the population or even higher. A Kermode Bear Stewardship Area is in the works with the Gitga'at First Nation, with the goal of ensuring a healthy population of kermode bears through land management on Gribbell Island and the north end of Princess Royal Island. It is

Mountains alongside Verney Passage.

unclear how that might eventually change recreation or camping opportunities along McKay Reach.

Place names: While surveying the coast in 1867, Captain Pender named this island after his brother-in-law, Rev. Francis Barrow Gribbell. He was a rector at St. Paul's in Esquimalt in 1869 and principal of the collegiate school in Victoria 1870–75. Kingcome Point is named after Captain William Kingcome, who was in charge of the Hudson's Bay Company barque *Princess Royal* 1862–63. He was master on the *Princess Royal* 1859–61 under the command of Captain J.T. Trivett (nearby Trivett Point).

The outer tub is the choice setting at Bishop Bay Hot Springs—even in a downpour.

Camping: N53°17.34'/W128°55.93'. This is my personal choice for one of the most picturesque coves on the B.C. coast, especially when waterfalls are cascading down the nearby cliffs after a recent rainfall. The cove is graced with a choice of beaches, with the nicest to the west. This is a scenic and strategically located camping opportunity at the top of Princess Royal Island.

Ursula Channel

This waterway linking Fraser Reach to Verney Passage has steep-sided mountains on both sides. The main attraction is the hot spring at Bishop Bay. It's not the only one—a little-known and undeveloped hot spring is located inside the north entrance at Goat Harbour (N53°21.55'/W128°52.96'). It issues from a 2.5-cm (1-inch) crevice and is a hot one: above 45°C (113°F).

Camping: N53°27.67'/W128°56.79'. Monkey Beach is the local name for a wonderful stretch of gravel and clamshell to the north of a small rock headland. Known as Q'weq'waksi'yas in Haisla, the beach has good upland sites, including the grassy top of the headland's neck. The forest adjacent to the neck is the site of a Haisla trapper's cabin, available for public use. This is a very pretty site.

Bishop Bay

Bishop Bay is almost 6 km (4 miles) deep. At the head is a dock with moorage for about four boats. During summer the dock will most likely be full by early afternoon. Late arrivals will have to anchor. This is a popular location, attracting numerous boats to the bay's protected shore for a chance to dip in the hot spring. From the dock a short trail leads to a covered picnic site and then to a bathhouse with two baths. One is in an enclosed room, but the choice location is on a wooden deck overlooking the bay. The water is just about the perfect temperature for a long and refreshing soak, courtesy of the spring, which issues 60 L (13.2 gallons) per minute at over 45°C (113°F). The facilities are maintained by the Gitga'at First Nation with a caretaker living on site. Amenities include a composting toilet. There is no charge for using the facilities.

Place names: Bishop Cove is a small indentation about 5 km (3 miles) north of the bay, and was named as early as 1867. By 1923 charts still weren't naming Bishop Bay, and it wasn't official until the 1930 B.C. Gazetteer. How the name was carried over from the cove to the bay is a mystery, as is the reference to the bishop. It is likely, however, in reference to Captain Charles Bishop who sailed the northwest coast of America from 1794 to 1799.

Camping: N53°28.20'/W128°50.27'. If you land at the dock and turn right on the trail instead of heading to the bathhouse, you will reach a selection of three large wooden tent pads. Unfortunately there is no beach for kayakers, but the sloping rock shore is thankfully quite forgiving. Be sure to have footwear with good treads, as the wet rock might be slippery. A good coating of seaweed at lower tides will protect hulls pulled up onto the rock.

Verney Passage

This long stretch of twisting water runs 35 km (22 miles) from Wright Sound to Devastation Channel. It is exceedingly picturesque mountainous terrain with the added advantage that it misses the most adverse winds that plague Douglas Channel.

Place names: Lt. Commander Edmund Hope Verney of the Royal Navy commanded the gunboat HM *Grappler* on the coast 1862–65. The steamer *Danube* (Danube Bay), operated by the Canadian Pacific

A Haisla cabin on the shoreline of Foch Lagoon.

Haisla cabins

The Haisla Trapline Association has created 34 cabins across traditional Haisla territory, from Bish Creek in the north to Monkey Beach in the south—and extensively along Devastation Channel and Gardner Canal. Individual Haisla trappers own the cabins, which are to a certain extent statements of Haisla rights to the land and resources. However, the general public and visitors are welcome to use the cabins on the condition they are left clean and undamaged. This sweeping invitation is unique, as many of the cabins are located on reserve territory.

The cabins are generally within sight of the water and are a standard design with four roomy wooden bunks, a table and in most cabins a wood stove. Due to just one small window they tend to be dark, but they are welcome in an area where rain is common and good camping beaches are rare. For information on the current availability of the cabins call the Kitimat Village Council at **250-632-9361**.

Navigation Company 1890–1904, was one of the first to pass through the Suez Canal. In 1873, while owned by the Scottish Oriental Steamship Company, the ship was selected to bring the body of Dr. Livingstone from Africa to Westminster Abbey. It struck a rock, later named Danube Rock off the Queen Charlotte Islands.

Camping: N53°29.57'/W129°05.82'. North of Jenkinson Point is a small bay on the west shore with a clean stretch of beach. The finest portion is on the northeast side. The setting is one of the most magnificent imaginable—mountains with huge granite cliffs on all sides.

N53°33.24'/W129°01.04'. Fishtrap Bay is a large, circular bay set to the north of the junction with Ursula Channel. A long spit extends off the east side of the mouth. The best camping is just north of the spit on the east shore of the bay. The beach is grit and rock. Portions of the beach will escape most spring tides, and a Haisla cabin is set slightly back in the woods.

Dorothy Narrows

Currents will run several knots through Dorothy Narrows. Passage is best planned for travelling with the current, though wind can channel up or down Devastation Channel, overriding the current. Kitsaway Anchorage is a popular spot for boats, and a Haisla cabin can be found opposite the entrance to the anchorage. A new logging road extends into Hawkesbury Island from the shoreline quite near the cabin. As well as being logged, the island has been mined over the years—for kyanite and aluminosilicate, two minerals used in ceramics.

Place names: Dorothy Anderson was daughter of Lt. Col. W.P. Anderson, a chief engineer with the federal government. He named the narrows while examining Kitimat Arm in CGS *Quadra* in 1898.

Gardner Canal

Many travellers consider this inlet one of the most scenic on the coast. It is also one of the longest; a trip to its terminus is a voyage of 91 km (56 miles), with an option to continue on into the Kitlope Heritage Conservancy. It is a steep-sided canal with calm waters and a constant ebb tide. While there may be pocket beaches here and there for kayakers, the area is strewn with Haisla cabins. Near the entrance they are located at Crab River, Collins Bay, Ochwa Bay and Triumph Bay. Farther along (off the regional map; consult a chart to locate these places) they can be found at McAllister Bay, both Hotsprings Bay and directly across from the bay, Kiltuish Inlet, Brim River and Kemano Village.

The first stop on the canal (or the last) should be at Europa Hot Springs. It is located in a small bay about 3.6 km (2.2 miles) southeast of Shearwater Point, marked on the chart by piles and booms. To the right of a small creek is the Haisla cabin. The rough wooden hot spring structure is visible from the water. It is located about 21.5 km (13.3 miles) southeast of the entrance to Gardner Canal (Staniforth Point).

The hot spring issues 484 L (106 gallons) per minute from a crevice 5 cm (2 inches) wide and several metres long. The temperature is well over 45°C (113°F). It was discovered by Vancouver's crew during their visit in 1793. Vancouver wrote: "Some of the seamen attempted to wash their hands in it, but found the heat inconvenient."

If you continue down Gardner Canal you will eventually reach the Alcan smelter and community at Kemano. The inlet ends at Kitlope River and the Kitlope Heritage Conservancy, renowned for its old-growth forests, Haisla heritage, array of waterfalls and incredible mountain scenery. It is a huge park covering 321,120 ha (1,240 square miles). Together with Fiordland and Tweedsmuir provincial parks and the Entiako Protected Area, it creates a corridor of protected land that extends 215 km (134 miles) into the B.C. interior from the ocean.

A great trip in Kitlope would be to paddle up the Kitlope River to Kitlope Lake. There are currently no developed trails in Kitlope.

Place names: Captain Alan Gardner, commander-in-chief of the Channel Fleet, recommended Captain Vancouver for the command of his expedition to the B.C. coast. Vancouver named the canal in 1793. Kitlope is a derivation of the name for the original residents of Gardner Inlet, with *kit* meaning people and *lob* meaning rock or stone, thus "People of the Rocks."

Camping: N53°12.86'/W127°50.63'. The Kemano Community Association maintains a cabin on the north side of Kitlope River.

There is a B.C. Parks cabin on the south side of the Kitlope River at N53°12.95'/W127°51.78'. Access is by water or plane only.

N53°07.68'/W127°46.71'. The Hill/Amos campsite is located on the east side of Kitlope Lake.

N53°06.30'/W127°46.41'. The Rediscovery campsite is located on the east side of Kitlope Lake.

Wright Sound

This waterway is the central point for the meeting of the waters of Douglas Channel, Verney Passage, McKay Reach, Whale Channel, Grenville Channel and Squally Reach. In most cases, though, it will seem less a sound and more a continuation of Douglas Channel.

Hartley Bay

This community was born in 1887 when 27 people decided to return to their own land rather than follow a missionary to Metlakatla in Alaska.

The original Gitga'at lived at Laxgal'tsap in Kitkiata Inlet in Douglas Channel during the winter months and resided in several other locations in Douglas Channel, Whale Channel, Wright Sound, Lewis Passage and Caamaño Sound in warmer weather. A second group, the Gitn'oogad'x, lived in an area around Aristazabal, Campania, Princess Royal and other smaller islands.

The arrival of Europeans meant the start of trade in the 1870s with both Fort Simpson (Lax Kw'alaams) and Fort McLoughlin (Bella Bella). About the same time, missionaries William Duncan and Thomas Crosby brought Christianity and the lure of a Christian community at Metlakatla (Prince Rupert). A split in the community in 1887 led Duncan and his followers to establish a new Metlakatla in Alaska; 27 instead decided to start a new Christian community at Txalgiu, named Hartley Bay around that time by surveyors, to take advantage of the growing steamer trade on the Inside Passage.

Today it is home to about 180 people. The band maintains a salmon enhancement project and a roe-and-kelp operation for employment. It is a unique community for being joined entirely by wooden boardwalks. ATVs, not cars, are the vehicle here. Hiking trails lead to nearby lakes, rivers and hilltops. A new community hall is just being completed, and the community boasts a school for kindergarten to Grade 10. Gas and water are available at the government wharf. Accommodation is available at two bed and breakfasts, while a store offers very basic foods such as snacks. The community honours its heritage with two traditional dance troupes and several carvers. Other plans include longhouses for use as accommodation, a feast house, a museum and a gift shop. The *Harbour Mist I* provides

Carved pole, Hartley Bay.

transportation twice per week from Prince Rupert. Daily plane service is provided out of Seal Cove in Prince Rupert by Harbour Air. The post office is V0V 1A0.

South of the community are Promise Island and Stewart Narrows. The narrows can have strong currents and is recommended for small craft only. Just west of Stewart Narrows is Coghlan Anchorages, with boat havens on both sides of the passage.

Travel notes: Hartley Bay made world news when it became the hub for the rescue of passengers and crew of the B.C. Ferries vessel *Queen of the North*. It sank on its Inside Passage voyage from Prince Rupert to Port Hardy by striking Gil Island on March 22, 2006.

Douglas Channel

North of Hartley Bay is one of the most challenging waterways on the coast. It is a trip of about 58 km (36 miles) from Cape Farewell to the end of Maitland Island where it becomes Kitimat Arm. Currents tend to be a constant ebb due to river runoff. Winds, meanwhile, heavily favour inflows, leading to choppy conditions on Douglas Channel. The wind can begin early in the morning and peak at mid-afternoon. Nanakwa Shoal provides the wind updates for this region on marine weather forecasts. The shoal is located just north of the confluence of Douglas Channel and Devastation Channel.

Douglas Channel.

Travel notes: I've been told the average wind in the channel is 28 km/h (15 knots). Douglas Channel is one of just a few that defeated me on the coast. Trying to get south to Hartley Bay from near Kitkiata Inlet, I left at 5 a.m. to catch the morning calm. But the wind had been blowing all night, and at 5:55 a.m. I was sure I would not make the 19 km (12 miles) to Hartley Bay that day. I turned back and it took 13 minutes to return to my campsite. I took advantage of the conditions to get a lift to Foch Lagoon and Gilttoyees Inlet for some photography, then headed down Devastation Channel and Verney Passage to leave the region after a side trip down part of Gardner Canal. When I crossed Douglas Channel to get to Hartley Bay four days later, the channel was dead calm—not so much as a ripple. It pays to have a flexible itinerary.

Place names: James Douglas (1803–77) was governor of Vancouver Island in 1851 and governor of B.C. in 1858. He joined the Northwest Company (later Hudson's Bay Company) in 1819 and became chief factor in 1840, taking over the Pacific operations in 1846. He founded Fort Camosun in 1843. It later evolved into Victoria.

Kitkiata Inlet

Here was the original winter village of the Gitga'a: Laxgal'tsap (Old Town), abandoned between the 1860s and 1880s for Metlakatla. The village was located at the mouth of a stream on the east side of the inlet. A portage from Quaal River in the inlet led to the Ecstall River, allowing trade between Laxgal'tsap and the Tsimshian of Skeena River. The river is still navigable for a considerable distance. On an island a mile up the river was a fishing station and war refuge called Qalahaituk.

Camping: This is traditional Gitga'at territory. The Gitga'at requests that anyone planning on camping or hiking in Gitga'at territory contact the development corporation for more information. The number is **250-841-2602**.

N53°40.29'/W129°09.54'. Halfway between Kitkiata Inlet and the entrance to Sue Channel on the northwest shore of Douglas Channel is a conspicuous beach. It is rough stone, as are all beaches in this area, but it is a good place to escape Douglas Channel if you need to pull out.

Place names: Captain Walbran wrote that it is pronounced *kitkart*, with *kit* meaning "people" and *kart* being the name of a stream in the inlet. The points at the inlet's entrance were named by Walbran in 1898 after Helen Gertrude Davies, eldest daughter of Sir Louis H. Davies, the minister of Marine and Fisheries Canada at the time.

KITIMAT ARM

Six provincial parks can be found along the waters near Kitimat, an indication of how much there is to see here. Others, such as Jesse Falls, have yet to be permanently protected. With mostly rough beaches along the arm, Haisla cabins fill the gap. Side trips into places like Gilttoyees Inlet and Kildala Arm will be rewarded with wonderful scenery.

Devastation Channel

Inflow winds can blow up this channel, creating particularly rough conditions where Douglas and Devastation channels meet. Currents will increase by as much as a knot in spring tides—a characteristic not shared by adjoining channels where the currents remain static through the month.

Place names: The six-gun paddle sloop *Devastation* was built in England in 1841 and served the B.C. coast 1862–65, where, in Captain Walbran's words, it "had an active share in the suppression of lawlessness among the Indians of the coast."

An unusual rock formation near the entrance to Loretta Channel.

Weewanie Hot Springs

The hot springs are set in a small cove just north of Weewanie Creek. At the head of the cove is a rough beach where a trail leads north along the waterfront to an enclosed bathhouse with two tubs. The first tub is for soaking, the outer one for washing. Two mooring buoys are provided in the cove for visitors. The hot water comes by way of a pipe that runs from a holding tank where the hot water from the spring can cool temporarily. The spring itself issues 60 L (13.2 gallons) a minute at 47°C (117°F).

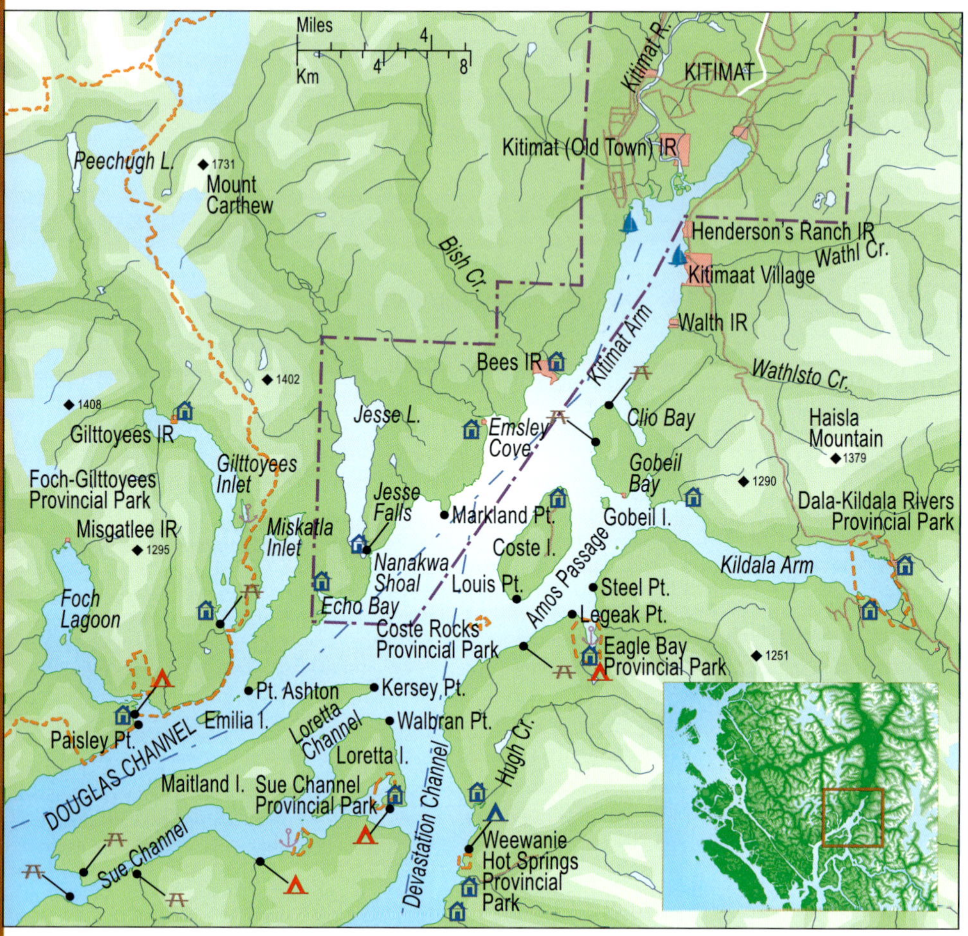

Camping: N53°41.78'/W128°47.41'. A picnic shelter suitable for camping is located partway along the trail from the beach to the hot spring. Kayakers will appreciate this come spring tides; at other tide levels most will probably prefer the beach, though driftwood takes up much of the useable space. Nearby camping alternatives include Hugh Creek or Weewanie Creek. The north bank of Weewanie appears to have lots of room. Haisla cabins dot the area.

Sue Channel

This twisting passage is a way to bypass about 17 km (11 miles) of Douglas Channel. Winds can still blow up this channel, but you'll avoid the worst here. There are numerous beaches along Sue Channel, but most are rough. Sue Channel Provincial Marine Park, one of the

A small cove is equipped with mooring buoys at Weewanie Hot Springs.

many new parks created here in 2004, is 209 ha (516 acres) and protects a safe anchorage. Branching off north of Loretta Island is Loretta Channel, a scenic route with steep bluffs along the shoreline.

Place names: H. Maitland Kersey was managing director of the Canadian Development Company in 1898. He was aboard the *Quadra* during the 1898 examination of Kitimat Arm.

Camping: N53°41.75'/W128°56.42'. This is the closest to a sandy beach in Sue Channel. It is located halfway along, on the south side.

N53°43.35'/W128°50.94'. A small, rough beach at the end of Loretta Island faces an islet. It is within the park boundary. There are clear spots here, as well as a cabin.

Foch Lagoon

Just outside the lagoon is a deep bay with a beach on the southwest side. Hidden farther up the bay is the lagoon entrance, which will run like a river when the current is in flow. It is known for overfalls, whirlpools and rapids with drops of 1 m (3 feet) or more.

A beach at the entrance to Foch Lagoon.

The lagoon is recognized bear habitat and winter habitat for Barrow's goldeneye, which are drawn to the rich meadows supported by the estuaries. There's an old mine site up the creek at the north entrance to the lagoon. A Haisla village was once located at the north end.

Camping: N53°45.69'/W129°01.77'. A beautiful little beach is tucked into the cove on the west entrance to the lagoon. A cabin is located behind the beach.

Gilttoyees Inlet

This is a narrow, curving inlet with cliffs backed by high peaks along much of its length. It ends in an estuary with an intertidal marsh and meadow. A Haisla village was once located here. A scenic anchorage can be found in the narrow bay midway along the inlet. Miskatla Inlet is not nearly so scenic, as it is surrounded by rolling forested hills.

Place names: This was originally Dawson Arm, and Gilttoyees Inlet was just the northerly branch. Dawson Arm was dropped in favour of Gilttoyees in 1946.

Gilttoyees Inlet.

Jesse Falls

This is a visual highlight of Douglas Channel. The waterfall drains Jesse Lake, a large body of water that can be accessed by a rough path on the east side. On June 30, 1793, an exploration party from Captain Vancouver's *Discovery* camped here.

Coste Rocks

This unassuming collection of rocks is off the south end of Coste Island in the middle of Kitimat Arm. What can be seen above water is the top of an underwater pillar that extends down 45 m (150 feet). This makes the rocks ideal for diving. Above water the rocks also teem with life. Marine birds, including surf scoters and sandpipers, find shelter here, and seals use the rocks as a haulout. The rocks are another of the new provincial parks created in 2004, and cover 29 ha (72 acres).

Place names: Louis Coste was chief engineer for the Canadian Public Works Department in 1898, the year he explored the head of inlets along the B.C. coast to select the terminus for the Yukon railway. Charlie Amos (Amos Passage) was the first Kitimaat to convert to Christianity.

Coste Rocks.

Eagle Bay

This large anchorage was made a provincial park in 2004 and protects 262 ha (647 acres). The bay is a holding ground for spring salmon. It's backed by a gravel beach suitable for both camping and walking. Be sure to look out for the wreckage of the Grumman Widgeon plane on the beach. There's also a trail to a lookout from the beach and a non-native burial site in the southeast waterfall's wall. A controversial issue here has been a proposed logging dump.

Camping: N53°47.98'/W128°42.36'. The gravel beach at the back of Eagle Bay is a strategic place to camp when exploring out of Kitimat. Other rough beaches line Kitimat Arm. One good candidate is located directly south of Louis Point.

Kildala Arm

This inlet has a wonderful skyline of mountains and snowfields. Its traditional use includes fishing salmon and oolichan from the Kildala River. Andalusite crystals believed to be of gem quality could bring mining to the head of the river—barring the success of preservation efforts. Three watersheds drain into Kildala Arm: the Dala, Dahlaks and Kildala. All three estuaries are recognized grizzly bear habitat, wintering bird habitat and migration staging areas. An old-growth stand of spruce abuts the Dala estuary.

Bish Creek

This is the site of Bisamut'is, an abandoned 30-ha (74-acre) Haisla village. The creek is backed by a long, sandy beach, behind which is a reserve. A Haisla cabin is set back from the beach.

Kitimaat Village

Kitimaat Village is a First Nations community that exists in tandem with Kitimat. It was originally known as Kitimaat Mission, while the post office mailing address is known as Haisla. Most amenities are found in Kitimat, which is set back several miles from Kitimat Arm. One of Kitimat's two main marinas is located on the north end of Kitimaat Village. Amenities here include a restaurant and laundry. Camping, oriented toward RVs, is located next to the parking lot.

Place names: The names of both Kitimat and Kitimaat are derived from a Coast Tsimshian word meaning "people of the falling snow." The river was called Hum ja cis xi X'a'islai, meaning "the dinner plate of all Haisla."

A view of Kildala Arm to Dala-Kildala park.

Dala-Kildala River Estuaries Provincial Park

This park was created in 2004 and protects 741 ha (1,830 acres). The estuaries are considered one of the key wetlands of the north coast. Coho, chinook and pink spawn in the rivers and in turn attract a range of waterfowl.

Fishing and industry—the staples of Kitimat.

Kitimat

Kitimat is largely a creation of Alcan, which built a smelter here in 1950 due to an attractive deep-sea port. Power came from a 60-km (37-mile) transmission line from the generating station in Kemano. Other industries were soon drawn, including Eurocan Pulp and Paper and Methanex, a petrochemical plant. A downturn in the aluminum industry has reduced the population, but the central spirit of the community remains intact. One charming feature is the wide, pretty walking trails that connect every neighbourhood in the city.

The heavy industrial base has made it a prosperous community with ice rinks, a recreation centre and gymnasium, a swimming pool, cross-country skiing and an 18-hole golf course.

It's a full-service community, even though much of the commercial base is centred in Terrace, 73 km (45 miles) north. But chances are you'll find everything you need in town, including a selection of hotels and bed and breakfasts, restaurants and stores. For the most up-to-date selection of services, visit **www.visitkitimat.com** or call **1-800-664-6554.**

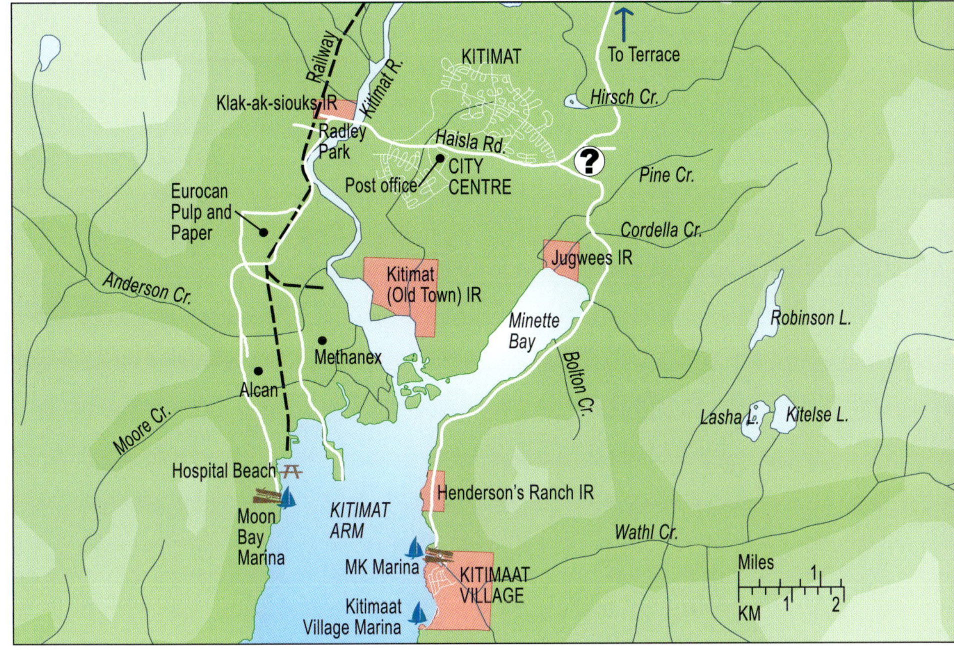

The city is split into the townsite east of Kitimat River and the industrial sector to the west of the river. The Alcan and Methanex complexes are highly visible from Kitimat Arm. It's not all industrial, though. To the south of Alcan is Hospital Beach, a recreation and picnic area along the waterfront. South of that is Moon Bay Marina, the more casual of the two main marinas in Kitimat. MK Marina is on the east side of Kitimat Arm. Because it is off the power grid, Moon Bay Marina has only basic amenities, which include a boat launch, parking, showers and camping in a pleasant area on the waterfront above the docks.

Continue past Moon Bay Marina for 7 km (4 miles) to reach the trailhead for the North Cove Trail and Recreation Site. A 1-km (0.6-mile) hike leads to the recreation site, which has three tables and views of Douglas Channel.

A view across Principe Channel from Banks Island.

The Northern Channels

CHAPTER EIGHT

A WOLF STEPPED ONTO THE ROCK BLUFF NEAR ME AT KEWAR POINT IN north Principe Channel. Rather than run away, it came down the bluff to get a better look at this strange creature in a kayak. A few hours later I found myself on a glorious white sand beach on the north end of Banks Island—just the first of many beautiful beaches I would find here.

Paddling down Grenville Channel some weeks later, I was about to cross from Stuart Anchorage to Kumealon Inlet when a splash caught my eye. I turned and saw a humpback slapping a fin against the water. Seeing it was in a playful mood I decided to take the time and paddle a little closer. For my effort I was treated to a 10-minute show of splashing and jumping before the whale finally headed north.

At Lowe Inlet I crossed into the little bay outside of Verney Falls to spy a grizzly taking advantage of the jumping salmon in the holding basin. It was a few moments before the grizzly saw me, roared its objection to my arrival, then disappeared into the forest.

Those are just a few of the many memories of this region.

There are two ways to see this area: the traditional route of the Inside Passage through Grenville Channel, or Principe Channel, a wider passage with a lower topography but a more convoluted shoreline. When deciding which way to go, there is no magic answer. Most boaters will probably prefer the established anchorages, carefree route and awe-inspiring mountain scenery of Grenville Channel. Kayakers and adventurous boaters will likely be drawn to the Outside Passage for its intricate island groups and varied shoreline.

Given what's out there, it's hard to go wrong.

See Prince Rupert, page 285
Gurd I.
PORCHER I.
Kitkatla Inlet
Ogden Channel
Rippon Pt.
Klapthlon IR
Stuart Anchorage
Calvin Pt.
Alpha Pt.
Alpha Bay
Bonwick Pt.
Goschen I.
Kitkatla Channel
Comrie Head
Captain Cove
KITKATLA
Dolphin I.
Strouts Pt.
Spicer I.
Connie Cove
Holmes L.
South Spicer I.
Beaver Passage
Noble Mtn.
879
Newcombe Harbour
BROWNING ENTRANCE
Elbow Pt.
Hankin Pt.
McCAULEY I.
400
Robinson Pt.
Baird Pt.
Morrison Pt.
Kewar Inlet
Mathers Pt.
White Rocks
Kewar Pt.
Petrel Channel
Larson I.
Deadman Inlet
Norway Inlet
Keyarka IR
Keyarka Cove
PRINCIPE CHANNEL
Solander Pt.
Sneath Is.
Laverock Pt.
Byers Bay
Colby Bay
Allerton Passage
Kingkown Inlet
Headwind Pt.
Kul IR
Bonilla I.
Antle Is.
Kirkendale I.
600
PACIFIC OCEAN
BANKS I.
600
Mount Gransell
619
277
Survey Bay
Carlo Range
Miles
4
Km
4
8
Wreck Is.
Foul Bay
Kooryet L.
HECATE STRAIT
Spearer Pt.

Mount Elwin
Kumealon Lagoon
Kumealon Inlet
McMurray Pt.
Baker Inlet
Watts Narrows
Pa-aat R.
GRENVILLE CHANNEL
Kxngeal Inlet
Knokmolks IR
Ecstall R.
Iakwas IR
Johnston L.
See Kitimat, page 243
Foch-Gilttoyees Provincial Park
1300
Quaal R.
Kitkiata L.
1000
East Inlet
Klewnuggit Inlet Marine Park
Harriot I.
Freda L.
Gavel L.
Hevenor Inlet
1000
Nabannah Bay
Evening Pt.
1100
Quaal IR
Kitkatha IR
Kitkiata Inlet
Wyndham L.
Batchellor L.
Simpson L.
Ormiston Pt.
Wilson Inlet
Saunders L.
Nettle Basin
Kumowdah IR
1000
PITT ISLAND
Lowe Inlet Marine Park
Cosine I.
Wright Inlet
Anger I.
Ala Passage
Sylvia L.
Gamble L.
Kiskosh Inlet
DOUGLAS CHANNEL
Belowe L.
Miller Inlet
800
Ralston Is.
Burns Bay
Red Bluff L.
Trade Its.
Patterson Inlet
Mount Frank
638
Union Passage Marine Park
Mink Trap Bay
Lundy Cove
HARTLEY BAY
Stephen Nelson L.
Hawkins Narrows
Tuwartz L.
Peters Narrows
Promise I.
Buchan Inlet
Leavitt Lagoon
Kooryet Bay
Toowartz IR
Payne Channel
Hinton I.
Port Stephens
WRIGHT SOUND
FARRANT I.
Monckton Inlet
Keecha Pt.
Tuwartz Inlet
Gale Pt.
Cridge Passage
Citeyats IR
Fin I.
270
Kitlawaoo IR
Cherry Its.
Principe Its.
Ring Pt.
Deer Pt.
Otter Channel
Terror Pt.
Sisters Is.
NEPEAN SOUND
Fanny Pt.
GIL I.
Breaker Its.
Block Is.
Otter Passage
Trap Is.
Campania I.
Trutch I.
See Laredo, page 209

Grenville Channel looking north toward Ormiston Point.

GRENVILLE CHANNEL

This is the legendary northern leg of B.C.'s Inside Passage, running 86.6 km (54 miles) from Rippon Point to Waterman Point. It's often referred to as The Ditch, and is the main route for cruise ships, ferries, barges, fishing boats, freighters and recreational boat traffic. It sounds bad, but the traffic isn't overwhelming (this is the remote coast, after all), and seeing a freighter pass close by can be part of the attraction.

The narrowest portion of the channel can have currents up to 2 knots. The ebb current will continue 1½ hours after the high water.

Travel notes: A huge freighter passed me just south of Lowe Inlet Marine Park. I expected to be sloshed around by the wake in the narrow channel, but there wasn't even a ripple. A little later B.C. Ferries' *Queen of the North* passed, causing a huge wake with rebound waves back and forth across the channel long after the ferry was out of sight. I can only guess that the greater speed of the ferry was the difference, though both seemed to be travelling at a good clip.

Place names: Baron William Wyndham Grenville was Speaker of the House of Commons and secretary of the Home Department in England 1789–90. He was a cousin of Prime Minister William Pitt. Vancouver named the channel in 1793.

A view from inside Union Passage looking toward Hawkins Narrows.

Union Passage

Union Passage is a scenic alternative for transiting between south Grenville Channel and Squally Channel. Along the way are two sets of narrows with currents as high as 8 knots. Slack water is 15 minutes before both high water and low water at Prince Rupert. Slack lasts 5 minutes. The current splits in Union Passage, with the ebb flowing north in Hawkins Narrows and south in Peters Narrows. Considering the speed of the current, a crossing is recommended near slack tide.

Inside Union Passage between the two narrows is a safe all-weather anchorage and an undeveloped trail along the east side of Farrant Island to a viewpoint at a low ridge. The interior of Union Passage is convoluted and GPS navigation may save a few turnabouts in dead ends.

An interesting place to visit is a beach near Peters Narrows in a bit of a cove on the south side of Union Passage. It gives access to an old logging road (N53°22.56'/W129°27.16') that leads well into the interior of the island and passes an old open-pit quarry. Don't fall in—it's steep and filled with water. Eventually the old trail splits into a choice of routes. I followed one logging road till it petered out, but other routes may cross the entire island.

Union Passage Marine Park

This park was created in 1993 and protects 1,373 ha (3,400 acres) between Pitt and Farrant islands. Numerous anchorages can be found in the placid bays between the two narrows. It's in the traditional territory of the Tsimshian and two known archaeological sites are located within the park boundaries.

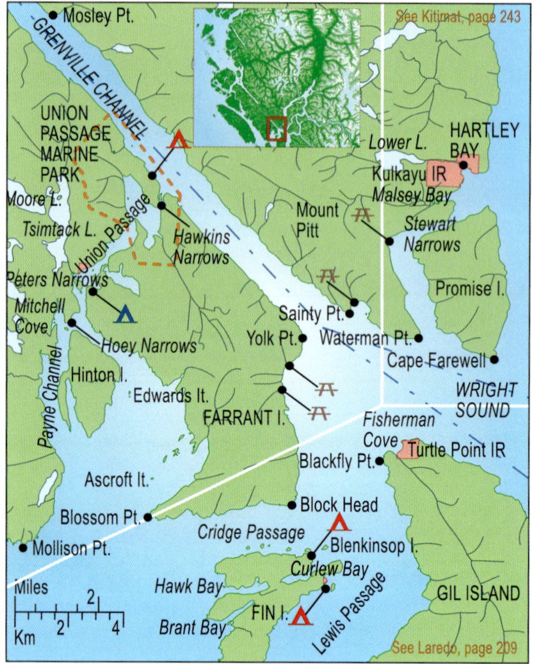

Place names: This was originally known as Matliksimtas Passage, but Union Passage was adopted in 1930.

Camping: N53°22.56'/W129°27.16'. Just inside Peters Narrows is a small cove popular with waterfowl. On the southwest shore is a grassy beach with a good upland clearing in a grove of alder trees. Be sure to pick the second beach—the first falls off steeply at lower tide levels. Behind the grove is the road to the old quarry.

N53°25.60'/W129°26.30'. In Grenville Channel just north of Hawkins Narrows is a long stretch of stone beach best used as a campsite during neap tides. It's preferable to Sainty Point across the channel to the south, which is a difficult rock beach.

N53°28.55'/W129°30.98'. Across from Mosley Point on the east side of Grenville Channel at Red Bluff Creek, about 9 km (5.6 miles) north of Hawkins Narrows, is a cove with beaches to both the north and south. The south beach is crushed shell at the top and rock below. The beach to the north is as good, but with less high tide clearance.

Lowe Inlet

This inlet extends about 3.4 km (2 miles) inland and ends at scenic Verney Falls. The waterfall is at the end of a deep, narrow basin that serves as a holding area for migrating salmon. They have to make their way past the 7-m (23-foot) falls to get to the spawning grounds in the Kumowda River. A trail runs from a rough beach north of the waterfall alongside the falls to Lowe Lake. The trail leads through a Tsimshian reserve. A formal arrangement for the trail has yet to be made.

Verney Falls.

Historical sites dot the area. One is a highly visible fish trap near the trailhead. Another is a fish cannery located on the north side of Nettle Basin. It operated from 1890 to 1934.

Rough beaches surround the inlet, but high, level areas are tricky to find. The Department of Fisheries and Oceans maintains a staff cabin here. Watch for the possibility of eddies in the vicinity of the inlet in Grenville Channel on an ebb tide.

Klewnuggit Inlet

Tall mountains press down on this multi-branched inlet, but the recreation highlight is probably the trail that leads from its southeast end alongside the river to Brodie Lake. From Brodie Lake the trail continues to Freda Lake, where there are views of rapids and a waterfall. The trail crosses through the tiny Iakgwas reserve at the trailhead. Use of the trail has yet to be formalized.

B.C. Parks reports the best anchorage is at the north end of East Inlet.

Lowe Inlet Marine Park

This park was created in 1993 and protects 555 ha (1,371 acres) of upland and 212 ha (524 acres) of foreshore. It's a popular anchorage for the Inside Passage. There are no amenities.

Inside Lowe Inlet looking toward Grenville Channel.

The tidal current splits in Grenville Channel near Klewnuggit. More precisely, the flood tide meets off Evening Point while the ebb tide separates 1 mile northwest. The exact location, however, is variable and subject to the influence of wind. North of the division the current will flood south; to the south the current will flood north. This makes Klewnuggit and Nabannah Bay strategic places to stop and await favourable tides.

Camping: N53°40.76'/W129°45.60'. A peninsula splits Grenville Channel as it branches into Klewnuggit Inlet. On one side of the peninsula is Nabannah Bay. On the north end is a gravel beach that is somewhat of an oasis in a stretch where beaches are rare. The beach is divided by a headland. If you go east around the headland you'll find a beach that appears grubby, but the advantage is stones at low tide instead of rocks. Small spots can be found in the uplands. The reward is beautiful views up Grenville Channel.

Baker Inlet

Watts Narrows, at the mouth of this inlet, causes strong currents and tide rips. Rough beaches can be found here.

Klewnuggit Inlet.

Kumealon Inlet

Strong currents and tidal falls can be encountered at Kumealon Narrows, which moderates the tide level within the lagoon. Inside is the sheltered Kumealon estuary. The estuary is important for salmon, waterfowl and grizzlies. An area of limestone creates a karst geology with caves.

Outside the inlet, Kumealon Island forms part of a bay with rough beaches possible for camping if the need arises. Two boat havens are located here, off the northeast shore of the island and in the small bay to the north.

Klewnuggit Inlet Marine Park: This park was established in 1993 and protects 1,733 ha (4,282 acres), including all of East Inlet, Brodie and Freda lakes and Freda Rapids, located between the two lakes. It is a key anchorage along the Inside Passage. There is a hiking trail to Brodie and Freda lakes, with the possibility of paddling with a portage.

Camping: N53°50.92'/W130°03.71'. The bay north of Kumealon Island has potential, but the best beach in the area is across the channel at Stuart Anchorage. Just south of the anchorage is a cove with a sand and stone beach facing east. There's good high tide clearance and the beach is one of the cleanest in the area. The nicest stretch of beach by far is north of Calvert Point, but unfortunately that's part of Klapthlon Indian Reserve.

PRINCIPE CHANNEL

Principe Channel, a key portion of the Outside Passage, is favoured mainly by the few boaters who wish to forsake the marine highway of Grenville Channel. Here the topography is flatter and the channel wider. Banks Island has few features along most of its length, but Pitt Island more than makes up for it with its numerous inlets, bays and island groups. For this reason kayakers are likely to keep toward Pitt Island. Three boat havens and a small number of campsites keep this formidable 75-km (47-mile) transit manageable.

The tide splits north of Anger Island. South of the island the current floods north; north of the island the current floods south. Currents will reach 3 knots.

Place names: Lt. Commander Jacinto Caamaño named this channel while using it for a southward journey on his search for the strait of De Fonti. The *Principe* was a Spanish packet boat built in 1767 and stationed in Mexico.

Monckton Inlet

Monckton Inlet extends about 8 km (5 miles) into Pitt Island. Slightly to the north is Port Stephens, backed by Leavitt Lagoon. The shore-

A view from Port Stephens looking to Principe Channel.

line here is unforgiving rock from Otter Channel to Lundy Cove—except for one beach just south of Monckton Inlet.

Heavy moss gives an indication of the amount of rainfall on Pitt Island near Monckton Inlet.

Camping: N53°18.24'/W129°40.84'. South of Monkton Inlet is a small cove, almost hidden. On its south end, between two rock headlands, is a curving beach of grit, pebble and scattered rocks. There's good room for campsites at the high tide level. For spring tides there's a natural moss clearing on the upland to the west of the beach. Several tents will fit in the clearing, and there are more sites farther up if you follow the trail—enough room for a sizeable group. The trail eventually leads to an old-growth tree. Two trees once grew together, but pioneering loggers cut down one (you can see the notches cut into the stump) and left the other, younger tree standing. Now it's almost as big as its connected sibling, when it was cut, probably 125 years or more ago.

Anger Island

This large island and the inlets, coves and archipelagos around it are a recreational highlight for Principe Channel. Larger boats are likely to give most areas a wide berth, as reefs and kelp abound, but paddlers and a few others will get to enjoy the intricate shoreline. A few convenient campsites allow for extended explorations of this area, which are essentially limitless. If there's a drawback it's the mundane nature of most of the shoreline. I found this particularly true east of Cosine Island in the area north of Anger Island, though by another measure it is a placid, protected area of pristine waterways. I found the Ralston Islands the most scenic, as well as the outer shore of Anger Island. A good paddling trip might be a circumnavigation of the island to take in the best of both worlds. Many of the island groups can serve as shelter should a northwesterly pick up in Principe Channel while you are paddling northward.

Boat havens/anchorages are located at Ire Inlet on the east side of Anger Island and in Curtis Inlet on the opposite shore of Ala

Ala Passage.

Passage. Boats will want to use extra caution transiting Ala Passage through the rocks to reach them. Kelp might also be a problem.

Across Principe Channel, Limestone Bay is a nod to the geological diversity of the region. Here a band of white and rose limestone and dolomite extends into the island in a 8-km (5-mile) wedge. It is undeveloped. The only developed prospect on the island is to the north at Donaldson Creek, which flows into Patsey Cove. Here pure white quartz has been found on the northwest side of Donaldson Creek. Reserves are estimated at 9,000 tonnes (9,921 tons) of silica. A garnet deposit is on record at Grief Point, and other limestone and dolomite outcrops dot the island (near Gale and Keecha points, for instance).

Place names: This area was surveyed by Captain Pender in 1867–69. Apparently it wasn't an enjoyable place to survey, given the Anger and Ire evident here. The islands to the north have a mathematical root. Cosine, Sine and Tangent islands are a tip of the hat to the methods used by the triangulation survey party that charted this area in 1921. A member of the survey party was P.M. Monckton (Monckton Inlet).

Camping: N53°27.97'/W129°57.49'. A tiny stone beach on the south end of the main island in the Ralston Islands group has a good, high back to escape spring tides. Look for clear upland areas near the grassy neck on the south end. This is a pretty site with views down to Lundy Cove.

N53°28.28'/W129°58.16'. Between the north end of the main Ralston Island and a semi-attached islet is a series of beaches. The best beach is to the very north of the main island. There are many choices for camping here, including a few upland sites. This has good group potential.

N53°31.59'/W129°58.86'. A wide cove sits north of Anger Inlet. Just outside the cove's west entrance, behind an islet, are three tiny crushed shell beaches that join into one at low tide. While unassuming in appearance from the water, they hide a lovely forest clearing that is an established campsite. It's a lush forest and moss setting

Rough shoreline at Ralston Islands.

with huge old-growth stumps, the notches of the pioneer loggers still visible. (Strangely some of the old-growth trees were cut and left.) This site is a perfect base camp for groups exploring the region. It can be exposed to northwesterlies.

South and West McCauley Island

South of McCauley Island are numerous islands and passages, though they tend to be unimpressive, with grubby and rough intertidal beaches—not somewhere to invest a great deal of time. This is generally true of the shore along McCauley Island as well. Most potential sand beaches are usually intertidal muck at closer inspection. Banks Island remains largely featureless until the first of the sand bays north of Keyarka Cove. Then the appeal of Banks Island changes drastically as it shifts towards an open-ocean environment.

A boat haven/anchorage is located in Colby Bay on Banks Island.

Camping: N50°37.41'/W130°26.01'. On Banks Island between Keyarka Cove and Deadman Islet is a small, unnamed bay with a terrific sand beach on the north side. It's one of the cleanest white beaches on the coast. There's no developed upland, but flat upland areas can be found.

Petrel Channel

This is a narrower and arguably more scenic alternative to north Principe Channel. Its charm, in large part, is the mountains of Pitt Island. Noble Mountain, reaching 696 m (2,283 feet), is made more interesting by its sparse tree cover and the prominent spines that drop toward Petrel Channel. It would make a great ascent for veteran hikers, affording clear views up the mountainside. Consider starting at a beach in Petrel Channel just north of Elbow Point. From there you can penetrate the lower thick forest to follow the spine.

Several waterways branch off Petrel Channel and extend deep into Pitt Island. The longest is Hevenor Inlet, which is further extended by Hevenor Lagoon for a total distance of 17 km (11 miles). Newcombe Harbour and Captain Cove are anchorages.

Comrie Head is a distinctive bluff at the north end of Petrel Channel. A fish farm is located at Petrel Point at the south end of the channel.

Several distinctive twists lie along Petrel Channel's length, with a narrow portion near Elbow Point. While charts mark the tide at 3 knots maximum, my guess is the water here can run several knots faster. If you're paddling through, time your trip to go with the tide or it will be a very long and tiring journey.

Don't expect much in the way of beaches in Petrel Channel. There are many by number, particularly in the south end, but they are almost all rock at the high tide and intertidal clam-bed muck at lower tides. A clean white-brown beach halfway between Comrie Head and Captain Cove makes a nice place for a lunch, but it is entirely intertidal.

Camping: N53°42.51'/W130°11.68'. On the south end of the turn at Elbow Point is a rough beach with a pleasant upland clearing. The clearing can be found behind a sandy patch near a creek, just north of a distinctively large boulder on the beach. There is room for a large group here.

North Banks Island

With its wind-stunted trees above rock bluffs and islets dotting the shoreline, north Banks Island is truly a special place, a must-see on any north coast itinerary. White sand beaches stretch along much of

Deadman Inlet.

the shore. Larson Island and its neighbouring archipelagos cry out to be explored, though the passage between Banks and Larson islands runs dry at low tides.

Deadman Islet and Baird Point are where the currents from Principe Channel and north Banks Island meet, as flood tides run north around outer Banks Island to collide here. Currents rarely go above 0.5 knots, but tide rips can be encountered near Baird Point.

Camping: N53°37.83'/W130°29.00'. Of the beaches along this stretch, Deadman Inlet is the standout. Since the inlet is almost entirely sand, you could camp anywhere, but the far end runs dry for a considerable distance at low tide. The best and most protected of the many choices is on the west side near the inlet's entrance. The upland is undeveloped, but there are level places to avoid spring tides if you look hard enough.

Beaver Passage

This is a wide and hazard-free passage between Browning Entrance and Ogden Channel. The channels around Spicer and South Spicer islands are interesting but there are rough beaches only. Currents can be several knots and swirl and clash in the area just outside Connie Cove.

Camping: N53°41.75'/W130°23.72'. Southwest of Hankin Point on McCauley Island are two coves. Between them is a narrow wedge of brown-sand beach. Rocks line the beach at lowest tide only. This well-protected site has a large clearing in the upland suitable for a group.

N53°43.36'/W130°21.84'. Midway along Beaver Passage south of Spicer Island is a small islet joined to McCauley Island by an intertidal tombolo. On McCauley Island the clamshell beach would survive most tide levels.

N53°45.23'/W130°17.33'. A long beach at the end of Connie Cove is adjacent to an estuary. The cleanest portion of beach is found next to a cluster of rock. The beach will become quite extensive at low tide. There are some small upland grass pockets near the rock pile.

Outer Banks Island

With names like Wreck Islands, Foul Bay, Grief Point and Terror Point, outer Banks Island has earned a reputation as a fiercely dangerous place to travel. It's about 81 km (50 miles) from the relative protection of Larson Island to the cover of Breaker Islets in Otter Passage, and all of it through exposed ocean strewn with reefs. There are very few protected beaches on the outside, so expect a long day of paddling, searching for places to stay, if you venture out this way. A run down the coast is recommended only for veteran mariners and paddlers alike. Kayakers must be especially careful on this route due to the long, exposed conditions and lack of shelter. Better than running the island might be an overnight trip from the shelter of somewhere like Deadman Inlet to Bonilla Island and back. If you decide to travel this stretch, plan for August when winds are at their lowest. Entry through Otter Passage on the south end can be difficult (see page 230).

Bonilla Island

Bonilla Island has the last lighthouse constructed on the B.C. coast (in 1960). It is still staffed. The 9-m (30-foot) fibreglass tower and associated buildings sit on a small islet just off the main Bonilla Island. It's a fair-weather place to visit only.

Sunrise near Larson Island.

If you make the crossing, it is about 12.7 km (7 miles) from the relative shelter of Larson Island to Bonilla Island, and all through exposed water. It's a crossing best made in the morning before wind and swell have a chance to build. The largest sand beach on Bonilla Island (N53°29.80'/W130°37.88') is adjacent to the lighthouse and protected from all seas, but is susceptible to a north or northwest wind (the prevailing summer wind). At low water you can walk to the lighthouse island from the beach.

Weather: Given the exposed location, it's not surprising that Bonilla Island has cool days, reaching an average daytime high of just 15°C (59°F) during July and August. That's not much warmer than the coldest point of the day, as summer temperatures rarely drop below 11°C (52°F). Hot days are just about unheard of. The warmest temperature ever recorded is 26.5°C (79.7°F) on September 8, 1989. That was an oddity. On average, only once every 10 years does Bonilla Island record a day in August above 20°C (68°F).

Precipitation isn't overwhelming here—just 2,120 mm (83.5 inches) per year. Most of that falls October to January. The driest month is July, with just 81.9 mm (3.2 inches). June and August are not far off with 102 mm (4 inches) each.

It is a windy place. Unfortunately details weren't available for the entire year, but June and July see an average of 23.7 km/h (12.8 knots) and 22.4 km/h (12 knots) respectively—considerably more than most other weather stations on the coast. (Remember, that's an average, so for every calm period there's a time when the wind is double the average.)

A view toward Porcher Island.

Prince Rupert

CHAPTER NINE

WHEN I FIRST ARRIVED IN THIS REGION A WIND PICKED UP IN KITKATLA Channel, and I ducked into a beautiful little campsite in Pelham Islands. This was followed by several leisurely days exploring the beaches outside Porcher Island. I bobbed on the water outside Fan Point and chatted with two boaters who happened by on skiffs. The odds of a prolonged conversation with passing boats on the open ocean might have seemed slim, but there it was—a perfect day on the water.

This was followed by stays at beautiful beaches on tiny isolated islands. I stopped at the dock at Lax Kw'alaams and had a hamburger at the little restaurant there and chatted with a friendly group of youths diving off the dock on a sunny summer's day. Then it was across Portland Inlet in the early evening in conditions so calm I could hear four separate whale groups surfacing several miles away, clear into Chatham Sound. Several groups would pass close by, including a pod of killer whales.

Stretches of beach could be found everywhere, one of the few places on the coast where the camping opportunities are every bit as beautiful as the surroundings. There is so much to see and do here it is definitely worth a return trip.

For many visitors from Alberta this area is as close as Vancouver. Only a few make the journey, however. During my time here a few kayakers and campers were making use of Oval Bay and the nearby beaches on Porcher Island. A family of boaters was darting around on dinghies, a yacht was anchored in Freeman Passage and a UBC archaeology group was on Dundas Island. Otherwise it was just the fishermen who always ply the coastal waters. It seemed remarkably underpopulated, but such is the nature of the B.C. coast.

A rarely visited beach on outer Goschen Island.

PORCHER ISLAND

Porcher Island's size is deceiving. While it appears to be a minor island on coastal maps, it extends 34 km (21 miles) from Cape George to Hunt Point and contains several mountain ranges and sizeable inlets. There are two communities in the area—Oona River and Kitkatla—but the majority of the island is undisturbed wilderness, ranging from intertidal wetlands sheltering large numbers of waterfowl to lengthy coastal cobble and sand beaches.

Place names: Commander Edwin Augustus Porcher commanded the gun vessel *Sparrowhawk* on the B.C. coast 1865–68.

Kitkatla

This tidy little community is in a cycle of improvement, with a new school and gym, band office and dock. Gas is available at the dock, but the pumps are closed on weekends. Several stores in the village stock very basic provisions, most notably snacks and pop. (These might be in short supply. During my visit one store had just three small bags of chips in its entire inventory. I purchased two, leaving one bag so the village wouldn't be destitute.)

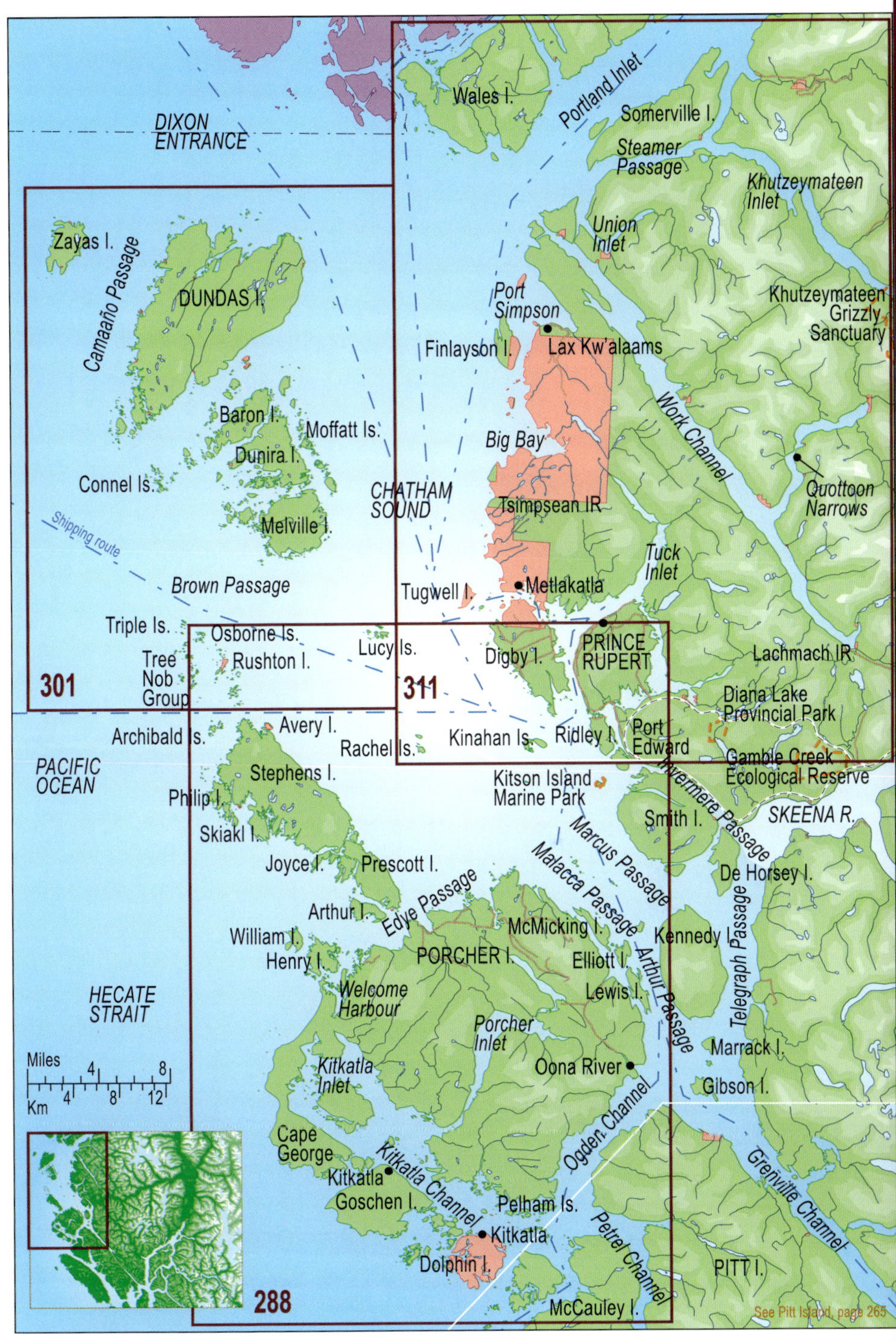
DIXON ENTRANCE
Wales I.
Portland Inlet
Somerville I.
Steamer Passage
Khutzeymateen Inlet
Union Inlet
Zayas I.
Camaaño Passage
DUNDAS I.
Port Simpson
Lax Kw'alaams
Finlayson I.
Khutzeymateen Grizzly Sanctuary
Work Channel
Baron I.
Moffatt Is.
Dunira I.
Big Bay
Quottoon Narrows
Connel Is.
CHATHAM SOUND
Tsimpsean IR
Melville I.
Shipping route
Tuck Inlet
Brown Passage
Tugwell I.
Metlakatla
Triple Is.
Osborne Is.
Lucy Is.
Digby I.
PRINCE RUPERT
Lachmach IR
Rushton I.
Tree Nob Group
301
311
Diana Lake Provincial Park
Archibald Is.
Avery I.
Rachel Is.
Kinahan Is.
Ridley I.
Port Edward
Gamble Creek Ecological Reserve
PACIFIC OCEAN
Stephens I.
Kitson Island Marine Park
Inverness Passage
Philip I.
Smith I.
SKEENA R.
Skiakl I.
Marcus Passage
Joyce I.
Prescott I.
Malacca Passage
De Horsey I.
Edye Passage
Arthur I.
McMicking I.
Kennedy I.
William I.
Telegraph Passage
Henry I.
PORCHER I.
Elliott I.
Welcome Harbour
Arthur Passage
Lewis I.
HECATE STRAIT
Porcher Inlet
Marrack I.
Miles
4
8
Km
4
8
12
Kitkatla Inlet
Oona River
Gibson I.
Ogden Channel
Cape George
Kitkatla Channel
Grenville Channel
Kitkatla
Goschen I.
Pelham Is.
Kitkatla
Petrel Channel
Dolphin I.
PITT I.
288
McCauley I.
See Pitt Island, page 265

Osborne Is.
Lucy Is.
See Prince Rupert, page 313
Digby I.
PRINCE
RUPERT
Rushton I.
Qlawdzeet
Anchorage
See Dundas Group, page 300
Archibald Is.
Avery I.
Rachel Is.
Kinahan Is.
Ridley I.
Port
Edward
Lelu I.
300
Qlawd
Hill
STEPHENS I.
Philip I.
China Pt.
Congreve Pt.
CHATHAM
SOUND
Kitson Island
Marine Park
Mount
Stephens
425
Skiakl I.
Smith I.
Stephens Passage
Lawyer Is.
Marcus Passage
Joyce I.
Minnie I.
Parry I.
PACIFIC
OCEAN
Prescott I.
Hunt Pt.
Malacca Passage
Creak Is.
Genn Is.
Prescott Passage
Arthur I.
Edye Passage
Refuge
Bay
Hunt
Inlet
Hammer I.
William I.
McMicking I.
Useless
Bay
Spillar
Range
727
Edwin Pt.
Henry I.
Chismore
Passage
Elliott I.
Arthur Passage
HECATE
STRAIT
649
Bell
Range
Salt
Lagoon
Lewis I.
OVAL
BAY
Welcome
Harbour
Chismore
Range
433
PORCHER I.
Serpentine
Inlet
Dries
Inlet
Porcher
Inlet
Oval Pt.
Oona Pt.
Oona River
Kitkatla
Inlet
Wilcox
Group
Fan Pt.
888
Gurd I.
Snass Is.
Porcher
Narrows
Porcher
Peninsula
Ness Is.
Ogden Channel
Alpha Pt.
Cape
George
Absalom I.
Coquitlam I.
Cessford Is.
Billy
Bay
Skene
Cove
Mount
Shields
630
Freeman
Passage
Nubble
Mtn.
292
Chief Pt.
Kitkatla Channel
Gladstone Is.
Joachim Spit
GOSCHEN I.
Comrie Head
Willis Bay
Gilbert I.
Pelham Is.
Kitkatla Is.
Shakes Is.
KITKATLA
Goschen Pt.
McCauley Pt.
Petrel Channel
Dolphin I.
Prager Is.
Schooner Passage
Spicer I.
Miles
4
Km
4
8
S. Spicer I.
McCauley I.
See The Northern Channels, page 265

A view toward Kitkatla, which hugs the shore of Dolphin Island.

Kitkatla is located on the north end of Dolphin Island, with the dock in a bay to the west of the village. The Tsimshian name for this village is Gitkxaahla, meaning "people of the salt," a reference to the ocean location. It's one of the oldest continually inhabited villages on the coast. Whereas other villages were abandoned to take advantage of trade opportunities with the Europeans, Kitkatla's population remained, keeping it one of the more isolated and traditional villages. The band membership is around 1,600; 440 live on the reserve.

Most employment is provided by a sawmill, boat building and salmon enhancement projects. Regular floatplane service is available, as is bed and breakfast accommodation.

Kitkatla Channel

Within this channel are delightful archipelagos of picturesque little islands, made all the better by a smattering of beaches. Northwesterlies can funnel through the channel, but otherwise it's quite calm. Shakes and Prager islands lie in the channel between Goschen and Dolphin islands. The complex maze is difficult to navigate due to strong tidal currents. The many reefs and shallow areas make this

Kitkatla Islands, Kitkatla Channel.

kayaking country. Currents are variable but tend to flood toward Ogden Channel in the east and ebb to the open ocean to the west.

Billy Bay is a rich intertidal estuary surrounded by islands that run together at low tides. At the heart of Billy Bay are expansive eelgrass beds that attract an array of birds, most notably surf scoters. As many as 30,000 have been recorded here.

Camping: N53°49.21'/W130°21.55'. On the southwest corner of Gilbert Island is a sand and pebble beach with a good, high back. For spring tides a headland on the south side leads to an expansive clear area. This is the choice beach among a number sprinkled throughout the Pelham Islands area.

Kitkatla Inlet

This secluded adjunct to Kitkatla Channel is rarely visited. It's most notable for its bird population; the flats attract western grebes, surf scoters, oldsquaws, great blue herons, gulls and Brant geese during their spring migration.

Intertidal areas are extensive, and the channels around Snass Islands, for instance, can run dry.

Camping: N53°51.53'/W130°31.56'. Most shore locations are intertidal in the inlet, and camping is not recommended for a couple of reasons. One is to avoid disturbing the birds; another is that the beaches are not particularly pretty. Long stretches of beach are located on the south side of Gurd Island; while they are perhaps not particularly clean, they would offer good views down the inlet. However, a pretty location is on a small islet in the northwestern string of Cessford Islands. The islet has accumulated the lion's share of crushed clamshell in the area, making for a white, high-backed beach. A level area is available on the point atop the beach, if needed.

One of the Prager Islets.

Freeman Passage

This passage leads between Cape George on Porcher Island and Goschen Island. It's protected on the northeast side by Absalom and Coquitlam islands, which together with a smattering of islets and reefs do an admirable job of blocking the passage for anything larger than a dinghy. With strong tidal currents—as high as 4 knots, with a northeast flood and southwest ebb—it is a difficult transit by paddle against the tide. The passage is most popular for its anchorage tucked into the north shore. An unusual feature of the area is Joachim Spit, which dries into an exceptionally long bar of boulders at low tides. At other tide levels it will appear as a line of breaking waves extending to a navigation buoy. This is an important herring spawn area.

Goschen Island is easily dismissed as a small adjunct to Porcher Island, but it's quite large (about 9.5 km/6 miles from end to end) and has some of the more colourful features. It has a half-dozen large peaks, with the distinctive and partially bald Nubble Mountain topping 282 m (925 feet). Much of the outer shore is rugged, wave-battered, granite bedrock, but between Goschen and Joachim points are a variety of beaches, from cobble to fine sand. This is a stretch for advanced paddlers only, given the open ocean. If you do stop for a visit, take a look at how far the driftwood has been thrown back into the forest—an indication of the violence of winter storms.

Freeman Passage from Joachim Spit.

Driftwood clogs most camping opportunities along this stretch. The best options are listed below.

Place names: Captain Absalom Freeman was in charge of the fishing steamer *Coquitlam* operating in Hecate Strait in 1894. A fishing station, where halibut were cleaned before being shipped south, was located in this pass at that time. George Joachim Goschen (Cape George, Joachim Point and Goschen Island) was First Lord of the Admiralty from 1871 to 1874 and governor of the Hudson's Bay Company from 1874 to 1880.

Camping: N53°49.32'/W130°37.68'. At Joachim Point is a long rock spit with a beach on either side that becomes progressively more jumbled with rock the lower the tide level. Look to the extreme east and west edges of the beach for clear paths at all tide levels. The tops of the beaches are sand and cobble. They are nicely high-backed. With views extending from the open ocean through to the mouth of Freeman Passage, this is an attractive camping area.

N53°48.52'/W130°37.74'. South of Joachim Point is a curving bay with a sand beach along a considerable portion. Camping is possible, but not without some difficulty. Rocks and boulders are evident at lower tides. Departures and arrivals are best planned for higher tides. While high-backed, camping areas could disappear in storms when waves might reach the drift log piles at the beach top. Otherwise this is a beautiful, rarely visited beach.

Oval Bay

This long, curving stretch with 2.3 km (1.4 miles) of beach is a recreational highlight for the region. Much of it is cobble, especially along the central portion. Some portions are also steep and prone to crashing surf, so use caution when landing. A trail near the centre, marked by a blue jug on a stick (N53°58.45'/W130°40.27'), leads through a boggy area. Another trail leads to Welcome Harbour on the northeast end of the bay.

This area is considered one of the best places to view killer whales on the coast.

Camping: N53°56.95'/W130°42.20', south side; N53°59.41'/W130°39.82', north side. Anywhere on Oval Bay is fair game for camping, but surf, cobble and steep beaches are all factors. The

Oval Bay, Porcher Island.

favourite spot is at the north end, where the curve of the beach provides some measure of protection. It's also easily accessible from the trail at Welcome Bay. Another area to consider is the extreme south end, where the beach is more sandy and quite high-backed.

N53°55.76'/W130°43.39'. Just south of Oval Point is another curve of beach rarely considered as a campsite. The beach is clean and high-backed. Surf may be a factor.

Welcome Harbour

This is a wonderfully intricate area where bays, islands and islets create a maze perfect for kayaking. Note that currents can run several knots through the harbour and into Edye Passage, which can have tide rips that run south from Arthur Island's east side. Nearby Useless Bay was named for its role as an anchorage (less than ideal); while it has a beautiful sand beach, it dries extensively. A residence is located at the back of the bay.

Welcome Harbour is the site of a forest recreation campground—a rare feature on the coast. It has picnic tables, outhouses and fire pits in a pretty forest setting. A short trail leads to Oval Bay. Two mooring buoys are provided.

Two mines, the Edye Pass mine and Surf Point mine, operated on Porcher Island between 1919 and 1939, yielding 639,000 g (1,410 pounds) of gold and 226,000 tonnes (249,122 tons) of silver. The Reward Mining Company built a 50-tonne-per-day (55-ton) mill in 1939 to replace a smaller one that burned down the previous year, but it closed soon after, probably due to Second World War staff shortages. The Surf Point mine is located near Welcome Harbour (N54°01.42'/W130°35.16') with Edye Pass mine 1 km (0.6 miles) north (N54°01.67'/W130°35.00'). History buffs might enjoy trying to find the ruins, if any, that remain.

Place names: Admiral William Henry Edye served as captain on HMS *Satellite* on this coast in 1869. William Island, Henry Island and Edye Passage are all named for him.

Camping: N54°00.15'/W130°39.76'. There are several tent clearings at Welcome Harbour.

N54°00.12'/W130°39.95'. This exclusive and intimate beach is set in a cove between Oval Bay and Welcome Harbour facing the southwest end of Henry Island. The beach is high-backed and surrounded by steep dirt banks. It's well-protected and very private.

An extraordinarily pretty campsite off Stephens Island.

Stephens Island

Combined with Prescott Island, this is an area of beautifully complex shorelines and passageways. Novice paddlers unsure of the open ocean should at least leave the sanctuary of Welcome Harbour to do a circumnavigation of Prescott Island via Prescott Passage and Stephens Passage. Numerous beaches dot the many coves. Distinctive white rocks add to the appeal. The more adventurous will want to explore the outer portions of Stephens Island.

On the west side of Stephens Island, intertidal and wetland areas draw an abundance of shorebirds and water birds. The east side is straight, steep and rocky, with numerous kelp beds.

On the north end, tucked in behind Avery Island, is Qlawdzeet Anchorage—a popular place for fishing boats to overnight thanks in part to an old floating dock where boats can tie up. It was here that Captain Vancouver and his crew aboard the *Discovery* and *Chatham* found refuge on the stormy afternoon of July 20, 1793. They were piloted in by the ship *Butterworth,* which had already anchored in the bay along with two other vessels, *Prince Le Boo* and *Jackall.*

Caution: A passage runs between Philip Island and the northwest corner of Stephens Island. It may seem like a pleasant passage to meander through, especially if the current is going with you. But listen closely. That roaring you hear in the distance is a tidal rapid. I discovered this by ignoring the sound until I was looking down on a significant drop of white water over rocks and was forced to paddle back against a strong current to get out.

Place names: Qlawdzeet is Tsimshian for "the place of the hissing sound," a reference to the sound of clams squirting water on the beach. "Zeet" represents the hissing sound. It acknowledges the abundance of clams here. Sir Philip Stephens was secretary to the British Admiralty. Vancouver named the island in August 1793.

Camping: N54°08.93'/W130°49.83'. If you're looking for an exotic campsite, this should deliver. On the outside northwest edge of Philip Island is a group of reefs and islets with just one narrow stretch of beautiful white sand and crushed clamshell. The beach is high-backed, and if you'd rather not camp on sand, you're in luck. Behind the beach is a lightly vegetated, level berm with views in both directions. This is a truly magical place and could accommodate a group.

A killer whale passes near Rachel Islands.

N54°08.05'/W130°46.45'. Inside the cove on the north end of Skiakl Island is a beautifully soft, clean sandbar. Look for a small clear area on the south side of the bar to escape high tides. It's unfortunate that most of the sandbar will disappear at high tide, as that is the main attraction.

N54°12.25'/W130°46.07'. On the south end of Qlawdzeet Anchorage is a nice sand and grit beach facing an assortment of reefs and rocks. There's a clear, level area back in the forest with a rudimentary cabin. There's space for a large group here.

Chatham Sound

This huge body of water lies between Dundas Island in the north, Stephens Island to the south and Tsimpsean Peninsula to the east. It's protected through most of its length on the west by large islands and small island clusters. Currents are minimal in the north portion of the sound, rarely exceeding a knot, with a flood setting north. In the southern portion the waters from Brown, Bell and Edye passages meet the flood north from Malacca Passage to create an easterly flow that can run 2 knots. In an ebb tide the reverse is true.

Several small island clusters are located within the sound, as are several major shipping routes. Rachel Islands is a small island group that shelters a sizeable marine bird population on the central cluster of rocks. The south island has a wonderful sand beach to the north that connects with a small islet. On the islet is a well-built cabin. A sign on it reads: "Welcome to this shelter, it was built for a safe refuge for everyone. Please take good care when you are staying here. It may depend on saving someone or yourself. Thank you, M. Maksymyszyn." It's well-provisioned and appointed on the inside, making it look more like a private residence than a shared cabin. Trails cross the island to various viewpoints.

Place names: John Pitt was the second earl of Chatham and the First Lord of the Admiralty 1788–94. He was brother of Prime Minister William Pitt. Chatham Sound was named in 1788 by Captain Duncan.

Camping: N54°12.12'/W130°33.60'. The beach near the cabin on Rachel Islands will survive most tide levels; the cabin occupies the clear, level upland area.

Place names: George Andrew Noble Kitson served on HMS Malacca (Malacca Passage) on this coast 1866–67.

Marcus and Malacca passages

This is a wide portion of the Inside Passage, and vessel traffic may go either side of Lawyer Islands. Due to their proximity to Grenville Passage and Skeena River, Marcus and Malacca passages are prone to some very odd and unpredictable tidal currents. Most traffic will want to avoid Telegraph Passage and the shallow sandbars that surround the mouth of Skeena River (these areas are off the regional map; see the main chapter map on page 287). In Telegraph Passage the floods will head north and reach 3 knots, and ebb south at 4 knots. The

Kitson Island Marine Park

This diminutive 44.7-ha (110-acre) island was protected in 1993 as a strategic recreation area for Prince Rupert. There are two brown-sand beaches here—a small one on the east side facing the industrial waterfront of Port Edward and the other facing south to Marcus Passage. A trail connects the two. Partway along the trail, closer to the south beach, is a tent clearing. There are no amenities. The actual island is owned by the Prince Rupert Port Corporation and leased by B.C. Parks

turn is 1 hour after high tide. High waves can occur at the junction of Marcus and Telegraph passages southeast of Parry Point on the south end of De Horsey Island. Marcus Passage floods east with currents of 3.5 knots, and an ebb flow reaches 5 knots.

Kayakers may want to duck into the cover of Chismore Passage, which runs between Porcher and the McMicking, Elliott and Lewis off Porcher's northeast side. It's pleasantly serene and out of the shipping traffic. Lawson Harbour, on the north end of Lewis Island, was once a community; the remains of the village can be visited behind the curving beach.

Flood currents set northwest in Malacca Passage and meet the flood setting northeast from Edye Passage near Hunt Point on the northern tip of Porcher Island.

Malacca Passage turns into narrow Arthur Passage alongside Kennedy Island and then opens into the confluence of Ogden and Grenville channels. The current through Arthur Passage floods north and ebbs south, and can reach 2.5 knots south of Hammer Island.

Place names: Arthur E. Kennedy was the governor of Vancouver Island 1864–66. Dr. Chismore was with the United States Army and stationed with the 2nd U.S. Artillery at Tongass Island, Alaska. When Captain Vancouver sailed through here in 1793, he named Raspberry Island at the mouth of Skeena River for the quantity of excellent raspberries there.

Camping: N54°02.50'/W130°17.29'. A great curve of beach in the south end of McMicking Island faces east. It's high-backed enough for most tides, with a few level, clear areas in the trees if needed. The beach is far above the quality of most others in this area and is a great campsite for either the beginning or end of a run up or down Grenville Channel.

Ogden Channel

In this channel between Porcher Island and north Pitt Island the flood current runs north and then divides, with one portion running southeast into Grenville Channel and another continuing north to Arthur and Telegraph passages. The ebb streams from Arthur, Telegraph and Grenville passages meet off the north end of Ogden Channel. The muddy water of the Skeena River is often distinguishable among the blue ocean currents.

The rugged western shore of Dundas Island.

At the north end of Ogden Channel is the Scandinavian community of Oona River, now home to about 40 residents plus a number of recreational cottages. A family-owned sawmill, woodlot and fish hatchery provide employment. There's a public dock. Logging roads and trails crisscross the island. Because of its proximity to road transportation at the head, Porcher Inlet's three tidal rapids have potential for use as a whitewater route.

THE DUNDAS GROUP

This cluster of islands off the northwest corner of the Canadian mainland coast features five main islands and a host of smaller island groups dominated by Dundas Island. This remote region requires a 13-km (8-mile) crossing of Chatham Sound or more than 8 km (5 miles) from the already isolated Triple Islands to the south. The various island groups offer a range of shorelines—from mundane but placid inner islands to the wave-battered outer islets and bays of west Dundas Island.

Primarily a fishing destination, the archipelagos here offer untapped potential for sightseeing, especially whale watching. Humpback, gray and killer whales are common.

Aranzazu Pt.
White Its.
Gnarled Is.
Arniston Pt.
Zayas I.
Boat Harbour
Goose Bay
Whitly Pt.
Holliday I.
207
Slab Hill
Brundige Inlet
Jacinto Pt.
Caamaño Passage
Grey It.
Green I.
DUNDAS I.
Mount Bonwick
401
464
Mount Henry
Channel Is. IR
Whitesand I.
Randall I.
Hudson Bay Passage
Clam Inlet
Baron I.
Nares Its.
Prince Leboo I.
Edith Harbour
Moffatt Is.
Dunira I.
Farwest Pt.
Connel Is.
399
Melville I.
PACIFIC OCEAN
Hammer Rocks
CHATHAM SOUND
Brown Passage
Triple Is.
Lucy Is.
Tree Nob Group
Osborne Is.
Miles
4
4
8
Km
Bell Passage
Archibald Is.
Avery I.
See Porcher Island, page 286

Hudson Bay Passage marks the division between Dixon Entrance and Hecate Strait.

Place names: Henry Dundas was treasurer of the navy 1783–1801. The island was named by Captain Vancouver in 1793.

Tree Nob Group

This is just one of a number of island groups that lie between Chatham Sound and Hecate Strait. Numerous rocks and reefs dot the area, and it's considered an excellent dive site. It's a substantial seabird colony for pelagic cormorant. The *Butterworth* hit a rock in this area—now called Butterworth Rock—in 1793, temporarily losing its rudder. Repairs were made at Qlawdzeet Anchorage.

Tidal streams are strong through all the islands.

A fortress-like lighthouse with a conspicuous helicopter landing pad is located on Triple Islands in an inhospitable area surrounded by reefs. Built in 1920, the original octagonal concrete tower is still in place.

Brown Passage

This waterway separates the Dundas Group from the cluster of tiny islands to the south. It's a marine artery for large vessels travelling Dixon Entrance or Hecate Strait to Prince Rupert. The main shipping route passes just north of Triple Islands. Tidal currents can be strong here and are variable in direction.

Triple Islands Lighthouse.

Travel notes: If you are crossing from Triple Islands to Dundas Islands, the sightline for ship traffic is generally good, but the passage is wide some ships could conceivably leave Prince Rupert Harbour and be in Brown Passage before a kayak could cross. Keep in mind that shipping traffic will run between Triple Islands and Hammer Rocks, conspicuous as a navigation buoy. The distance between the two is about 4.8 km (3 miles). A shorter crossing is between a navigation buoy at Osbourne Islands, southeast of

Lucy Islands.

Triple Islands (N54°17.20'/W130°51.19'), to a whistle buoy south of Hammer Rocks (N54°18.35'/W130°48.54'). This crossing is just 3.5 km (2.2 miles). After that you are safe from most shipping traffic, though fishing and recreational traffic may pass on the outside of these buoys.

Place names: Captain William Brown of the *Butterworth* met Captain Vancouver at Qlawdzeet Anchorage, Stephens Island, on July 21, 1793. Brown provided valuable information about the nearby waters, including Portland Inlet. They would meet again in Nootka Sound.

Lucy Islands

This is a beautiful cluster of little islands smack in the middle of Chatham Sound. A highlight is the wide bar of sand that connects the two main islands. A good way to approach is from the north, as the north beach is protected by a nearby islet. An old lighthouse is located on the east side of the island atop a rock bluff. It is no longer staffed. A trail leads from the lighthouse to the beach on the far side of

A rhinoceros auklet.

the island. The boardwalk is maintained by the Prince Rupert Rotary, in part to keep the public on the boardwalk and off the nesting sites of rhinoceros auklets.

Lucy Island is home to the largest rhinoceros auklet colony on the B.C. coast. The birds nest in burrows across the island, but can be disturbed by recreational use. The auklets can be seen fishing in the water around Chatham Sound during the day and returning at night to feed the young.

Melville and Dunira islands

These islands are part of a closely knit cluster that includes several other island groups. The outer Connel Islands to the southwest feature the most dramatic shorelines, as they take the full brunt of storms in Hecate Strait.

A central charm of the whole region is the twisting channels and islets, which are exceptional between Melville and Dunira islands. Sand beaches also cover much of Melville's south and west edges and many of the outlying islands.

A wreck is located between Baron and Dunira islands—a reminder of the hazard boats face from unmarked rocks.

Travel notes: Many of the passages between islets can be choked with rock at lower tides, and I found west Melville Island unappealing because low tide revealed expanses of unattractive brown-black intertidal rock that blocked routes. Frequent kelp beds also made travel awkward. To avoid this, keep to the main passages or travel at higher tides.

Place names: Henry Dundas (1742–1811) was treasurer of the Royal Navy 1782–1801 and in 1802 was named Baron Dunira and Viscount of Melville. *Connel* is a Gaelic word meaning "roaring flood," and could be referring to strong currents or foul conditions around the islands.

Camping: N54°22.43'/W130°46.97'. Good beaches can be found along the west side of Melville Island; three especially prominent beaches are in close proximity south of a reef-strewn headland. The easternmost beach of the three has the fewest intertidal reefs and submerged rocks at the entrance. The high-backed beach is rock, with sand patches at lower levels and fine sand at the top. There are undeveloped but level areas in the uplands. Wolf prints dotted the beach when I was there in 2005.

N54°26.24'/W130°44.46'. On the east side of Dunira Island a clean gravel beach stands out. A slightly developed and level upland is available, though it may be overgrown.

Hudson Bay Passage

This waterway separates Dundas and Baron islands and also marks the division between Hecate Strait and Dixon Entrance. It's home to three separate island groups—Nares Islets and the Dundas and Channel islands. This stretch seems to have more beach than the entire central coast combined; just about every nook on an islet boasts an expansive beachfront. Note that the Channel Islands are a Tsimshian reserve.

Hudson Bay Passage is generally more placid than Caamaño Passage on the outside of Dundas Island, but southerlies and westerlies can still wreak havoc at the entrance near Prince Leboo Island, especially when currents and wind directions clash. Currents flood to the northeast and ebb southeast, reaching 1.5 knots.

Camping: N54°28.53'/W130°50.02'. With so many beaches there are simply too many choices. Consider making a base camp at the beautiful sand beach on the north side of Baron Island opposite the Nares Islets. From here you can pick and choose among a dozen other fine candidates.

Prince Leboo Island

There are two channels north of Prince Leboo Island. The longest and narrowest of the two (the one adjacent to Dundas Island) widens on the south outlet to create Edith Harbour. This is a popular anchorage, with beaches on the northeast (Dundas Island) side. The beach is a Tsimshian reserve. The channel itself can become a tidal rapid just northwest of the harbour. It would be unsafe to travel the channel at lower tides given the many rocks.

Islets dot the channel closest to Prince Leboo, but it's otherwise clear and deep. The largest kelp bed in the region, off Prince Leboo's southern tip, is a productive area for rockfish, salmon, urchins, abalone and seabirds. The nearby rocks are a popular sea lion haulout, and they can be seen there year-round.

Prince Leboo Island and the associated nearby islets are a Tsimshian reserve.

Place names: *Prince Leboo* was a vessel Captain Vancouver encountered at Qlawdzeet Anchorage, Stephens Island, in 1793. It was commanded by a Captain Sharp. The namesake Prince Leboo was a scholar—the first from Palau—who sailed with Captain Henry Wilson on HMS *Antelope* to London in 1783. On your next visit to Palau, look for his statue.

Dundas Island

This sprawling island features a number of large mountains, including Mount Henry, the island's tallest at 464 m (1,522 feet), and Slab Hill, a distinctive flat-topped island near the north. The east shore is free of bays, inlets or beaches north of the Channel Islands, and while the north shore of the island has bays and anchorages, the beaches—of which there are many— are almost all choked with rock below high

Dating Tsimshian history

Archeological evidence has uncovered about 4,500 to 5,000 years of habitation of the north coast by the Tsimshian. But such a short history seems odd, as archaeological evidence shows about 9,000 years of habitation in the Queen Charlotte Islands, on the south coast of Alaska and at Namu in Heiltsuk territory. In other words, the Tsimshian are surrounded on basically all sides by seemingly older cultures.

Archaeologists have reason to believe the Tsimshian culture is just as old, and it is just a matter of finding the evidence. A recent University of British Columbia cultural survey of archaeological sites may have found that.

The survey is taking place 2005-2007 and in the first year examined about 50 archaeological sites on Dundas Island. The hope of the study is to eventually map all the sites in the Dundas Group, suspected to number about 200. It is a low-impact study based on surface evidence plus core sampling and augering. This will leave the sites largely undisturbed.

The archaeologists began their survey with a hypothesis based on the Queen Charlotte Islands experience. There some of the oldest sites were found well above sea level, a result of the tilting of the island—the east side has been rising and the west side dropping over the last several thousand years. Consequently it is believed older sites on the west coast of the Charlottes are now submerged.

Did Dundas Island undergo the same tilt? Based on mapping and where the shoreline might have been, archaeologists looked for sites on high ground—and found them. At the time of writing the core samples were in the process of being carbon-dated, with a good possibility these may be among the earliest Tsimshian sites. This poses an interesting convergence of archaeological findings and Tsimshian oral history, which spoke of the existence of these ancient sites.

Should these sites not be as old as anticipated, the likelihood of finding one is probably just a matter of time—and then the Tsimshian can rewrite their history to be among the most ancient people of the coast.

tide levels. Set in the back of the bay southwest of Whitly Point is Haa-Nee-Naa Lodge, a sports fishing resort. Residences and cottages are located along Goose Bay.

Travel notes: I was told not to travel to Dundas Island due to the blackflies. Tales are told of how bad these nasty biting creatures are—stories like the yachtsman dropping his anchor and being unable to see it for blackflies as it hit the water. It has even been speculated the island is devoid of deer due to the high number of these flies. The story has almost reached mythical status. However, both fishing lodges and residences seem to manage, and I can say that during my several days here I was undisturbed by blackflies. That doesn't mean they can't be bad, but don't assume the worst. For more on managing bugs, see the introduction, page 45.

Petroglyphs are a prominent reminder of Tsimshian culture, but it is impossible to determine their age because they cannot be carbon-dated.

Place names: Henry Dundas, the Royal Navy treasurer 1783–1801, was a staunch opponent to reconciling with the rebellious American colonies while serving in Parliament. Captain Vancouver named these islands in the belief they were all one island.

Camping: N54°37.42'/W130°55.05'. This is a good high-backed beach set between rock bars just west of Goose Bay. It's accessible at all tide levels if you watch for a few rocks and reefs at lower tides.

Green Island

This tiny island is off the northeast side of Dundas Island in the area between Dixon Entrance and Hecate Sound. It's a staffed light station, at one time the most northerly in Canada. Grey Islet is located 1.35 km (0.8 miles) northeast and is an automated weather station. The two tend to duplicate services, but public pressure in the late 1980s stopped all the staffed Pacific coast light stations from closing and being replaced by automated stations. So now both the automated and the staffed weather stations operate in tandem.

Weather: Like many weather stations on the B.C. coast, Green Island records generally mild temperatures with average daily maximums in July and August of 17.3°C (63°F). Average daily minimums hover around 11.8°C (53°F) in the same months. Temperatures rarely go above 20°C (68°F)—only about 8 or 9 days a year. Temperatures do drop below freezing here regularly over the winter, on about 30 days per year.

Precipitation is 2,447 mm (98 inches) each year, with the heaviest rain in October at 360 mm (14 inches). In June and July it will average 107 mm (4.2 inches) per month and considerably more in August—about 153 mm (6 inches). In September it increases yet again to an average of 240 mm (9.5 inches).

Expect some amount of rain about 17 to 18 days each of the summer months, with moderate rain of 5 mm (0.2 inches) or more on 6 to 8 days and heavier rain of 10 mm (0.4 inches) or more on 3 to 4 days during June and July and on five or six days in August.

In 2005 wind averaged 33 km/h (18 knots) south and southeast; 37 km/h (20 knots) southeast and northeast in July; 18.5 km/h (10 knots) south and southeast in August and 22 km/h (12 knots) south, southeast and southwest in September.

Looking across Caamaño Passage from Zayas Island.

Lightkeeper Serge Pare reports that in recent years the winter wind has changed to come just as often from the south, southeast and southwest, whereas it used to come from the northeast due to the winter outflow winds from Portland Inlet. The winter wind is generally 55 km/h (30 knots) to as high as 92 km/h (50 knots).

Caamaño Passage

Separating Dundas and Zayas islands, this passage is along the exposed side of Dundas Island. While swell can be intimidating, the complex shoreline of Dundas makes for an incredible area to explore. Smalls bays litter the shoreline. Catch this area on a day of light winds and moderate swell, and you'll be treated to a breathtaking show of the power of the ocean as the waves explode onto the reefs and islets. Be warned that many of the perfect sand beaches in the various bays, especially just north of Prince Leboo Island, are likely on Tsimshian reserve land.

Place names: Lt. Commander Jacinto Caamaño was in charge of the Spanish corvette *Aranzazu* that explored this coast in 1792. It was named by Captain Learmouth of HMS *Egeria* in 1908 while surveying Zayas Island.

Zayas Island

Situated on the west side of Caamaño Passage, this small island can be exposed to heavy weather. The best beaches are on the east shore, while the most dramatic shoreline is at Aranzazu Point at the northwest tip and Jacinto Point to the south. Despite the exposure, the rest of the shore is not particularly outstanding.

Camping: N54°37.14'/W131°03.04'. Northeast Zayas Island has an excellent curve of sand beach. Portions are high-backed, with the ruin of a cabin and its outbuildings prominent on the south end. Other beaches of varying quality are located on the southeast shore of Zayas.

Long lines of rocks extend well offshore at low tides from most points of Tsimpsean Peninsula—including an unlikely resting spot for a boulder.

TSIMPSEAN PENINSULA

Prince Rupert is set in the shelter of a deep harbour, while most of the outer coast of Tsimpsean Peninsula is owned by Lax Kw'alaams and Metlakatla. Just a short jaunt across Portland Inlet lies Alaska, and kayakers could find themselves in the Alaskan Panhandle within a day's paddle of leaving Prince Rupert. Portland Inlet has its own attractions, particularly the grizzly bear sanctuary at Khutzeymateen Inlet.

Port Edward

This industrial waterfront along Inverness Passage south of Prince Rupert is accessible by Highway 16 and supports a population of about 770, though most visitors from the water will just see the grain terminal and the bulk coal loading facility dominating the waterline on Ridley Island.

The port's roots go back to 1908, when it was picked as the terminus of the Grand Trunk Railway; land speculators bought parcels, only to have the plans for the railway shift to Kaien Island instead. Early development was mainly fish canneries; the North Pacific Cannery, built in 1889, was designated a National Historic

ALASKA (U.S.)
Pearse Canal
Safas Is.
Wales Harbour
WALES I.
Wales Passage
Winter Inlet
PEARSE I.
Maklaksadagamks IR
PORTLAND INLET
Start Pt.
Yakaskalui Pt.
Somerville Bay
Kwinamass Bay
Talahaat IR
Miles
Km
Tongass Passage
Ksadagamks IR
Manzanita Cove
Proctor Is.
Ksadsks IR
Truro I.
SOMERVILLE I.
Spakel IR
Welgeegenk Pt.
Haystack I.
Boston Is.
Wales Pt.
Tracy I.
Me-Yan-Law IR
Steamer Passage
Crow Lagoon
Elliott Pt.
Kumeon Bay
KHUTZEYMATEEM INLET
Walskakul Pt.
1100
Tsamspanaknok Bay
Father Pt.
Hogan I.
Maskelyne I.
UNION INLET
Union L.
Tymgowzan IR
Mouse Cr.
Parkin Its.
Flewin Pt.
Union Bay IR
Ksabasan IR
1300
Mount McNeil
Birnie IR
Grassy Pt.
Trail Bay
PORT SIMPSON
Zumtela Bay
Worsfold Bay
Gordon Pt.
Khutzeymateem Grizzly Sanctuary
LAX KW'ALAAMS
420
Mount Griffin
615
Mount Ben
Finlayson Island IR
Eagle Bight
Knamadeek IR
CHATHAM SOUND
593
Leading Peak
Legace Bay
WORK CHANNEL
Ensheshese IR
Meyanlow IR
Mist I.
South I.
Georgetown Cr.
Grave Bay
Ndakdolk IR
Thulme R.
BIG BAY
Swallow I.
Simpson Pt.
Spanaknok IR
Quottoon Narrows
Trenham Pt.
779
Sharp Peak
Wilskaskamel IR
Tree Bluff
TSIMPSEAN IR
Nishanocknawnak IR
1420
Thulme Peak
Jap Pt.
Tuck Pt.
Osborn Cove
Quottoon Pt.
Bill Lake IR
Swamp I.
900
Kasika IR
Mission Mountain
Ryan Pt.
Duncan Bay
TSIMPSEAN IR
TUCK INLET
METLAKATLA
Tugwell I.
Venn Passage
Leverson L.
Prince Rupert Harbour
Shawatlan L.
Pike I.
Maganktoon IR
Devastation I.
Grindstone Pt.
Fern Passage
PRINCE RUPERT
Davies Lagoon
Pillsbury Pt.
TSIMPSEAN PENINSULA
Cridge I.
DIGBY I.
Fairview Pt.
708
Butze Pt.
Lachmach IR
Casey Pt.
Mt. Hays
Morse Basin
KAIEN I.
Delusion Bay
Denise Inlet
Martin I.
Wainwright Basin
Kloiya Bay
Lima Pt.
Rachel Is.
Ridley I.
PORT EDWARDS
Diana Lake Provincial Park
Gamble Creek Ecological Reserve
Kinahan Is.
Lelu I.
See Porcher Island, page 288

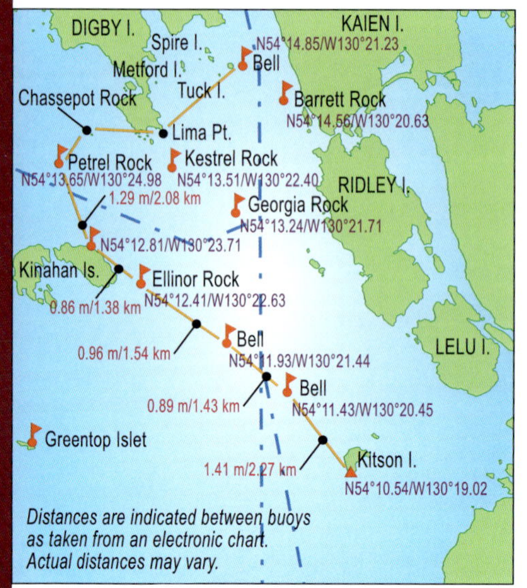

Site in 1985. It's now operated as a living museum. The North Pacific Fishing Village offers performances, tours and exhibits. It's located across from Tatenham Point on the north end of Smith Island (just outside the regional map).

The North Pacific Cannery was just one of seven salmon canneries scattered around the Skeena River estuary in the 1890s. The area's industrial nature is destined to continue. As Vancouver's port reaches capacity, Prince Rupert is being eyed as an alternative, and a major container-shipping

Transiting Prince Rupert shipping traffic

Kayakers could face a particularly stressful time in the waters around Prince Rupert due to commercial traffic. Ships exiting the harbour down the narrow channel between Kaien and Digby islands include freighters, cruise ships and ferries. They move quickly and may head south or may turn suddenly and head north. You won't know by sight alone until the turn is made. So you may see a ship apparently heading south toward Malacca Passage only to have it turn to Kinahan Islands and head north.

The trick for kayakers is to stay close to navigation buoys.

If you are travelling north from Kitson Island, for instance, and want to avoid the harbour and go around the outside of Digby Island, the shallow banks around Kitson Island will help you by allowing you to get closer to Kinahan Islands through an area where ships won't go. The outside limit of the bank is marked by a navigation bell 2.3 km (1.4 miles) to the northwest of Kitson Island. All shipping traffic will pass west of this buoy. Once at the buoy check for the all-clear, then aim for the next navigation buoy/bell 1.4 km (0.9 miles) to the northwest. Traffic will generally pass east of this buoy. Once at the second bell you can cross to Ellinor Rock and Kinahan Islands.

Between Kinahan and Digby islands is another major shipping lane. Ships will pass south of Petrel Rock, which is marked by a navigation bell. The distance between Petrel Rock and Kinahan Islands is about 2.1 km (1.3 miles). If you aim for the bell your exposure in the shipping lane should be about 20 minutes at a moderate paddle. This is still a long period considering the lack of sightline, so monitoring Channel 71 or contacting Prince Rupert traffic control is always an option for peace of mind. Vessels leaving Prince Rupert Harbour are required to call in at Pillsbury Point and give an estimated time of arrival at Petrel Rock, Greentop Islet, Holland Rock, Lawyer Islands or Genn Islands, depending on their route. This should help alert you if a ship is about to cross near your path.

terminal expansion is planned that would see Prince Rupert capable of handling 80 per cent of Vancouver's capacity. It already has the advantage of lying on the shortest trade route between North America and Asia. Plans could include filling in the waterway behind Ridley and Lelu islands.

Launches: The District of Port Edward maintains a boat launch at Porpoise Harbour, the body of water behind Ridley and Lelu islands. From here it would be possible to head directly south, avoiding the traffic of Prince Rupert Harbour. Other amenities at the launch include a temporary moorage, washrooms and a fish-cleaning table.

Prince Rupert Harbour

Prince Rupert is a colourful and energetic city that augments its industrial base with a cosmopolitan tourism industry spurred on in large part by the growth of the cruise ship industry and by Prince Rupert's role as a hub for ferry traffic. As a result, in the area surrounding the cruise ship terminal, you can find everything from cute cafés to scooter rentals. For current information on amenities call **1-800-667-1994** or visit **www.tourismprincerupert.com**.

The Atlin Building and dock in Prince Rupert.

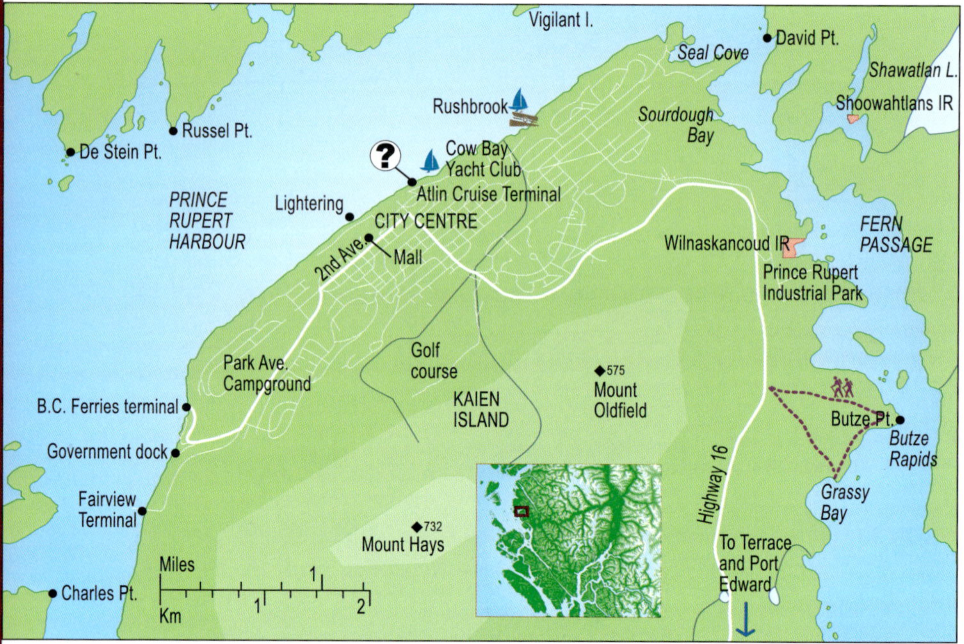

Those entering Prince Rupert Harbour by water will see the industrial nature of the area first, with views of the commercial fishing docks and container terminal at Fairview Point. This can be a busy place, with fishing boats unloading their catch for processing right at the waterfront.

Shipping plays a huge role in Prince Rupert's economy. It's considered the third-largest ice-free harbour in the world and one of the largest natural deep-sea harbours. It's also close to Asia, cutting about 700 km (435 miles) from a trip when compared to other North American ports.

Canadian National's northern transcontinental line ends here. A rail line skirts the waterfront from Prince Rupert to Port Edward.

Tucked into the commercial docks north of Fairview Point is a distinctive red government dock. Note that it's in an industrial area, and the only amenities near the dock are the few services offered at the nearby ferry terminal; otherwise it's a lengthy walk or a taxi ride to the downtown area.

The cruise ship terminal is located at the Atlin dock, and this is where the tourism and service sector begins, including the city's marinas. The tourist information centre is located on the waterfront in the Atlin building—a converted halibut-processing plant. Also

Commercial fishing boats line Prince Rupert Harbour.

in the same building are tour operators and art galleries. Food and shelter of all varieties are located nearby, from hotels to several tidy new hostels.

Prince Rupert's population is about 14,000, with roughly two-thirds of First Nations' ancestry—a mixture of Haida, Gitsa'at, Tsimshian and Nisga'a. The first railway building was a tool, shed built in 1906, and by 1910, the year the city was incorporated, the population was 4,000. Canneries further boosted the area's fortunes, and in the Second World War it became a strategic transportation link for the Pacific. The town was fitted with a seaplane base, new docks, a military hospital and a road to Terrace. In 1949 a pulp mill was added south of Kaien Island, and by 1972 the Port of Prince Rupert was established to spearhead the port's development.

Place names: Prince Rupert of the Rhine (1619–82) was the cousin of King Charles II. In 1670 he was granted the charter for "The Company of Adventurers of England Trading in Hudson's Bay," making him the Hudson's Bay Company's first governor. The Grand Trunk Railway held a contest to name the town, and Eleanor MacDonald of Winnipeg won, earning herself $250.

Launches: The city's main boat launch is at Rushbrook, northeast of the city centre. For long-term parking options, contact Prince Rupert Visitors Information at **1-800-667-1994**.

Camping: For those arriving at or leaving Prince Rupert and in need of nearby camping options, a good bet is Prudhomme Lake Provincial Park. The park is located just east of Prince Rupert off Highway 16. It has 24 vehicle-accessible campsites. There are no reservations. It's popular with vehicles using the Inside Passage ferry service or en route to or from the Queen Charlotte Islands.

Fern Passage

This is considered a dangerous stretch due to strong tidal currents and is probably best enjoyed from land. A trail leads from the highway to an observation point for watching the whitewater at Butze Rapids. This is an easy 5.4-km (3.3-mile) walk over boardwalk and gravel.

Tuck Inlet

Tuck inlet is located at the northeast end of Prince Rupert Harbour. A barge landing at the head of the inlet provides a road connection to Lax Kw'alaams via barge or band-run ferry. The Tuck Inlet Road is currently being improved, and the feasibility of a fixed link is being explored.

At Tuck Point is Tuck Narrows, which has strong tidal currents. The area is relatively sheltered, with a steep shoreline.

Venn Passage

This is a key route for boat traffic out of Prince Rupert Harbour. It's convoluted, with numerous navigation markers to guide boats through the maze of islands, bays and tidal flats. There are many beaches along here, but the entire stretch is part of Metlakatla's Tsimpsean Indian Reserve. The tide floods into Prince Rupert Harbour, so departures are simplest during falling tides. The current can run as high as 3 knots and will turn 1 hour before high water. At the west entrance, sizeable sandbars become exposed at lower tides.

The village of Metlakatla is located on the north shore of Venn Passage and was once the principal village of the Tsimshian before Port Simpson was developed in 1834. The residents returned in 1862, but in 1887 it was vacated again due to a division along religious lines. Missionary William Duncan refused to allow converts to take Holy Communion. In a dispute with the bishop over the matter he moved his mission and about 800 residents to New Metlakatla in Alaska.

The shore of the passage is dotted with petroglyphs, including the famous Man Who Fell From Heaven (see below). Venn Passage is considered one of the major archaeological sites of the coast, with the waters once home to about 8,000 people in 15 winter villages.

The Man Who Fell From Heaven

Probably the most significant and distinctive petroglyph on the B.C. coast is The Man Who Fell From Heaven, the name for a full-sized human figure etched into the granite bedrock at the second small point immediately west of Robertson Point (N54°19.26'/W130°24.36'). Note it is on reserve land, considered private property, and is not visible from the shore. Dozens of other smaller petroglyphs dot the point. To avoid trespassing, take a kayak tour offered by the Tsimshian-run Seashore Charters. Call **250-624-5645**.

The Man Who Fell from Heaven.

The carving is considered significant not just for its size but also because it would have taken the artist years to create. Castings of the image can be viewed at the Museum of Northern British Columbia and at the Atlin Building at Seashore Charters where the tourist information centre is located. A third casting is in Lax Kw'alaams. The following is the Tsimshian story about the petroglyph.

"The nearby First Nations have many legends of how the petroglyph came to be. One of our favourite tales concerns a young tribesman who was expelled from his tribe for misconduct.

This young tribesman desired to be readmitted to the village, so he cast about for some time, attempting to regain his lost prestige. In those days men who could perform feats of magic were always sure of a ready welcome, so the young man returned home with a tale of magical prowess almost beyond belief.

He told the villagers of a trip to heaven and of the wonders he found there, but said sadly, he had accidentally fallen out and plunged to earth. Deciding that their one-time neighbor was imagining things, the villagers were about to reject him when the tribesman replied he had proof. This engaged the villagers and they demanded he show them his proof.

So the tribesman escorted the villagers down to the beach and showed them the impression of his great impact, where he hit the earth. With his physical evidence before their eyes, the tribe was quick to acknowledge his genius, and long weeks of secret carving were rewarded with recognition as the number-one magician in B.C.

The rock was called The Man Who Fell from Heaven, and is still known as that today."

Tour guide and Metlakatlan Eagle Crest prince John Haldane points out a petroglyph to a youngster on Pike Island.

Petroglyphs can be found at Crippen Cove (a little cove west of Grindstone Point on Digby Island), Metlakatla and Wilgiapshi Island.

Place names: Metlakatla is a derivation of the Tsimshian word *Metla-kah-thla*, which means "a passage between two bodies of water." This refers to Venn Passage. When the name was made official in 1905 it put to rest many versions of spelling, which included Metlah Catlah, Metla-Catlah, Metla-kathla, Metla Catla and Metla-Katla. William Duncan named the passage after Reverend Henry Venn (1796–1873), the honourary secretary of the Church Mission Society from 1841 to 1873. In 1913–14 Lionel Crippen ran a fish plant at Crippen Cove producing "Crippen's boneless kippered herring."

Pike Island

Pike Island (Laxspa'aws) is a unique touring opportunity offered by the Metlakatla band. It'is considered the centre of the traditional Tsimshian territory and boasts five archaeological sites. Three of these are village sites, and two are suspected of being last inhabited 1,800 years ago. The other village was inhabited by the Giluts'aaw tribe, who lived here until the Skeena River Tsimshian moved from Metlakatla to Lax Kw'alaams in the 1840s to take advantage of Fort Simpson. The village once had about 30 houses supporting a population estimated at 500.

Two clusters of petroglyphs are on the island's waterfront, and there are more than 100 in all.

Visitors are welcomed to the island as part of tours that run almost daily during the summer from Prince Rupert. The half-day trips include a boat trip to the island, a guided tour of some of the archaeological highlights, a trip through a forest trail with explanations of native use of the forest environment and a unique musical finale at a reconstructed longhouse. For tour information call Metlakatla's Seashore Charters at **1-800-667-4393** or visit **www.seashorecharters.com**.

Lax Kw'alaams is backed by Mount Griffin.

Place names: Laxspa'sws means "island of sand." Commander John William Pike captained the paddle sloop *Devastation* on the B.C. coast 1862–64.

Big Bay

This bay extends about 6 km (3.8 miles) into the Tsimpsean Peninsula and features a number of beautiful beaches. The mouth of the bay is a large, shallow intertidal zone considered one of the most important intertidal wetlands on the north coast. As many as 400,000 wate birds have been recorded here during the herring spawn in April, while several thousand overwinter here. Migratory birds include several hundred thousand surf scoters, swans, snow geese and Brant geese. The herring spawn supports the largest herring roe fishery on the coast. The annual harvest is about 2,463 tonnes (2,715 tons).

The ruins of Georgetown Mills, a water-powered sawmill, can be seen at the mouth of Georgetown Creek.

Port Simpson

The Port Simpson trading post was established in 1834, and First Nations villages in the region—with the exception of Kitkatla on Dolphin Island—were abandoned in favour of a new village at the port, known at the time as Lach Goo Alams. It became famous for its carved houseboards and painted housefronts before more traditional

Commercial fishing vessels dot Portland Inlet.

housing replaced them, and a collection of the carvings was shown at the Philadelphia Centennial Exhibition in 1876. The fort itself was a trade shop, a warehouse, officer's quarters, a mess hall, houses and shops inside stockade walls. Two bastions, each supporting four guns, were placed on a palisade of thick cedar. The last buildings from the fort burned in 1915.

Today Lax Kw'alaams is a well-established community of about 1,300 people located on the south side of Port Simpson. It celebrated a major step forward in October 2005 with the completion of a swimming pool, youth centre, elders centre and refurbished gymnasium. The community itself has a small hotel, store, restaurant and marina. A government dock is located near the fish cannery—a major employer for the town. A boardwalk trail leads around the headland at the south entrance to Port Simpson.

Place names: Captain Emelius Simpson served in the Hudson's Bay Company; he died the year Port Simpson was founded at Port Nass. The band changed the community name from Port Simpson to Lax Kw'alaams in 1986. Lax Kw'alaams means "place of small wild rose bushes."

Portland Inlet

This inlet is famous for its storm-force outflow winds, but fortunately only in winter. During the summer season it's far more pleasant. Portland Inlet leads inland 35 km (22 miles) to Observatory Inlet, which then branches into Alice Arm and Hastings Arm. Attractions near the entrance include numerous side routes into areas like Work Channel and Wales Passage. The entrance is also an excellent place to view humpback whales, especially in August and September.

Rough water can be encountered at the confluence of Portland Inlet and Work Channel.

Place names: The inlet was named Brown Inlet by Captain Vancouver in 1793, but officially became Portland Inlet in 1924. Portland Canal was originally Vancouver's name for Pearse Canal to the north. William Henry Cavendish Bentinck (1738–1808) was the third duke of Portland.

Camping: N54°36.49'/W130°26.35'. Southeast of Flewin Point is a sand and gravel beach interspersed with rocks. Clear areas can be found at most tide levels. At the head of the beach is a stretch of nice brown-red sand. Clear and level but undeveloped camping areas can be found in the forest upland.

Work Channel

This channel extends 48 km (30 miles) from the entrance of Portland Inlet along the length of Tsimpsean Peninsula to Lachmach Indian Reserve. Quottoon Inlet extends another 16 km (10 miles) off the south end of the channel. Many consider it and the waterfall at Thulme River to be one of the most beautiful places on the coast. Tidal streams here can reach 4 knots, with tide rips at Sager Rocks near the entrance.

Work Channel is steep-shored and can have currents of 3 to 4 knots. The main access was a boat launch with a campsite, located at Lachmach on the south end of Work Channel, but the forest recreation site has since been permanently closed due to the risk of landslides.

Khutzeymateen Inlet

This inlet is accessible by Steamer Passage, which is composed of steep shorelines and granite cliffs. Kumeon Bay is the site of the Kumeon Cannery, which operated 1918–20. A Tsimshian village was located here in the 1800s.

Khutzeymateen is a deep, sheltered fiord extending 28 km (17.4 miles) into the B.C. interior. A large estuary at Tsamspanaknok Bay attracts grizzly bears. The Khutzeymateen Inlet area is used by about 50 grizzlies along with mountain goats, marmots, beavers, seals, wolves, porcupines, wolverines and otters. The estuaries support waterfowl, eagles, owls, grouse, woodpeckers and kingfishers.

Crow Lagoon, located near the mouth of the inlet, is surrounded by vertical walls with an intertidal flat of volcanic sand. It's notable for being a caldera—a large crater created by a volcano that collapsed into a bowl-shaped depression. The caldera has been breached by the tidal waters of Work Channel, and consequently can now be entered by small boat.

Wales Passage

This narrow channel runs between Pearse Canal and Portland Inlet, with a historic vestige of the days when the Canadian border ended at Portland Inlet, not Pearse Canal. An old cement block house at Manzanita Cove is one of the four original cabins built for the surveys of the Alaskan border in 1896. A boundary tribunal in 1903 would see the border shift northward.

Manzanita Cove is both an anchorage and a possible camping area.

Place names: Mr. William Wales was the mathematical master at Christ's Hospital and an astronomer on Captain Cook's *Resolution* when Captain Vancouver was a junior officer 1772–75. Captain Vancouver named the island and passage in 1793, crediting Wales with the instruction that allowed him to navigate the B.C. coast.

Khutzeymateen Grizzly Sanctuary

Officially it is the Khutzeymateen/K'tim-a-Deen Grizzly Sanctuary—the first Canadian park officially designated to protect grizzlies. It was created in 1995 and protects 44,000 ha (108,000 acres) and habitat for an estimated 75 to 143 grizzlies in an area of old-growth forests, coastal wetlands and peaks as high as 2,100 m (7,000 feet). The only access is from Khutzeymateen Inlet, but the park's strict conservation mandate discourages land-based visits of any type. Water-based viewing is recommended. A seasonal ranger station is located off the north shore at the head of the inlet. Additional information is available there.

In 2005 two guides were licensed to offer tours in the park—Ocean Light II Adventures (**604-328-5339**) and Sun Chaser Charters (**250-624-5472**). All guided tours must be accompanied by a licensed guide.

Grizzly and black bear viewing

A black bear forages for grub.

Grizzly bears are common along B.C.'s north coast. Their usual habitat is valley bottoms in areas with salmon streams. They tend to stay in self-contained populations often broken by natural barriers such as mountain ranges or lakes. Human barriers such as highways further isolate the populations. In the north coast the highest concentration is found in the area of the Khutzeymateen Grizzly Sanctuary near Prince Rupert (see previous page).

The sanctuary, the first of its kind in B.C., is significant due to the falling number of grizzlies in North America. Once found in all areas of B.C., they are now rare in the south and south-central parts of the province. Humans and grizzlies seem incapable of co-habiting: when humans move in, grizzlies must move on.

The best season to view grizzlies is May to July, when they graze on sedges in the intertidal zones before berries, salmon and other foods are available at higher elevations. During salmon season they spread out along the rivers. This reduces the odds of seeing a grizzly, especially if you are limited to viewing from the water.

The good news is that the bears may congregate at river bottoms to catch salmon, making August an ideal time to watch for them along salmon rivers where waterfalls and salmon holding basins are near the ocean.

Some of the primary tidal areas for viewing grizzlies are Khutzeymateen Inlet, Green Inlet, Khutze River, Canoona River and Koeye River. Viewing should be restricted to marine areas unless accompanied by a certified guide. Guided tours are recommended to minimize disturbance.

Pearse Canal

The boundary between Alaska and Canada runs down the centre of Pearse Canal, which turns into Portland Inlet at the north end 40 km (25 miles) away. The entire waterway extends 152 km (94 miles) through the Alaskan Panhandle to end at the border community of Stewart, B.C. There can be strong inflow and outflow winds and moderate tidal currents in the inlet. Various islets dot the length north of Wales Island, and attention must be paid to ensure you don't stray onto American soil—unless Alaska is your destination.

Place names: Captain Charles H. Peirce commanded a detachment of the 2nd U.S. Artillery stationed at Fort Tongass, Tongass Island, 1868–70. It was the first United States military post in Alaska after its purchase from Russia in 1867 for $7.2 million. The canal and island were named by Captain Pender during his 1868 survey, but the spelling error was never corrected.

Tongass Passage

This passage runs down the west side of Wales Island and shares the border with Sitklan Island in Alaska to the west. Two small but very pleasant island groups lie in the passage: the Boston and Proctor islands.

Camping: N54°42.33'/W130°33.60'. The outermost cluster of islands in the passage, Boston Islands, hides a fine sand beach facing Wales Island. Spring tides would be problematic here.

N54°44.27'/W130°35.87'. On the second of the Proctor Islands from the north facing toward Wales Island is a beautiful high-backed beach. There's also a high, grassy upland bank for shelter at spring tides. This is a very pretty location.

Connecting to Alaska

For those transiting the Inside Passage, it's approximately 80 km (50 miles) to Ketchikan, the southernmost Alaskan community on the coast. Visiting vessels should visit Customs there. The route is via Revillagigedo Channel.

A view towards Porcher Island.

Bibliography

"Account of Clio voyage" (*Victoria Colonist*, January 5–6, 1866).

"Akwé: Kon, Voluntary guidelines for the conduct of cultural, environmental and social impact assessments regarding developments proposed to take place on, or which are likely to impact on, sacred sites and on lands and waters traditionally occupied or used by indigenous and local communities" (Secretariat of the Convention on Biological Diversity, 2004).

"Appendix V: Revised Study Areas Descriptions—Goal 1, The Central Coast Protected Area Strategy Report," K. Lewis, J. Crinklaw and A. Murphy (Resource Management, May 1997).

Archeological Survey on the Northern Northwest Coast, Philip Drucker (Smithsonian Institute, Bureau of American Ethnology, Bulletin 133, 1943).

A voyage of discovery to the North Pacific Ocean and round the world, in which the coast of north-west America has been carefully examined and accurately surveyed, undertaken by His Majesty's command, principally with a view to ascertain the existence of any navigable communication between the North Pacific and North Atlantic oceans, and performed in the years 1790, 1791, 1792, 1793, 1794 and 1795 in the Discovery, sloop of war, and armed tender Chatham, under the command of Captain George Vancouver, George Vancouver, G.G. and J. Robinson and J. Edwards (1798).

Bella Coola-Kwakiutl-Nootka-Salish, A Photographic History (Archaeological Survey of Canada and National Museum of Man, Ottawa, 1972).

"Beyond Nakwakto Rapids," Réanne Hemingway-Douglass and Don Douglass (*Pacific Yachting*, December 1999).

"Purpose Statement, Byers/Harvey/Conroy/Sinnett Island Ecological Reserve" (Environmental Stewardship Division, Ministry of Water, Land and Air Protection, July 2003).

"Cruise of Grappler" (*Victoria Colonist*, December 4, 1863).

"Current Conditions Report: North Coast Land and Resource Management Plan," Greg C. Tamblyn and Hannah Horn (prepared for Prince Rupert Interagency Management Committee, Smithers, March 2001).

"Ecosystems of British Columbia," Del Meidinger and Jim Pojar (Research Branch and Forest Sciences Section, B.C. Ministry of Forests, February 1991).

"Estuaries of the North Coast of British Columbia: a Reconnaisance Survey," MacKenzie, Remington, and Shaw (Wetland and Riparian Ecosystem Classification Program, B.C. Forest Services Research Branch, 1999).

Exploring the North Coast of British Columbia, Blunden Harbour to Dixon Entrance, 2nd edition, Don Douglass and Réanne Hemingway-Douglass (Fine Edge Productions, 1997).

"Forest and Fisheries Tourism Opportunities Study for the North Coast Forest District Project Report," Clover Point Cartographics Ltd. (Tourism Policy and Land Use Branch, Tourism and Corporate Policy Division, Ministry of Small Business, Tourism and Culture, March 2000).

"From Ceremonial Object to Curio: Object Transformation At Port Simpson And Metlakatla, British Columbia In The Nineteenth Century," Joanne Macdonald (*The Canadian Journal of Native Studies*, Vol. 10, No. 2, 1990).

"Gamble Creek Ecological Reserve Management Direction Statement" (Skeena Region, Environmental Stewardship Division, Ministry Of Water, Land And Air Protection March 2003).

Indian Petroglyphs of the Pacific Northwest, Beth and Ray Hill (Hancock House, 1974).

"Kalum Land and Resource Management Plan" (Skeena Region, Ministry of Sustainable Resource Management, May 2002).

"Kitson Island Marine Park Direction Statement" (Skeena District Management, Environmental Stewardship Division, Ministry of Water, Land and Air Protection March 2003).

"Klewnuggit Inlet Marine Provincial Park Management Direction Statement" (Skeena District, Environmental Stewardship Division, Ministry Of Water, Land And Air Protection, March 2003).

Lewis & Dryden's Marine History of the Pacific Northwest, E.W. Wright (Lewis Dryden Print Co., 1895).

"Management Direction Statement, Dewdney and Glide Islands Ecological Reserve" (Skeena Region, Environmental Stewardship Division, Ministry Of Water, Land And Air Protection (March 2003).

"Management Direction Statement, Diana Lake Provincial Park" (Skeena District Management, B.C. Parks Division, Ministry of Environment Lands and Parks July 2000).

"Management Direction Statement, Klewnuggit Inlet Marine Provincial Park" (Skeena Region, March 2003).

"Management Direction Statement, Lowe Inlet Marine Provincial Park" (Skeena Region, March 2003).

"Management Direction Statement, Lowe Inlet Marine Provincial Park" (Skeena District, Environmental Stewardship Division, Ministry of Water, Land and Air Protection, March 2003).

"Management Direction Statement, Prudhomme Lake Provincial Park" (Skeena District Management, Direction Statement, Ministry of Environment Lands and Parks, B.C. Parks Division, July 2000).

"Management Direction Statement, Union Passage Marine Provincial Park" (Skeena Region, WLAP, Environmental Stewardship Division, March 2003).

"Moore Mckenney Whitmore Islands Ecological Reserve Purpose Statement" (Environmental Stewardship Division, Ministry of Land, Water and Air Protection, July 2003).

"Nuxalk First Nation Community Profile, Bella Coola, BC," Rhonda Carriere (Simon Fraser University Community Economic Development Centre, Burnaby, January 1999).

Pacific Yachting's Cruising Guide to British Columbia, Vol. II, Desolation Sound and the Discovery Islands, Bill Wolferstan (Evergreen Press, 1980).

Prince Rupert Port Cruise Industry Handbook, undated.

"Protected Areas: Supporting Information" (North Coast Land and Resource Management Plans Government Technical Team, October 2003).

"Rapid Transit," Jett Britnell (*Globe and Mail,* page T2, May 17, 2003).

"Resource Analysis Report, Recreation," Denise Stoffels (updated by Denise Stoffels and Van Raalte for the Land and Resources Management Plan North Coast Government Technical Team, March 2003).

Sailing Directions, British Columbia Coast, North Portion, Volume 2, 12th Edition (Department of Fisheries and Oceans, Ottawa, 1991).

"Socio-Economic & Environmental/Marine Base Case: Final Report, Central Coast Land and Coastal Resource Management Plan" (Ministry of Employment and Investment Economics Branch, November 2000).

Studies in Bella Bella Prehistory, James J. Hester and Sarah M. Nelson (SFU Archaeology Press, 1978).

"Surf: The Forgotten Town," Angela Dorsey (*Northward Magazine,* Fall 2001).

The Dig, George F. Macdonald (National Museum of Man, 1976).

"Tourism Opportunity Strategy for the Mid Coast Forest District of British Columbia, Final Report" (Ministry of Small Business, Tourism and Culture, July 2001).

"Union Passage Marine Provincial Management Direction Statement" (Skeena District, Park Ministry Of Water, Land And Air Protection Environmental Stewardship Division, March 2003).

"Unit Descriptions" (Chatham Sound Coastal Plan Planning, Resource Management Division, Ministry of Sustainable Resource Management, 2003).

"Whiskey smugglers appeal" (*Victoria Colonist,* January 11, 1866).

The following websites were also used to research this book:

B.C. Ferries
www.bcferries.com

B.C. Parks Conservation Ecological Reserves
www.env.gov.bc.ca/bcparks/eco_reserve/ecoresrv/ecoresrv.html

B.C. Parks Recreation
www.env.gov.bc.ca/bcparks/explore/explore.html

Bella Coola Tourism
www.travel-british-columbia.com/cariboo_chilcotin_coast/bella_coola.aspx

Cariboo Chilcotin Tourism
www.travel-british-columbia.com/cariboo_chilcotin_coast/cariboo_chilcotin_coast_information.aspx

Communications and Electronics Branch, National Defence, World War II Ground Radar
www.commelec.forces.gc.ca/organization/history/branch/anxc_e.asp

Environment Canada Weather Office climate normals
www.climate.weatheroffice.ec.gc.ca/climate_normals/index_e.html

Great Canadian Rivers
www.greatcanadianrivers.com

Heiltsuk First Nation
www.heiltsuk.com

Klemtu Tourism
www.klemtutourism.com

Ministry of Energy, Mines and Petroleum Resources MINFILE Capsule Geology and Bibliography
www.em.gov.bc.ca/cf/minfile/search/search.cfm?mode=capbib&minfilno=103H++027

Ministry of Energy, Mines and Petroleum Resources Programs and Services Geology Map
webmap.em.gov.bc.ca/mapplace/minpot/bcgs.cfm

Ministry of Agriculture and Lands B.C. Geographical Names Information Service
ilmbwww.gov.bc.ca/bcnames/g2_search_by_name.htm

Prince Rupert First Nations Education Services
www.sd52.bc.ca/fnes/smalgyax.html

Radio Detachment historic page
www.pinetreeline.org/misc/other/misc5b3.html

Simon Fraser University Nuxalk First Nation Community Profile
www.sfu.ca/cscd/research/forestcomm/fcbackfile/communities/bccp.htm

Raincoast Conservation Society
www.raincoast.org

Index

Numbers in italics indicate the best map for locating the entry.

N

O

P

Q

R

S

T

U

V

W

Y

Z

Notes

ABOUT THE AUTHOR

John Kimantas is an editor and writer with 18 years of experience at newspapers in Ontario, Manitoba and British Columbia. His credits include five awards for environmental writing. He is an avid outdoorsman and kayaker and is currently working on his third volume in The Wild Coast series, covering the Gulf Islands, Desolation Sound and the B.C. south coast. His kayaking adventures can be followed at **www.thewildcoast.ca**.